D1231218

Little Giant

THE LIFE AND TIMES OF SPEAKER CARL ALBERT

Little Giant

BY CARL ALBERT
With Danney Goble

University of Oklahoma Press
Norman and London

Permission is acknowledged for the use of photographs on the following pages: Carl Albert Collection in the Carl Albert Congressional Research and Studies Center, University of Oklahoma, pages 6, 14, 72, 88, 152, 154, 168, 169, 187, 197, 204, 249, 250, 261, 282, 303, 314, 322, 328, 363, 369, 377; Western History Collections, University of Oklahoma Library, pages 10, 12, 15, 42; Dev O'Neill, pages 228 and 364; National Park Service, photograph by Abbie Rowe, page 209; and KNOE-TV, Monroe, Louisiana, page 259.

Library of Congress Cataloging-in-Publication Data

Albert, Carl Bert, 1908–
    Little giant : the life and times of Speaker Carl Albert / by Carl Albert ; with Danney Goble.
    p.   cm.
    ISBN 0-8061-2250-1 (alk. paper)
    1. Albert, Carl Bert, 1908–   .   2. Legislators—United States—Biography.   3. United States. Congress. House—Biography.
4. United States. Congress. House—Speaker—Biography.
I. Goble, Danney, 1946–   .   II. Title.
E840.8.A36A3   1990
328.73'092—dc20
[B]   89-29013
                                                                CIP

The paper in this book meets the guidelines for permanence and durability of the Committee on Production Guidelines for Book Longevity of the Council on Library Resources. ∞

Research and writing for this book were made possible through the generous support of
W. Lee Brown and the National Bank of McAlester
Jack T. Conn
Mrs. Tom Garrard
Elmer Hale
Walter Neustadt, Jr.

Contents

Illustrations

Little Giant

Albert Is My Name

On May 22, 1927, a single head-
line streamed across the entire front page of Oklahoma's largest
newspaper. "WEARY AIRMAN CONQUERS PARIS," it announced tri-
umphantly. The lead story's first sentence captured the magnitude
of Charles A. Lindbergh's achievement and gave him the heroic
nickname he would never lose: "A lone eagle, flying without radio
or signalling devices of any kind, winged his way from the American continent Saturday on the long hop to Paris."

No fewer than ten other stories plastered the front page of that
day's *Daily Oklahoman*. Collectively, they gave a hungry audience
such details of the flight as Lindbergh's fuel cost ($175), mileage
(ten miles to the gallon), and diet (five sandwiches and two can-
teens of water). Only one other story ran on the front page. Only
one name other than Lindbergh's appeared in a headline. It said:
"CARL ALBERT GOES EAST."

I was leaving Oklahoma and going to Washington. There I
would speak on the Constitution of the United States. It was
twelve days past my eighteenth birthday.

What put a high school from McAlester, Oklahoma, up there
with the company of the Lone Eagle was a contest sponsored by
the *Daily Oklahoman* and forty-nine other metropolitan newspapers. In 1924, the papers had launched the National Oratorical
Contest on the American Constitution. Open to any high school

3

student in the country, the contest divided the nation into seven regions. In each, preliminary and state competition would identify every state's best orator on the Constitution of the United States or the work of an individual associated with it. The seven regional contests then pitted champions of neighboring states against one another. The prize for seven regional winners was a trip to Washington for the national finals, to be judged by justices of the United States Supreme Court. Each of the seven also received an award that it had been my ambition to win for years: an expense-paid, three-month summer tour of Europe.

That prize was almost beyond the comprehension of a boy who had seen little more than the farm fields and coal mines of Pittsburg County, Oklahoma, but the contest's requirements were perfectly fitted to me. Each contestant—three million entered the initial eliminations that year—would write and deliver a ten-minute oration. Other than that, the rules were brief: "The only requirement is that he do his best."

By 1927, I had done my best three times. As a sophomore, I entered the district contest at Ardmore. I placed third. There were three in the contest. As a junior, my best was better. I won both the district and the state eliminations and fell just short of capturing the regional championship at Kansas City. Finally, in 1927, untold hours of work and dreams paid off. I won the contest at Kansas City, and Carl Albert went east.

I took with me my first real suit, a gift from some proud hometown merchants. On my wrist was a brand new Bulova President, a fifty-dollar gold watch donated by Newton's Jewelry Store. Suitably outfitted, I left McAlester with my high school principal, R. L. McPheron, aboard the Texas Special on May 23. We rode all night to Saint Louis, where we took the Baltimore and Ohio's best train, the American.

When that train pulled into the Washington station, two men met us. One was my official sponsor, the *Daily Oklahoman's* Washington correspondent; the other was Senator Elmer Thomas. I had seen Mr. Thomas the year before during his campaign when he spoke at the McAlester courthouse. This was my first time, though, to meet him. New to the Senate—he was then beginning his third month in office—he looked just as I thought a United States senator should. Six feet, four inches tall, weighing a sturdy 240 pounds, Thomas had steel-gray hair combed sleek, and his attire was immaculate. Little wonder, then, that Oklahomans elected to the Senate for four six-year terms, a record of service still unequaled. When I met him on my very first day in the capital, I began a friendship that would stretch over that entire time and beyond.

The next morning, I put on my new suit and watch, left the Raleigh Hotel, and went with the other contestants to the White House to meet the president. Calvin Coolidge sat relaxed and comfortable at his desk in the Oval Office. Because there were no color photographs, I had an unsuspected surprise: the president had red hair, like my own. I was not surprised by his greeting. As each of us was introduced to him, all we got back was a mild handshake and a quick and quiet "Pleased to meet you." Afterward, President Coolidge said not a single word, not even as he joined our group to record the occasion with an official photograph behind the White House. Silent Cal certainly lived up to his nickname that day.

Mrs. Coolidge proved to be much different. As she took us through the White House, she charmed us all with a graciousness and warmth that made me wonder how such a deadpan president could have earned such a charming first lady. In time, I came to know every first lady after her. All have been lovely, but few so impressed me as did the dour president's wife who so fully earned her name, too: Grace Coolidge.

That evening, we were all the guests at the mansion of John Hayes Hammond, a multimillionaire and old hunting buddy of Teddy Roosevelt. His home, destined to become an embassy, looked even bigger and better than the White House. For such an occasion, I put on my first tuxedo and took a cab right to the front door. Determined to make a suitable impression, I walked right up to the gentleman in tails who stood at the open door. I confidently extended my right hand, softened my Oklahoma accent, and solemnly announced, "Albert is my name." He took no pains

President Coolidge said not a single word. Carl Albert, second from the right, on the White House lawn with President Coolidge in 1927, with the other finalists in the National Oratorical Contest sponsored by forty-nine newspapers.

at all with his perfect English accent. Bowing almost to the floor, he rose to declare, "I am the butler."

As I recovered my pride, I made my way past the stairway into a large living room that featured a magnificent grand piano. At its bench sat Mr. Hammond's daughter. She sized me up perfectly but gently. As I stood there, barely five feet, two inches tall, she smiled at me and said, "You are so tiny and cute, you simply look like a doll in that dinner jacket." She did not look like a doll in her gown, but she looked very good to me just then. It turned out to be a wonderful evening for a McAlester boy in the Hammond mansion. For one thing, they gave me the best meal I ever ate.

Sixty years since that night, I remember that meal. I remember even more clearly my return to the hotel. To my surprise, Senator Thomas was there, ready to show his young constituent the sights of Washington. He drove me in his car up Independence Avenue. Ahead of us was the United States Capitol, awash in lights. It was my first glimpse of that magnificent building. As the senator parked his car, I stood on the sidewalk to the right side, the House side, of the West Front. I had never seen such a view. I stood there, my eyes drawn to one window. In time I learned that the window belonged to the office of the majority leader of the United States House of Representatives. Standing there that warm evening, I already knew that of all the places on earth I could ever be, this would always be the most special.

We had the contest the next evening. We spoke before a full audience at Constitution Hall in the stately building owned by the Daughters of the American Revolution. Seven high school students—seven out of the three million who had entered the eliminations—came to the stage, each a little nervous, all mighty proud. I spoke first, opening with the words that I had rehearsed thousands of times: "Our Constitution, in the course of its existence, has weathered many storms arising within and without our country."

I was just a boy, and I was a long way from home. Home was and always would be Oklahoma, but I would return to Washington many times. Always I would have something of the feeling that I had experienced on a spring night in 1927, when I knew that of all the things I could ever want to do, this was it. I would meet more presidents, know more first ladies, visit more mansions. In my last months there, I would greet the queen of England. For thirty years, I would make the House side of the Capitol my workshop. For nine of those, I would look through the majority leader's window from the other side. For another six, I would occupy the Speaker's chair. I would be there as our Constitution weathered its most severe storms since the Civil War.

This is the story of how I came to be there.

CHAPTER ONE

We Had Everything but Money

When I was a boy, I often heard my grandfathers speak of territorial fever. It was a condition that had stirred my family for generations. My earliest Albert ancestors came from Germany's Rhine Valley to Pennsylvania in the early 1700s. My mother's people were of Scottish, English, French, and German descent. Whatever their origin, they were of common pioneer stock. Most of them reached America before the Revolutionary War; all were here by 1800. They fought in each of America's wars from the Revolution onward. All went west at early dates, and all continued west, part of the human waves that settled the continent.

The particular fever that my immediate kin experienced occurred as the last of those waves swept across the nation's final frontier. As the nineteenth century ended, virtually all of the North American continent had been settled, its soil plowed, its resources applied. Everywhere this was true, except for a large hole that most maps still labeled "The Indian Nations." Now Oklahoma, those lands lay as a patchwork of Indian domains, each assigned to a different tribe, each closed to all but a trickle of white pioneers, all ready for the next outburst of territorial fever.

For the Choctaw Nation, which occupied eight million acres in the southeast corner, the fever rose just after the Civil War with the discovery of coal. After 1872, when the Missouri, Kansas and

Oklahoma's first industrial city. McAlester in 1904.

Texas (MK&T or Katy) tracks reached the coalfields, the fever became an epidemic. Within a generation, nearly fifty mining companies opened more than one hundred mines in the area. Rich veins of what was called the "best steam coal west of Pennsylvania" ran two to eight feet thick and produced three million tons of coal annually. The town of McAlester lay at the center of the bustling activity. Named for J. J. McAlester, a storekeeper and Indian trader who had opened the first commercial mine, the sleepy village of 646 people in 1900 was Oklahoma's first industrial city ten years later with 12,000 residents.

My own family was part of that increase and typical of it. My grandfather, Granville Albert, had been a farmer most of his life. He had farmed in Kansas for a while but was living in Barry County, Missouri, when he heard about the Choctaw country. In the late 1880s, he took his entire family there. My mother's people crossed the Red River about the same time, coming north from Gainesville, Texas. The men on both sides did work related to mining. My mother's father, Robert Carlton Scott, and his brother, Charles, were carpenters who built houses and mining tipples for the coal companies. Grandfather Albert briefly fired the boiler at the Number Nine mine in Krebs before he opened a hotel down the MKT line at Savanna. Mostly, though, they did what they always had done. They farmed, hoping to get better land, better crops, and better markets.

My father, Ernest Homer Albert, was my family's first to work underground. He began mining coal at sixteen and became a well-paid, highly skilled miner. An old Scotsman taught him to be a gasman, a job that fully earned him his pay and demanded his skills, for it was one of the most dangerous in the industry. Before the mine opened each morning, he would go alone into each dark entry and room. Armed only with a tiny lamp to register lethal gases, he would probe each cavity, checking for fire, air circulation, and accumulated gas. A good gasman could turn a potential tragedy into a routine day. On the other hand, a gasman's error could bring grief and disaster to an entire community.

That happened not once but many times. There were ten major mine disasters in the McAlester area before statehood. On average, the blood of thirteen men stained every million tons of coal mined. One of those men was Lewis Durman, one of my uncles, who was the victim of a rock fall in the Number One Samples mine. After my uncle's death, Mr. Samples gave Aunt Minnie some leftover lumber, and some of her kin used it to build an extra story on the house she owned. With the added space, she could take in boarders to eke out a living for herself and her three small children. The only other thing Mr. Samples gave her was the right to dig around the slate dump for any scrap coal that might have fallen into the

I was named for my mother's father.

pile. He offered to pay three dollars per ton for what the widow and orphans could scrape together. That was her compensation for a husband killed working in the world's deadliest mines.

My father was boarding with Aunt Minnie when he married my mother, Leona Ann Scott, on March 2, 1907. After their wedding, my parents moved into the Bolen-Darnell mining camp. They lived in a cheap, unpainted, four-room house. It was a company house, and it sat across the street from the company store. Beside it ran the Katy spur that carried coal from the Big Bolen mine, which lay two blocks west.

It was in that company house in that mining camp that I was born on the tenth day of May in 1908. Those who recall the occasion better than I remember that it was about eight o'clock on a bright and beautiful spring morning when my father rushed to the company store to summon Dr. Virgil Barton. Three miners' wives helped the doctor, my mother—and me. I was named for my mother's father (Carl being a shortened form of Carlton) and my father's brother, Bert.

My earliest memories go back to the Bolen camp. Most are trivial, such as being sent across the street to buy a loaf of bread and returning from the company store with a sack of candy. Another was a horrifying event: the fatal shooting of a man near our front yard. Frank Miller had black, curly hair and was a great favorite of mine. He boarded with our next-door neighbors. One morning the man of the house unexpectedly returned home early to find Miller in bed with his wife. The neighbor grabbed his gun as Miller dashed out the back door and headed for our house. The first shot missed as Miller passed through our yard. The second killed him instantly. My mother was looking through the window and saw the fatal shot. She was a witness at the trial. The jurors acquitted the neighbor.

More substantial events left less-permanent impressions. I do not at all recall the birth of my brother, Noal, in February of 1910. I do know that I and everyone else have always called him Budge. Only later did I learn that the nickname came from my own babyish efforts to say "brother." Budge it is.

The "Little Bolen" mine, opened by Carl Albert's father about 1910.

With two babies, my mother became very fearful of the dangers of my father's mining. Those fears were nearly realized while my father was working in a mine in Baker, a tiny community three miles west of McAlester. Working underground one day, my father was hit by a large, falling rock. Had not another miner been there to roll it off him, he likely would have died. My mother had had all she could take, so she laid down the law: my father had to get out of the mining business. That is how I came to live in Bug Tussle.

Bug Tussle is not a city. It is not even a town. It is (or was until 1968) a rural school district. It lies along Gaines Creek ten miles

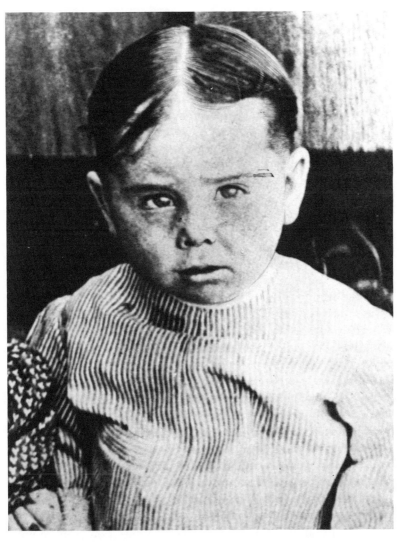

My earliest memories go back to the Bolen camp. Carl Albert, aged two.

northeast of McAlester and runs about four miles east and west, five miles north and south. When we moved there, my Grandfather Scott already lived in the community with about fifty or sixty other families. Like other rural communities, its center and most important feature was the schoolhouse. Before statehood, there were no public schools in the Indian lands. Subscription schools, usually charging each pupil a dollar per month, were about all there were. There were at least two subscription schools in private homes before 1900, when parents volunteered to put up a schoolhouse. It, too, was a subscription school until statehood gave it public, tax-supported status. About 1912, it was replaced by a new two-room school built one mile to the south.

Both buildings were not only schools but community centers, sites of preaching, singing, and holiday festivities. The story is told that it was at one of these that the school and community acquired their memorable name. Thousands of insects would swarm around the kerosene lamps that lit the building for night use in the early 1900s. Particularly during the summers, the insects were fearsome. One resident, a rowdy young man whose own name was Ran Woods, took to referring to the place as a real bug tussle. Bug Tussle it is.

Since all my father had ever done was mine coal and farm, if he had to leave the mines he had to find a farm. That was hard because the allotment of the Choctaw lands just before statehood left land difficult for a farmer to buy. Most were tenant farmers renting from landlords who had acquired the Indian allotments. For instance, Grandpa Scott's family was renting land owned by the country doctor who served the community. We initially rented a farm owned by Kyle Tennant, the doctor's daughter. After a year there, my father rented a large piece of bottomland a quarter-mile east. Because it was too large to work by himself, he went in with his father and his brother. The three of them rented and farmed the land for four years.

The Bug Tussle community had few people of wealth. J.J. McAlester had a country home, large ranch, and several thousand acres of land, but that lay four miles north of us in the community known as Reams Prairie. In Bug Tussle itself the resident gentry were families like Robert Sawyer's. Mr. Sawyer had a large ranch, cattle, a fine white frame house on Fish Creek, and the distinction of owning the community's first automobile. Otherwise, most of the families there were like ours: poor dirt farmers. John Virden, who grew up there with me, later described the place as "poor as gully dirt, the land *and* the people. Not just *kinda* poor, but real poor, the kind of poverty you can not only see, you can *feel it,* and *taste it,* and *smell it.*" How we all made it I will never know. But because my father was the hardest-working man I have ever known, we always had enough to eat. While our clothes were few and sometimes patched, my mother saw to it that they were always clean. As Budge says, we did not think we were poor. We had everything but money.

One of the things we had was family in abundance. All of my living grandparents lived nearby. Grandpa and Grandma Albert lived on our place, and my father's only brother lived two hundred yards away with his own two children. Grandpa Scott and my mother's stepmother lived a quarter-mile up the road. My mother's only full sister, Myrtle, lived in a town called Alderson, just a few miles away. Dozens of other relatives lived nearby. Our family ties were strong and deep.

The nearness of my grandparents was especially important to me because they provided a living link to my own roots. Grandpa Scott would tell me about his own parents, grandparents, and even great-grandparents. Grandma Albert—her name was Mary Jane, but everyone called her Mollie—was always pleased to have me ask about my ancestors. She loved to talk about her own childhood in Kentucky. One day she was washing dishes and I wiped for her. She told me about her own father, a really bright man, small in stature like herself. Her mother's name had been Ash, and she told me that she had an uncle named Green Ash. Then she laughed.

Grandpa Albert hardly ever talked about his ancestors. His own grandparents had died before he was old enough to know them.

Also, Grandpa Albert did not talk about much of anything. He was a very quiet person who always attended to his own business and never bothered anyone else. My brother and I would sometimes work with him in the field. He would never raise his voice, not even to his horses. Neither I nor anybody I have ever asked once heard him raise his voice to anything or anybody. He was a devoted Baptist, but he kept his religion and his politics to himself.

Grandpa Scott shared his own opinions, particularly on religion, with everybody. He was well read, very witty, and always talkative. He got religion late, for in his younger days he was very high tempered. Not long after he had come into the Choctaw lands, he and his brother Charles killed a man in Krebs. In June 1896, a man named Frank Newburn shot and killed their oldest brother. Granddad ran out with a shotgun, and Newburn started shooting at him. He tried to shoot back, but the shotgun was empty, so he hit him in the head and knocked him down. As Newburn started to get up, Uncle Charlie took the pistol out of his hand and shot him between the eyes. He lay there next to their brother, two dead men lying two feet apart.

My grandfather and great-uncle buried their brother in the McAlester cemetery. A federal marshal arrested them at the graveyard right after the funeral. He also arrested their father, who was just an innocent old man. The marshal took my grandfather and uncle over to the federal court in Fort Smith for trial. Because my grandfather had two little girls, the authorities let him post bond. Uncle Charlie had no children, so he stayed in jail until the trial. It was ten months before they were acquitted for acting in self-defense. After the trial, my grandfather met up with the marshal who had arrested them all. He pulled him out of a store and offered to fight a duel with guns. He put a chip on his shoulder and dared the lawman to knock it off so he could kill him. He meant it, and the marshal knew it. My grandfather had to satisfy himself with beating the man senseless.

It was later that Grandpa Scott got religion, and when he found it, he truly was born again. He turned completely around. He never met a person he did not try to convert. He preached in nearly every church and school building as well as in many homes in the area. He was an unrelenting missionary for the Lord.

His wife shared his zeal. My mother's own mother had died when she and her sister were children. My grandfather remarried and had three more children. His second wife was a small, dark-complected Texan whose maiden name was Mary Elizabeth Clark. Owing to her looks, everyone always called her Pedro. She had gone to college and was the only one in the family or the community with much formal education, but she was a literalist on the Bible, particularly in its prophetic and apocalyptic visions.

My grandfather's religious prejudices ran deep, but his own convictions were sure. I know that I was satisfied that everything he talked about was correct until I was about thirteen. For instance, because he believed so strongly in divine healing, I believed it was almost a sin to take medicine. Once when I suffered from fever and chills, the only cure I wanted was Grandpa Scott's prayer.

Grandma Albert believed in Sloan's Chill Tonic. She most certainly did not believe in Grandpa Scott's prayers. Her own religious convictions were just as strong as my grandfather's, and her prejudices ran just as deep. She was a Baptist, and she rejected every doctrine and every belief that did not square with Baptist teachings. This included faith healing.

She tried to push her beliefs on to her own children. When they were young, she would haul my father and his brother to Baptist services twice on Sunday as well as Wednesday nights. My father went no further in school than the fourth grade. He probably would have gone longer, but the family moved to Krebs. The only school there was operated by the Catholics. When he came home one day carrying a catechism, his mother jerked him out of school and never let him go back.

Aside from her religious prejudices, Grandma Albert was one of the most remarkable persons I ever knew. She and Grandpa Albert lived in a two-room log shack, but after they had lived there a few months one would have thought it had been touched by a fairy's wand. Tiny, quick, and industrious, she could do more for a run-down cabin and weed-ridden yard than anyone I ever saw; and she could do it with practically nothing. There were flowers all over her yard. There was never a stick or a tin can out of place. She had little money for niceties, so she made them. Her hands turned old rug strips into bright crocheted coverings. Her fingers knitted and sewed and made beautiful lace curtains to adorn the old windows. She dusted her furniture daily, and she scrubbed her wooden floors at least twice a week.

My father inherited his mother's zeal for work though not for religion. It seems that my grandmother's passions had burned any significant beliefs out of him. Like most of my people, he was small in stature. His own father stood five feet two, his mother five feet. He himself was a very stocky five feet, five inches. With muscles like pine knots, my father was known through the community for his wrestling talent. Even more was he known as a worker. With no education to speak of, he never doubted his ability to get his family through good times and bad. He never gave us cause to doubt it either.

I respected my father; I loved my mother. Where he gave strength, she gave love. She was small, too—about five feet two, and one hundred and ten pounds. That hardly measured the love she gave her children. They were her life, her devotion. She would clean us up for school, comfort our petty hurts, and worry over our mischief. Like my father, she had no more than a fourth-grade subscription-school education, but she read books, particularly the Bible, to her children. She read Scripture with the same fundamentalist convictions as Grandpa Scott, her father. Her concern for our welfare prohibited drinking, dancing, and gambling. If my father smoked, he would have go to off somewhere to do it. She would not allow anyone, including our father, to smoke in front of her children, and he respected her beliefs. We were nearly grown before any of us saw him use tobacco.

While we were on the farm that my father and his kin rented, we lived in a house typical of the Bug Tussle community. It was a double log cabin: two log rooms separated by a dog trot (an open breezeway) running north and south. Attached to the eastern room was a small lean-to that we used as a kitchen. A frame smokehouse sat to the rear on the north side. Drinking water came from an old well near the house.

In the backyard stood the universal and indispensable instrument of life in rural Oklahoma: a huge, black iron boiling pot, its three short legs resting on rocks. In the summer, it heated water for shoeless children to wash their feet nightly. In the fall, it converted ashes and hog fat into lye soap. Year round, it boiled our clothes, which my mother then washed with the lye soap on a scrub board set in a No. 3 washtub.

The barn was about thirty yards to the west. Surrounding it were cattle and horse lots, pigpens, and chicken coops. My father usually kept ten to twelve hogs. Cows provided milk and a few calves to butcher. We always had horses for farm work and riding. Mine was that shade of gray that gave him the name Blue. Adjoining the barn lots was a large garden that produced our vegetables. Fruit came from the orchard of trees and berry vines east of the house. My father kept the corncrib filled with corn, the shed with hay, and the smokehouse with hams and bacon.

Inside the house, there was no sign of luxury. A wood cookstove and family dining table occupied the lean-to. The children slept in the west log room. My parents slept in the east room, which was also our living room, where we gathered around the potbellied stove that was our sole source of winter heat. Other than the Bible, there were never many books. Newspapers covered the walls. They were all we could afford for wallpaper.

All in all, that layout was about average in Bug Tussle. Few Bug Tussle people had more worldly goods than we. Several had much less.

We were living there when my sister was born exactly two weeks before my fifth birthday. As I left my bed and entered the breezeway, I saw a strange horse and buggy in the front yard. They belonged to the community's doctor. He carried his black pill bag out of my parents' room. When I came in, I saw my mother lying in bed. Grandma Albert was washing the pink baby in a galvanized dishpan. My parents named her Kathryn, and she grew to be a beautiful girl with my mother's black eyes and black hair. She was to be the one girl in the family.

My extended family continued its nomadic ways. Grandpa Scott moved out of Bug Tussle to a farm near Adamson. In 1916, Grandpa Albert moved into the house where Grandpa Scott had been living. Uncle Bert followed his wife's people out west that same year to grow cotton in Beckham County. For a year, we were all that were left on the big farm that we once had all worked together.

In January 1917, we moved, too. It was about a mile west. My father rented 120 acres from Guy McCulloch. Mr. McCulloch put up a barn on the place and hired a well driller to drill us a well. Grandpa Albert selected the site, as he did for most of the wells in the community. He always used a peach-tree water witch; good water came in at eighty feet.

Our new house was one of the Bolen camp houses that Mr. McCulloch moved onto the place. It was similar to the one in which Budge and I had been born. Two more Albert boys would be born there. Homer arrived a month after the United States entered World War I. My youngest brother, Earl, was born on December 7, 1921. Thus, all four of us were born in unpainted coal mining camp houses. Only the last was born in one that we owned. My father had bought the place from Mr. McCulloch in 1918.

Earl would always be the family's baby and precious for it. His birth was a blessing to all of us. Homer was a determined and fearless boy. He would often frighten our youngest brother by taking him through the little country cemetery. Even as a small child the blackest darkness held no terror for him. His life was cut short by wounds suffered in Normandy on June 9, 1944. When I heard of his fate, I remembered my mother's unusual sorrow after his birth. One day she had called me to her side. She said that she just could not stop crying. She had brought a boy into the world at war. She was consumed with dread at the sadness and horror that might await him. Her own early death spared her the knowledge of

Homer's fate in another world war, the one that began on Earl's twentieth birthday.

All four of us kids called our parents Mama and Papa. Their generation used Ma and Pa, the terms they themselves used to address our grandparents. Words like Daddy were unused until my own children's generation. To us, that term sounded babyish, and Mother and Father were too formal for ordinary speech. My parents were Mama and Papa to me as long as they lived.

While we all lived together in Bug Tussle, we shared the family's labor. Mama and Papa worked tirelessly. The home was my mother's domain. She kept her scant furnishings orderly and clean. She did the same for her children, too. From time to time, my father would add to the family's income by working in the coal mines. This occasionally meant that he would toil underground in distant mines through the week before riding the train home for weekends with the family. The farm, though, remained his major work. At times, Papa would hire an extra hand; always, he made full use of ours.

Each of us worked before and after school. Daily we would collect and haul the wood and water that my mother would use for heating, cooking, and washing. Budge and I usually fed and watered the animals. Milking was another of our daily chores, done morning and evening. Cows, unlike boys, did not mind cold weather. It seems that my hands were never colder than when on a cow's udder on a typical January morning.

Our seasonal work moved with the natural rhythms of the crops. Spring and summer meant chopping (weeding) cotton, an activity calculated to tire every muscle and blister every finger. Summer's hottest days seemed reserved for baling hay and threshing oats. In the one-hundred-degree heat, it was all one needed to know of hell. But fall was worst of all; then hell became real. It was cotton-picking time.

The long rows of fleecy cotton plants stretching across a wide field were an awesome sight. The thousands of stalks must have been designed by Satan himself to foretell of the bottomless pit. The short plants would not allow a boy to pick from his knees. In a few hours they numbed, rendering him unfit to walk. Stooping merely transferred the agony to the lower back, quickly making it impossible to stand. The cursed burrs pricked my fingers until the blood ran. This surely was the temporal form of the eternal damnation of Grandpa Scott's sermons.

For all of the pain it inflicted upon us, the Bug Tussle farm made us a good living. A succession of good crops and decent prices had provided us the money to own at last a place of our own, and when they continued, my father would actually have money in the bank. At a minimum, the farm sustained us.

All our basic food was homegrown. Gardens gave us the vegetables that Mama served fresh in season and canned for year-round use. In a wood-burning oven she baked biscuits every morning, corn bread every two or three days. Wheat bread—what we called light bread—was a once-a week luxury. The pigpens gave us our basic meat: pork, ham, bacon, and sausage, all of which we prepared ourselves. Without refrigeration, beef was less common. About once every three or four weeks, we or a neighbor would butcher a calf and divide it with the community.

In other ways, we had to meet our own needs. The swarming insects that gave our community its quaint name had no charm at all in the summer, when clouds of mosquitoes brought malaria. Most kids caught it every summer. It is a wonder more did not die. The only way we had to fight it was with tin cans of burning oily rags to keep the mosquitoes at bay. They were about as useless as old Doc Tennant's little bag of pills.

More routine childhood diseases also required home remedies. Doc Tennant's treatment of mumps, for instance, was mare's milk. When I had the disease, we happened to have a mare nursing a new colt. I took one drink of the milk and declared that I would rather have the mumps.

There was no cure at all for the seven-year itch that afflicted the state during World War I. That common label was only slight exaggeration, since the malady persisted for months. Like others', my body was covered with sores that I scratched until they bled. Even Doc Tennant could not treat it. All we ever found that would ease the suffering was sulphur. For a while, everyone smelled like a sulphur well.

The international outbreak of swine flu after the war stretched its deadly hand into our little community. For that, we had no defense at all. Several of our neighbors died, one of them the brother of my good friend John Virden.

Johnny Virden's family was poor, even by Bug Tussle standards. He had lost his mother at an early age, and his father was an old man to have such a young child. Several of his older relatives were already living in Bug Tussle when Johnny moved into our old log house on the Kyle Tennant place. Years later, he would describe his first recollection of me. As he remembered it, I was walking down a country lane that ran due north of the Bug Tussle school. By then I was in school, so I was reading a book. According to John, I was oblivious to the world as I walked along, intently reading, my bare feet kicking up a great cloud of red dust. He recalls that I was dressed in the best Bug Tussle fashion:

> blue and white striped overalls with mismatching blue denim patches on the knees. [I] wore a hickory shirt and a broad-brimmed straw hat that had "shot up to seed" from being rained on too many times. And that was all. . . . We said "howdy" and told each other our names, and shook hands with the one-pump handshake peculiar to country kids and fullblood Indians.

Johnny and I became fast friends, perhaps because we shared a capacity for innocent mischief. One such incident occurred at the local swimming hole on Bucklucksy Creek. In the summer's drought, my father had rolled his farm wagon into the creek's shallow side, where the creek's water would soak the wooden wheels and keep their iron tires snug. Johnny and I decided that it would be great fun to pull the wagon over to the other, deeper side. We did. We had a good laugh as it disappeared beneath ten feet of muddy water.

A week or so later, we smiled—to ourselves—when my father stopped by Mr. Virden's place to ask if Mr. Virden had seen his wagon. It seemed he could not find it, and he thought Johnny's father might have borrowed it. He had not. But he did have an idea. With us boys in tow, Mr. Virden took Papa down to the creek. The men stripped and waded in. It was Johnny's father who found the wagon—when he stepped on its tongue. It took the two men and the two boys to pull it out. Only the boys saw the humor in it. John Virden can finish the story:

> Once the wagon was hub-deep and snugged to a tree with a rope, each father cut a limb that looked as big as a hoe handle. For the next three minutes any passerby would have thought somebody was killing a yearling in that thicket, the hollering and bellowing was that loud.

In time, Johnny's father wandered away from Bug Tussle, taking him to the little community of Ulan. I lost track of him after that, only to meet him again when we were both students at the University of Oklahoma. He was studying journalism, but what he really wanted was an appointment to West Point. He could never find a sponsor, so he went into the Army Reserve and built a career as a newspaperman. Eventually, he landed on Dwight D. Eisenhower's staff. He served as Ike's public relations officer when the general headed America's North Atlantic Treaty Organization forces. Since his Bug Tussle days, when ability counted, John Virden had it. He won several army citations for a superior performance.

John Virden was largely self-educated. As soon as he got near a library, he started reading. He taught himself more about the Civil War than any man I ever knew. He knew strategy, tactics, and details by the thousand, particularly about the Battle of Gettysburg. His grandfather had been an unsung Confederate soldier there, and John became so expert on it that he laid the wreath honoring the Southern dead at the battle's centennial ceremony. It was U.S. Grant's grandson who laid the Northern wreath. In time, John Virden would be invited to lecture at the school he could never attend: West Point.

I always think of Johnny Virden whenever anyone wonders

how a notable person could come from a place as obscure as Bug
Tussle, Oklahoma. That tiny, rural community with the curious
name had within it people who were just like Carl Albert and John
Virden. They are people I have known and respected all my life.
There was certainly nothing special about the two of us then
or there.

Even our innocent escapades were typical. They helped lighten
the heavy routine of farm work. Fishing and hunting helped, too.
It seemed that every boy had a .22 rifle and single-barrel shotgun.
Abundant quail and rabbit were our game. If there was a hunting
season, we did not know it; we certainly paid no attention to it.

Staying overnight with a friend was always a great treat, particularly if that friend was Bill Anderson. Our friendship stretches
beyond my memory; I cannot recall not knowing him. His mother
was Mama's dearest Bug Tussle friend, and his family was almost
as close to me as my own. When he was a boy, Bill Anderson was
loaded down with more names than any person I ever knew. For
some reason, his teachers always called him Charlie. All of his
friends called him Mook. His father called him Smook. When he
finally got to high school in another community, he ended the confusion—or maybe added to it—by declaring that his name was Bill.
His birth certificate gave his name as William Kitchell Anderson. If
he was ever called William or Kitchell, I never heard of it.

I loved staying over with him (under whatever name) and his
older brothers, Roy and Ray. We were known to swipe water-
melons in season and hunt out of season. Later, I enjoyed playing
with his little sister Ruth and brother Howard, who was called
Happy and now goes by the name James.

More organized entertainment came in such special events
as the annual Pittsburg County Fair. The fair was partly good-
natured competition between folks for the best livestock and
finest produce. To a country kid, it was also a special world of mechanical rides, thrilling side shows, and exotic foods. It was also
the one time of the year that I could count on getting a dollar bill.
Folding money just naturally made one feel rich, especially when
earned by chopping a farmer's cotton for a day. I always hated to

break a dollar bill, so I would survey the entire fair's offerings before doing it.

Bug Tussle afforded more frequently social events, but most were off-limits to Mama's children. Her moral disapproval of smoking, drinking, and gambling extended to dancing. Thus, we were spared the excitement of the occasional dances held at some of the farmhouses. Sometimes those dances were exciting. Young rowdies, their blood heated by moonshine whiskey and local Choctaw beer, often disrupted the dances with fights. Gunfire was not an unheard sound amid the country band's tunes.

Religious meetings may have brought some of this type to repentance. To us, they were social events as well as spiritual gatherings. When I was a boy, I hardly knew that formal denominations even existed. Occasionally, someone would teach a Sunday-school class, open to all, at the schoolhouse, and almost weekly we would attend gospel singing conventions at the Bug Tussle school or in one of the nearby country districts. Without a preacher, Sunday-night singings were our regular services. They were well attended and attracted the best singers from the entire area, even extending into Arkansas. The local residents joined in enthusiastically through the aid of shape-note hymnals. By reducing every possible note of any song into one of eight different shapes, these hymnals made it possible to create instant four-part harmonies.

Summers brought revivals. Some were held in brush arbors along Bucklucksy Creek, right below our house. More often, we would drive up to Reams Prairie, just north of us. Country preachers, including Grandpa Scott, exhorted far into the night. Their congregation included no idle pew-warmers. The people's own testifying, singing, shouting, and praying for the sick were very much a part of the service. The preachers expounded a holiness version of Christianity. Many believed in and practiced glossolalia. Speaking in tongues was the highest form of religious expression, for it gave tangible evidence of the baptism of the Holy Ghost that followed salvation and sanctification.

The sinner's conversion marked only the start of that process. It was made manifest and celebrated by baptism. A good preacher could get ten to fifteen baptisms at a time. The number would include repeaters, for many would redo the process from time to time. It seems that there were a lot of backsliders among us. The sacred site was a big hole in a creek under a culvert near the highway.

Coal Creek was the scene of one quite memorable baptism. Brother Alexander was a Freewill Baptist preacher up at Reams. One of his converts was a little old lady who was raising a mentally retarded daughter. Beulah, the child, was a large girl of sixteen. She would walk faster than a horse, swinging her arms, looking neither left nor right. For church, she had her own seat in the Reams schoolhouse. If anybody got there first, she would just knock him or her right out of it.

As the crop of converts came down to the creek, Beulah rose on both legs, staring wildly. Every time Brother Alexander dipped one under, she would shout, "Oh!" Then came her mother's turn. The preacher blessed the old lady in the name of the Father, the Son, and the Holy Ghost. As he put her under the water, Beulah yelled, "Damn you!" The girl pulled her mother out, threw her over her knee, and proceeded to beat the Devil out of her. Brother Alexander stepped in to save the poor woman. Beulah beat him, too.

I remember an even more notable conversion that occurred in a nearby community. It involved a woman who was fairly notorious for her activities, not only with her husband but with other men of the town. Her husband was arrested for luring a small girl down in a cellar and taking indecent liberties with her. He was thrown in jail, due to be charged with statutory rape.

During this time, the town was holding a camp meeting. The wife was so upset that she sought solace in the Almighty. She went to the meeting, made her way down to the mourners' bench, and met the Lord. She said she was saved. She said that the Savior wanted her to confess all her sins, and she was ready to tell it all. She confessed that she had done many evil things with many men in the community. She promised that she would recount them all at the next night's meeting. Before the next night came, some of those community men, including some who were county officials, released her husband and dismissed the case. The sinful couple quietly slipped away.

Aside from such events, our family's relief from toil largely consisted of visiting its kin scattered across rural Oklahoma. Grandparents stayed close enough for regular visits. Other relatives wandered farther away—far enough away to make a trip an adventure, given the primitive transportation. Henryetta can be reached in an hour by automobile now, but in 1913 it required a farm wagon, two railroads, a rented hack, and an entire day. That was what it took to reach the home of my mother's only full sister and her husband, a man whose 1876 birth date was commemorated in his name: Liberty Centennial Williams. That was an adventure.

It was adventure enough to whet my appetite for travel. Even in Bug Tussle we had heard of the *Titanic's* sinking. I was fascinated by the gigantic ship and those like it. I thought of them as floating cities, moving across dark seas to strange lands. For hours I would sit holding to my ear some sea shells that Grandpa Scott had picked up in Galveston. I heard the ocean's roar, and I wanted to be on it. I wanted to be on one of those ships. I wanted to reach through a porthole into salt water. I wanted to meet different people. I wanted to see a world larger than I knew.

For the time being, though, I had to content myself with what came to us. A good crop and war-induced prices in 1916 gave us enough money to see some of the world at home. We went to the Ringling Brothers Circus. It was a marvelous sight for a country kid; African lions, Asian tigers, Arabian horses, Indian elephants, Japanese acrobats, Chinese rope walkers—it seemed that the world had come to me.

Ringling Brothers came once. Gypsies came through every month or so. From as far back as I can remember until the time that I was grown, they plied their trades from Mexico City to Chicago along the old dirt trail that used to be the Texas Road. Later it was the Jefferson Highway. Today it is U.S. 69. It runs through McAlester, where the Gypsies used to camp on a stream just outside town. They were remarkable people. They had strange accents, strange clothing, and they had cultivated thievery into an art.

I watched once as they worked over a store about a mile and a half from our house. The owner had stacked five cases of soda pop outside the store. Every bottle disappeared in fifteen minutes. Yet not one native had seen any Gypsy take a single bottle. While the band outside performed its magic, the Gypsies inside were ravaging the store. I slipped in to watch. They alternated between predicting the owner's coming good fortune and prophesying his imminent doom. One old woman picked up a jar of pickles and asked the owner if she could have it. He answered bewilderedly that he could not just give things away. She warned that if he did not, his barn would burn that very night. He told her to take the pickles. I do not know whether what the owner respected was the Gypsies' habit of arson or their claim to prophecy, but they certainly had a gift for larceny. The barn did not burn, but the store was stripped.

They really were remarkable. I would have liked to visit their camp, but I was afraid. It was said that Gypsies stole children, too.

The area's resident population was surprisingly cosmopolitan. The coal mining boom that had summoned my grandparents to Indian Territory had been heard literally around the world. Especially after 1890, immigrants came to make up a large share of the mining population. Italians were the largest single group, but Russian, Mexican, Syrian, and Bulgarian accents were also common sounds to my boyhood.

A caste system, informal but real, had developed around the mines. Americans and some Englishmen generally managed the mines and held the highest-paying jobs. The dirty and dangerous job of digging the coal usually fell to the "foreigners." This caste system also carried over to the social life of the miners and their families. I remember that some of the people in my community would not even vote for a well-qualified Scotsman for mine inspector because of his "funny" accent. I also remember visiting my relatives in Krebs, Alderson, Bache, and Dewar, where kids would make fun of other children whose parents could hardly speak English.

These habits, reinforced by the identification of different towns with different aspects of the mining industry, resulted in the concentration of definite ethnic groups in certain communities. At statehood, McAlester's population was one-quarter immigrant stock, but in the surrounding towns, where the actual mining occurred, immigrant families made up a much larger share. In both Krebs and Hartshorne, for instance, they comprised a majority of the population.

These ethnic identities have proved to be quite durable. To this day, Hartshorne has a richly diverse population. Late in my congressional career, I addressed its high school commencement; the senior class included several full-blooded Indians, as well as graduates of Russian, Italian, Polish, and Mexican descent. A black girl was valedictorian. Hartshorne also is one of the few places west of the Mississippi to maintain a Russian Orthodox church.

Thinking about these towns later in my life, I recall the time I got a call from Manlio Givonni Brosio, the Italian ambassador to the United States. He said he had been looking through a congressional directory and it appeared that Krebs, Oklahoma, was in my district. I told him that it was, and he asked if I would accompany him to Krebs. "Nearly all the mail I get from that state," he explained, "comes from Italians there who want to bring their kinfolk from Italy to Krebs, Oklahoma." I agreed and contacted King Cappo, who lived across the street from me in McAlester. He was a prominent figure in the Italian community. He and his Italian friends planned to give the ambassador a regular Oklahoma wingding.

I introduced Ambassador Brosio at a large reception. He began speaking in English; after a few minutes he shifted entirely to Italian. I was walking through the crowd to gauge its reaction. A small Italian man about seventy-five years old, with a visored cap on, came up to me. He asked in a strong accent, "Are you Carl Albert?" I said, "Yes." He said, "I knew your papa. I worked with him in the coal mine a long time ago."

"That big shot up there," the old man continued. "him your friend?" I said that he was. He said, "You know what, Carl Albert? Him a-talka Italian better than me, I think."

Back in Bug Tussle when I was a boy, there were only a few Italian families living on farms. There were also some Choctaw families in the community, but the largest ethnic minority was the blacks. Several families lived there, and there were more living across Gaines Creek. Quite a few lived to the north of us. One of them, Joe Thomas, was a frequent childhood playmate. Fletch Tilford and his family ran a garage and country store—the store ravaged by the Gypsies—just down the road from our house. I used to play with his kids and with the Scott boys, whose father farmed in the community. Often I would start walking to school with the Tilford and Scott kids. When we would get to Kyle Tennant's meadow, I would angle off left to the Bug Tussle school. The black kids turned right.

Like every other school district in Oklahoma, ours had rigidly segregated schools. It was required by the state constitution. The Scotts and the Tilfords and about fifteen to twenty other black kids went to a school about a mile west of ours. Like the law's demand, it surely was separate; unlike the law's claim, it hardly was equal.

Theirs was a little old one-room schoolhouse on the creek bank. Its sessions were no more than six months, with school let out to send the black kids into the fields to pick cotton. They had one teacher, a young girl whose only education was through the eighth grade in a similar school up in Reams. They could not do better. The constitution required that the black schools be financed by a different—and lesser—tax base from ours. They could pay only sixty dollars for each of the six months. I was just a boy who was himself part of the world, but I knew even then that those black kids never had a chance. I felt that it was unfair, un-human, and un-Christian. I promised myself that if I were ever in a position to do something about it, I would.

Our own school was blessed, not only in comparison with the separate black school but with most rural schools in Oklahoma. The Missouri, Kansas and Texas Railroad was the largest taxpayer in Pittsburg County. About five miles of its track ran right through the Bug Tussle district, and we got a good share of its property tax. Ours was a two-room schoolhouse, quite enough for our needs, sturdily enough built that it is still used as a community center. We had a full nine-month term. We paid the lower-room teacher (the one with the first four grades) $75 to $100 a month; the upper room (grades five through eight) had its own teacher, usually the principal. The job paid $150 per month, a sizable sum at the time and equal to that paid in the largest city systems. In addition, a teacherage, a separate, well-built dwelling, adjoined the school and afforded the principal year-round, rent-free housing. Thus, while the black kids (and many rural white kids) had a poorly prepared teacher with at best a state third-grade certificate, Bug Tussle could demand teachers with a first-grade or lifetime certificate. The result was that all of our teachers were unusually well prepared. Most had normal-school or four-year-college training.

My own parents had very little education. Their subscription-school education had lasted only a few months a year, and none at all after four years. They hoped that their children could do better, but I doubt that they ever had any idea that any of us would ever go beyond high school, if that far. My parents never once required me to open a book. No one ever checked my schoolwork. But they sent me to school. And I wanted to go.

I started school in the first week of September 1914. For the first day, Papa drove me to the schoolhouse in a buggy, but he showed me how I could walk through the woods to and from school. I carried a brand-new aluminum lunch bucket that Mama had carefully packed. I also had a satchel. I had insisted on taking it, although the only thing in it was one little red book that my father had bought the week before. It was the primer that we would use. I had been looking forward to this day for some time. Six years old, I expected it to be the greatest day of my life.

It turned out to be a disappointment. Mrs. Lottie Ross taught the first four grades; her husband, Charles C. Ross, had the upper room. Mrs. Ross helped me pick out a desk near the center of the room. She told us what we would be doing and what she would expect of us over the year. Then she dismissed us. I did not know what to do until Ray and Roy Anderson told me I could go home. Bill Anderson went back with his older brothers. I started back through the woods alone. I made it home, and I remember that my mother met me, saying, "Are you home already?" I started crying and said, "I went to school but they didn't give me time to eat my dinner." I was not very impressed with my first day of school.

The second day *was* one of my life's greatest days.

I opened my primer to find a story about a little boy and a goat. I looked at the pictures a few minutes, then I went to Mrs. Ross's desk and asked her to read it to me. I stood by her, watching the words as she read them. She read the story slowly, carefully, and with great feeling. Every once in a while, I would look up at her and we would smile at each other. I went back to my seat a very happy boy.

When the morning recess came, the other kids ran out to play. I went to Mrs. Ross's desk and asked her to read the same story again. She did, pausing to let me talk about the boy and imagine what he was like. At my desk, I went over the story again and again, maybe fifty times in all. By the noon lunchtime, when I asked Mrs. Ross to read it for me again, she said, "I believe you can read the story to me now. Try and see if you can." I did, getting every word perfectly.

I took the book home and showed my mother and my father that I could read. Then I started going through the book's other stories. I found that I could recognize every word that had been in the goat story. With Mama's help on the new words, I could read those stories, too. At bedtime, I told my mother that I did not want to go to bed. "I want to sit up and read."

I have never had quite the feeling that I had when I finished that little red primer. I know I cannot describe it. I had learned to read. I was so thrilled that I literally sat up and clapped my hands. I had discovered a new world. It was a world that stretched beyond Bug Tussle, beyond Pittsburg County, beyond Oklahoma. It was a world without boundaries and without end, and I had the key to open it. Born that day was a joy and love of learning that would take me to four degrees in two universities. But I would never learn more than I had at Lottie Ross's side on the second day of first grade at Bug Tussle School.

I was blessed with a succession of good teachers all through my Bug Tussle years. Mrs. Ross not only taught all of the first-grade subjects, she did the same for the second, third, and fourth grades, all of us together. The school day ran from nine in the morning to four in the afternoon. Fifteen-minute recesses, one before and one after noon, helped break up the day. An hour gave us time to eat our home-packed lunches and run off some surplus energy.

Mrs. Ross was obviously an organized teacher, as well as an important one to me. However, she never did get used to the school's most ungenteel name. One fine spring day in 1915, she announced that Bug Tussle was an ugly name. Buttercups and daisies blanketed the little mound upon which the school sat. With meadowlarks and other songbirds accompanying her words, she declared that henceforth the school would be known as Flowery Mound. In time, that became its official name. Those who grew up there, however, still cling to the more rugged title that Ran Woods had first given it.

Lottie Ross taught the next year at Mountain View School, a suitably delicate name, though it was only the country district immediately south. Bessie Kelley replaced her. Hers was a remarkable ability to tell stories, long, involved fairy tales that kept our attention for weeks until another would begin. Mrs. Ross returned for my third year. A fine Syrian girl, Salima Moussa, from Krebs started me on my fourth-grade year. Halfway through it, I was advanced into the fifth grade. The teachers and my parents believed that the lower grade had little challenge for me. Though I was now in the upper room, I found it not much more challenging.

Fanny Ross, stepmother to Charles Ross, taught that grade. She also served as the school's principal and was one of the first women to hold public office in Oklahoma. In 1918, while serving as my teacher, she won election as Pittsburg County superintendent of schools.

The sixth and eighth grades each had challenge enough. In those years, I had two of the finest teachers I would ever see. I would have distinguished professors who knew more than they, but I probably never would have better *teachers,* not even at Oxford, than Walter Gragg and Robert Craighead.

Walter Gragg was my sixth grade and first male teacher. He was proficient in all subjects. He was absolutely inspiring with language; I doubt that a better grammar teacher ever lived. He would have us parsing sentences and conjugating verbs for hours—and loving it. Later I would learn Latin, Spanish, and Japanese. I never had to study their rules of grammar or the structure of their language. Walter Gragg had taught me all I would ever need to know of those.

Robert Craighead was a born teacher. He loved to teach children, especially those hungry for learning. He would stay after school; he would even invite a student to the teacherage at night to pursue a worthy idea. He came to us after several years of teaching country schools in Missouri and Oklahoma. He brought a wide range of experiences with him. He had been a rail splitter in Texas, he had fought in the Spanish-American War, he had lived three years in Puerto Rico, and he had attended a fine little college in Missouri.

Of course, he had long since mastered the subjects that he taught. He was in full command of all of the fundamentals of elementary education. He also knew and loved great literature. He was a fine speaker who often read poetry to us in his melodious voice. With his own money, he brought literary masterpieces into the school. He introduced me to the wealth of the English language and taught me about those who spoke and wrote it best.

It was just a little country school, and despite Lottie Ross's efforts, we persisted in calling it Bug Tussle. However, it provided a basic education exactly as excellent as any child might make it. Its subjects were the universal ones. I enjoyed and did well at them all. I was especially fond of geography, for it opened the world about me. American history enthralled me, and my best teachers always seemed to love it and teach it well. They taught it as a grand story, a pageant of heroes marching past for our inspiration and as our models.

I still remember the very first history lesson in our little American-history text. It was about Columbus persuading Queen Isabella to finance his trip to India by sailing west. When he was confronted by doubters of his belief that the world was spherical, my history book said that he took out an egg and dared them to make it stand on its end. They could not do it and asked him how. Columbus cracked the egg on its point and set it on the table with that end down. One of the ministers snorted that he could have done that if he had thought of it. Columbus answered, "Yes, but I thought of it."

History for me was full of such heroes—men who had thought of it and had acted upon that thought. I became a great admirer of men like Washington, Jefferson, Jackson, and Lincoln. After I had read every biography of them at the little school, my parents gave me more for Christmas. I read and reread them, moved each time by their subjects' bravery and achievement. Lincoln's story was especially inspiring. The boy who had read by a log cabin's firelight to prepare himself for the presidency meant a lot to a kid living in a log cabin, even if he was reading by kerosene lamps.

The Bug Tussle school not only served to educate the community's children, it also was the center for community festivities. Particularly at Christmas, it was the site of a grand community party. The children received small gifts and treated their parents with skits and recitations. My talent for memorization landed me such prize assignments as "The Night Before Christmas," the one sure favorite in those days. Under Mr. Gragg's and Mr. Craighead's influence, I also recited such memorable orations as Theodore Roosevelt's "The Strenuous Life" and Woodrow Wilson's speech recommending war. More forgettable was the occasion in which the schoolchildren dressed as fruits and vegetables. I sang out, "I am a little onion, O!" It was not all serious.

We made our own playground games with minimal equipment. Baseball, basketball, and blackman were favorites. Track—races of every distance and variation—was common. I inherited some of my family's wrestling ability. I was also a pretty good runner, but only a fair baseball player. Lyman Pope, a full-blooded Indian boy, had us all beat. He was our local Jim Thorpe. He could outrun and outhit any other boy in the school.

Bug Tussle's one prosperous family provided my first boyhood crush. Ruth Sawyer's father was a cattleman with extensive land holdings. His daughter was a sparkling child with black eyes and black hair. I was convinced that she just had to be the prettiest girl in the world. It took no small act of courage for me to bid on her pie at a community pie auction. I kept enough courage to stay in the bidding until I won the pie and the right to share it with her. That was my bravery's limit. We ate the pie silently, neither daring to glance at the other.

My schoolwork came easily for me. Sometimes it came too easily. In a few minutes I could grasp any assignment well enough to get by. Only when I had an excellent teacher—and I had some— did I reach for excellence myself. I suppose that it was precisely their ability to make me better that made them the best.

I also came to appreciate the teachers' likes and dislikes. On through high school and college, I seldom saw a teacher without a personal slant, prejudice, or theory. I would instinctively give them and the class their own views when I answered questions. In other words, I told them what they wanted to hear.

This was a trait that was to serve me well all my life. As a young congressman, it helped me win the attention of men like Sam Rayburn. Later, it helped me gather the support and goodwill of powerful legislators. I have not always been sure that it was the most intellectually honest approach; on the other hand, I have seldom seen reason in the ordinary course of affairs for a person always to bow his neck and insist on his own point of view. After all, I have never known a mule to get very far in life.

For whatever reason, my teachers always seemed to be especially fond of me. Lottie Ross once confided to my mother, "He's going to make a great man someday." She remembered that Mama laughed and replied, "He'll have to. He's too lazy to work." I was not lazy and Mama knew it, but I did learn early on something of the tangible value of an education.

Perhaps the only thing that ranked below my affection for farm work was my ability at it. In particular, I was one of the sorriest cotton pickers that ever lived. Papa had a rule, though: "Don't come in until you pick a hundred pounds." Budge could almost do it by noon; I was lucky to get there by sundown.

My father usually hired pickers to help. During World War I, these were two little black boys, Joe Scott and Nathaniel James, who lived just down the hill from us. They could pick even faster than Budge. So every morning we would line up, each assigned a row. They raced ahead while I straggled farther and farther behind.

Then I started to tell them stories about the war. I would start one as soon as we got going. I might tell them that I had read that the government was going to draft little boys. We were going to have .22 rifles, but instead of lead bullets, we would shoot cotton seeds. That way we would not kill the little German boys, but we would keep them back. Another tale was that the government was going to build a big lake and put little ships on it. Boys would serve in the navy, wear blue uniforms, and sail the ships.

Every time we lined up to start our rows, I would start my story. They got ahead of me, but they kept listening. Then I would talk in a lower and lower voice. When they stopped picking to hear, I would stop talking. I told them that I could not talk loud enough for them to hear me, that I would have to quit until I caught up with them. But they wanted to hear the story, so all three of them—Budge, Joe Scott, and Nathaniel James—would turn and pick back to me in my row.

The only trouble was they were putting the cotton in their own sacks. I explained that that would not do. Papa would wonder why my rows made so much less cotton than theirs. They would have to put it into my sack. Their fingers a blur, they would pick and put it in my sack so I could keep up. As long as I told my story, they would keep me up with them. I stretched that story out the whole season. That is how I picked my hundred pounds.

That may have been my most immediately valuable use of education. The most enduring came in 1914, my first year in Bug Tussle School. The Honorable Charles D. Carter, member of Congress from the Third Congressional District of Oklahoma, came out to Bug Tussle in a buggy. He was a mixed-blood Chickasaw Indian and our district's original congressman; he was also one of the most handsome men I had ever seen, the most articulate I had ever heard. I had seen and heard some of our county's politicians, but never anything like him.

He spoke to the student body at Bug Tussle school. He told us about meeting with President Wilson. He talked about Congress and how it worked. Then he said the words that burned into my soul, leaving a life's fire: "You know, I'm an Indian boy, and it's wonderful in this country that a man who's a member of a minority can be elected to Congress. A boy in this class might someday be the congressman from this district." I was sitting in the same seat where I had just learned to read. And I knew. I had no doubt. Mr. Carter was talking to me. I was that boy.

That was in the fall of 1914, the same school year in which the same student body assembled again for its group portrait. I stood exactly in the center of the front row with the other first-graders. My hair tousled, my head cocked to the side, I knew that day what I would know every day of my life thereafter. This little boy is going to Congress.

I told nobody. They would probably laugh and shrug me off. But that is why I studied history so intensely, finding inspiration

Exactly in the center of the front row, ... this little boy is going to Congress.

in the lives of great public men. That is why I loved and worked so hard at language, grammar, and oratory. Those were the tools of public men. That is also why Robert Craighead was so important to me.

Mr. Craighead was from Callaway County in Missouri's Ninth Congressional District. He was a constituent, admirer, and friend of Champ Clark, the district's congressman and the current Speaker of the House of Representatives. He told us of Champ Clark's life, the life of a poor boy, born—like Lincoln and many of us—in an unpainted log cabin. He told us of his devotion to the House, how he had turned down an appointment to the Senate after the incumbent's death. Mr. Craighead told us how close Clark had come to winning his party's presidential nomination and certain election, only to have them snatched away by Wilson in the 1912 Baltimore convention.

Perhaps because of his devotion to Champ Clark's career, Mr. Craighead knew a lot about the office of the Speaker. He explained how Clark and the great Republican rebel George Norris had led the fight to smash the rule of Speaker Joseph G. Cannon, the czar whose power nearly reduced the democratic body to one-man rule. As Speaker, Champ Clark modernized the House of Representatives. He used his power, but he did not abuse it. He was a Speaker who respected the rights of the minority and of individual members. He made legislative policy in the Democratic caucus, not in the Speaker's Rooms. He had done more to make the House of Representatives the people's branch than had any man since the Constitutional Convention.

Robert Craighead convinced me that Champ Clark was a great man. He convinced me, too, that being Speaker of the United States House of Representatives would be a great goal. That ambition, however, was tempered by Champ Clark's own counsel: "The Speakership is the hardest office in the world to fill, and the hardest to get." I later learned just how right he was. Even at the time, I sensed it. Politics had already cost me one of the finest teachers I had ever seen.

John Perteet headed one of the biggest families in the community. His father had lived there since the original land allotments, and the old man's many children had families there, too. John Perteet's eight children attended the Bug Tussle school, which was about two hundred yards from their home. One was Henry, a boy a little older than I, who was the school's champion speller. He also was crippled, and sometimes Henry Perteet would have to crawl to school.

For some reason, John Perteet came to dislike Mr. Gragg. He maneuvered to get himself elected to the school board. He was determined to fire my sixth-grade teacher; in fact, he came by our house and talked to my parents about it. He even asked me if I would not want to have Mr. Charles Ross back at the school for my seventh grade. I did not answer. I loved Mr. Gragg. We all did. But it counted for nothing. The school board dismissed Walter Gragg at the end of the year. Mr. Ross, stepson of Fanny Ross, county school superintendent, took his job.

By that time, I had also learned something of politics on a larger scale. We had greeted the news of Europe's World War with initial indifference. The immigrant miners must have felt loyalty to their homelands, as well as concern for their relatives there. Most people in our community, however, had no direct stake and little personal interest in the fighting. Our inconveniences were slight. For instance, we could not get German-made blue dye. But aside from the steady bleaching of our overalls and chambray shirts, Europe's war was not Bug Tussle's.

Germany's sinking of the *Lusitania* in 1916 did stir up considerable indignation. It was a principled resentment: a German submarine cowardly had attacked an unarmed British passenger ship. Our concern, however, was still neither immediate nor personal. Though Americans had died, none were our neighbors or relatives. Nonetheless, many greeted America's declaration of war in April 1917 with relief; at last the indecision of our country's role was resolved. Now, American forces would quickly settle the score and permanently resolve the issue. They would make the world safe for democracy.

We boys were certainly ready. Our newspapers told us that the Germans were a cruel and evil people. Their soldiers bayoneted Belgian babies and machine-gunned French civilians. Their wicked Kaiser plotted to rule the world. General Pershing's doughboys must return the help of Lafayette's brave men who had won us our own freedom. We sang with the departing troops, "Goodbye Broadway, hello France, we are going to pay our debt to you."

We only regretted that we could not go, too. We all wanted to be soldiers. In fact, we youngest boys formed ourselves into a military company. We marched through the woods, the fields, and the schoolyard, our chins high, our backs straight, sticks firmly held to our shoulders. Because one of Papa's hired hands had taught me the commands of his National Guard drills, I was their captain, and I put them smartly through their paces. For Christmas 1918, I received the grandest present I ever had: a tiny toy cannon that shot a rubber shell. Budge got a set of soldiers. We played that winter with my cannon blasting away at his charging infantry.

Otherwise, the war's immediate effect on my family and most of the community was economic. War demand ran cotton prices up to forty cents a pound, three and four times their customary level. We all wore better clothes. My father's bank account climbed, for the first time, to four figures. Papa bought a new horse-drawn hack, a poor man's surrey, and it was a great improvement over the secondhand buggy and Springfield wagon. Mama finally decorated the house with store-bought wallpaper.

Then the bodies started coming home. The first was Claude Tedrick's. He had been one of those young men—Claude was about twenty—who had come by the farm, looking for work. My father had hired him, giving him meals and a roof until the crop work began and his pay started. Claude was like a lot of people there; he could neither read nor write. He told me once how much he admired Doc Tennant. Claude said that he did not "know 'A' from a pig track," but the doctor "could make all them little crooks" without even looking at the paper.

He wanted something better and bigger than farm work, so he joined the army and served on the Mexican border. He went to Europe with Pershing's troops, one of Bug Tussle's first men to enter the war. Claude Tedrick died in a French ditch. By the time another of Papa's hands went to war, we did not hear as much about our debt to Lafayette. Carrying their draft orders, boys were leaving every week. There was crying, not singing, when we drove our new hack into McAlester and put Dave Williams on the train for Camp Robinson.

We boys, too young to fight or to understand, kept our war fever high. I was one of them. But it was obvious that war weariness was rising. People resented wartime regulations. Abstract principles gave way to personal fear for our sons and our friends and the future. My mother was not the only one to feel it. A rebellion of antiwar sharecroppers and tenant farmers erupted not far north, in the Canadian River valley.

The self-styled patriots were alarmed. Maybe they had cause to be. Oklahoma's governor, Robert L. Williams, created a state council for defense, and county councils appeared in most of the state. These were nearly hysterical where the foreign-born population was large, where poverty had eroded community bonds, and where patriotism had lost its lust.

Pittsburg County was just that kind of place. Our county council sought out the rebellious, and we had some. It vigilantly searched for slackers, and we probably had a few of those, too. The trouble was that the council could not tell the difference and it did not know how to handle either.

Grandpa Scott, as independent and as opinionated as any man who ever lived, was no slacker, but the local patriots thought any man so contrary just had to be one. They called on him, demanding that he nail a flag to his house to prove his loyalty. He showed them that he already had one flying from his mailbox. He also showed them the medal that his own father had won as a Civil War soldier fighting for that same flag. Grandpa invited them to nail up all the flags they wanted. They left.

They came back. This time, they wanted him to sign a card swearing loyalty to the president and everything it took to go into a war. They asked this of a man who had stood trial for murder, a man who had beaten the officer who arrested him, and a man who had found apocalyptic religion. He would sign no card. He would give his country his loyalty. But he would not swear to any man. In fact, he would not swear at all. In his view, swearing violated the Commandments, and that card was the mark of the beast, Revelation's symbol of fealty to the Antichrist.

So they arrested him and threw him into the Pittsburg County Jail. There a gang of patriots, joined by common drunks and thieves, bound him, and whipped him, two hundred lashes in all.

Grandpa Scott, as independent and as opinionated as any man who ever lived.

Grandpa Scott asked the Lord to forgive him and signed the card. He did it with his soul's reservation that he would recant if the Lord asked it of him. The Lord must have understood.

Through such experiences, I came to know and understand something about my community. Nature had blessed it abundantly. Beneath its soils ran the rich coal veins that had called our people forth. The hills and valleys received the gentle rain that nourished the daisies, buttercups, wild roses, and lilies of our fields. Spring sparkled with their brilliant color. Red oaks, hickories, sweet gums, maples, and evergreens renewed nature's palette in the fall. Yet for all of nature's wealth, most of our people were poor. Only a few owned their own farms or had any hope of ever owning them. For many miners, life was dirty, brutal, and short. Few country kids had decent clothes. Most went barefoot until winter. Some of the adults did, too.

McAlester, only a few miles away, was the area's metropolis, and many of its founders still lived there. Most of the coal companies had their headquarters there. Local promoters had built a school system that was envied across the state. They also had won for it the state institution that gave the place a reputation and the community a large and steady payroll: the Oklahoma State Penitentiary.

Most of our people believed in the old-time religion. They also believed in the old-time politics. In what was already called Little Dixie, that meant the Democratic party. Two hundred Democrats were registered to vote in our precinct; there were six Republicans, though no one knew why.

Outside our immediate area, a good number of people were turning to Socialism. Socialists governed Krebs, and a Socialist represented the working-class section of McAlester on the city council. Pittsburg County gave Eugene V. Debs, the Socialist party nominee, exactly one-fourth of its presidential vote in 1912. From the year of my birth through 1914, Socialists controlled the United Mine Workers.

Though my father was a union man, he was never a Socialist. He continued to believe in a man's hard work, not the overthrow of society. Considering what he had achieved with so few advantages, it was a reasonable belief, one that I could share.

That was, perhaps, the greatest lesson I learned in Bug Tussle. We lived no differently from most of the people there. I never thought myself any better than anyone there, yet I knew that there had to be something better than growing cotton or mining coal for a living. My family and my life had given me the means to see that. A visiting congressman traveling in a buggy had defined what it was. My teachers had shown me the path to it.

That was why I took so hard the news of 1922. In the spring, my father grew a good crop of cotton and our little class passed the county examinations with ease. We had a fine and moving graduation ceremony at the schoolhouse, for the Bug Tussle school went no higher than the eighth grade. If a student went to high school, he or she would have to go away. McAlester, only a few miles away, had a splendid high school. But cotton prices collapsed during the summer and Papa could find no way to get me there. He could not afford a car, and it was too far for me to ride Blue. There was no money to board me. So when other kids were ready to go to high school, I went to the cotton patch. I could not yet leave Bug Tussle.

In a sense, I never would.

CHAPTER TWO

A Little Giant

No one could have convinced me of it at the time, but the dropout year that followed my graduation from Bug Tussle School was one of the most important I ever had. The year gave me plenty of time to think about what I wanted to do with my life.

One thing I wanted had not changed. My disappointment only steeled my resolve that I *would* go to Congress one day. In that dropout year I decided to do everything possible to get me there. I would go to high school. I would go to college. I would take a law degree. I would excel in all my studies. Along the way, I would also master debate and oratory to prepare myself for public life. For the same reason, I would study government, and I would travel to study the world.

What kept me out of school breathed purpose into those ambitions. The collapse of farm prices—a collapse that began two decades of agricultural depression—briefly hurt me, but it nearly ruined my father. It did ruin thousands. In southern and eastern Oklahoma, the rout of prices occurred on a battlefield. For years most of our farmers had struggled in a hostile marketplace, their greatest foe the sharecropping system, their only weapon cotton stalks. Now, men less energetic or merely less fortunate than my father slid into bankruptcy or deeper into tenancy.

I watched as the colors faded from their clothes and the hope from their eyes. I saw their kids (not one of my classmates could go to high school that year either) take up hoes and plows to start lives that would lead to—I did not know where. But I did know that if our people were ever to go anywhere, government would have to help them. My classmates and their parents deserved better, and there was nothing else that could get it for them. The recent world war enlarged my awareness. I had seen the bodies come home. I had heard my mother's fears. I had touched my grandfather's scars. I believed that if war ever were to be prevented, it would have to be government that did it.

Binding these convictions together were bands of my own experiences. There were teachers who taught our history as a tale of individual struggle and achievement. There was Representative Charlie Carter, who told us kids that Congress could make a difference. Robert Craighead had explained how that institution worked and how important personal integrity was to it. I had, too, the examples of my father's persistence, my mother's devotion, and my grandfather's resolution. All of this summed to a boy's determination that his life would have a moral impact upon his world, his country, his state, and his community. This is what I learned that year. It is what I wanted to do and why I wanted to do it.

In the meantime, there were cows to be milked and crops to be tended. I did that, but I also tried to keep up with my education. Mr. Craighead, my eighth-grade teacher, knew how sharp my hurt was and one way to treat it. He gave me some books and lessons on English composition and ancient history. With his encouragement, I began to teach myself elementary algebra.

I also found work to do on my own. I had loved grammar. In fact, I had found it exciting for its order, its precision, and its ability to lift one beyond circumstances. I honestly did not understand why so many other kids found it difficult, boring, and irrelevant. So, I wrote an English grammar for twelve-year-old children.

I had two grammar books, one from the sixth grade, the other from the eighth. I compared them subject by subject. I then set out to express the grammatical rules in the simplest language, language that any kid could understand.

I wrote that our language could be reduced to a few simple rules. For instance, in all of English there were just eight different kinds of words. These were called parts of speech. Every word anyone would ever use belonged to one of these eight groups. I gave many examples for most parts. Of course, I mentioned that there was but one common expletive, the word *there,* as in "There was a boy who had a goat." From words, I moved to phrases, from phrases to clauses, from clauses to sentences. I used two whole Big Chief tablets fixing up that grammar.

My zeal was not shared by my family. When Budge and I were in school together, I usually sat in the front row, where I could listen to everything. He sat in the back, where he could have a little fun. No one in my family—and, aside from the teachers, no one in my community—had any education to speak of. Still, my mother's love stretched to embrace any ambitions her children cherished. My father, however, thought that eight years of schooling were plenty. Sometimes he would fuss when I studied so much. For all his fussing, though, he was the one who helped me to do it. My mother had persuaded him to leave the mines for her children. For us children, he now knew he must go back.

A revival of mining had opened new jobs in the mines. Mine owners sought out my father, knowing that he could do anything around a mine from digging coal to supervising a crew. The owners also knew of his skill in the two most dangerous jobs underground: gasman and shot firer.

Papa returned to the mines in August 1923, working as both a gasman and shot firer. He also finished the year's harvest, and he would keep and supervise our farm thereafter, though others would work it. As a very skilled miner, he sometimes made more than four hundred dollars a month, an unusually high wage at the time. He earned every penny of it. There would be one stretch of seven years in which he would work on the night shift seven nights a week, every night save one for seven years. The one time

Papa returned to the mines. Carl, Homer, Leona, Earl, Kathryn, Ernest, and Noal Albert.

that he had to take off sick, the mine exploded, killing eighteen men. It was another one of the Samples mines. My father always believed that had he been at work it would not have happened.

As soon as we could, we would have to move closer to the mines and give the farm's renters our house. Until then I was able to start school, thanks to Mr. Craighead. He bought a brand new Model T. He had a son, Edwin, about my age. Edwin drove into McAlester for high school, and I rode with him. In September, we bounced over the country roads into McAlester to enroll for high school.

The school that I was starting was more than just a high school. In the first place, high school itself meant far more then than it does today. Only a minority of the American population at the time had earned high school diplomas. In rural southeastern Oklahoma, it was a rather small minority. Then, high school was a *high* school, roughly equivalent to a community college today.

McAlester High School was at least the equal of a very good community college. The city was home to some of Oklahoma's outstanding lawyers, engineers, accountants, and businessmen— educated professional people with pride in their city and expectations for their children. The school system they built and supported was one of the state's finest; McAlester High School was its crowning jewel.

The building itself was nearly new. Sitting high atop a hill overlooking the business district, its architecture of red brick and white limestone was flanked with columns and turrets to follow the day's collegiate style. Almost all of its teachers were university graduates, and several had done considerable work beyond the baccalaureate. What other school would have a teacher like Arthur Coole, who coached the football team? In his spare time, he studied Mandarin Chinese to prepare himself for a subsequent career as a missionary to China.

He was also a pretty good coach. The school took its athletics seriously. In fact, one of its students, Tom Poor, had gone to Europe recently as a high jumper with the United States Olympic team. It was the competition, the triumph of excellence, that gave the school's athletics significance. It gave athletes a certain status, but one no higher than that of debaters, orators, or scholars. McAlester High School was known for entering just about every competitive speech and academic contest in the state. Its teams did not often lose. Its graduates were stars of the best universities in the region. Shirley Buell, who came up through the school system and was salutatorian of my class, remembers it just right: "At that time, in that town, in that school system, of that state, there were giants."

Everyone in the school—everyone in the town—knew just who

the giants were. Academic achievement was greatly respected, and the record that she had compiled even before entering high school already made Shirley Buell one of them. It gave her and a dozen other students a popular stature equal to Tom Poor's. I knew who they were even before I started school. Like everyone else, I respected them. In fact, I was in awe of them. I was a country kid, barely five feet tall. It would be hard for me to be a giant, too.

My enrollment underscored that. English and algebra were required ninth-grade subjects. Edwin and I had agreed upon ancient history and Latin as our electives. When we handed in our enrollment cards, the principal, Mr. McPheron, told us we could not take Latin. He would not allow freshmen from the country schools to take it because they were not prepared well enough for it. We masked our feelings and signed up for the first alternative, public speaking. The teacher happened to be in the office with us, and she redeemed something of our day. "I want these two boys," Miss Perrill Munch laughed. "I may not teach them to speak Latin, but I will bet you they speak good English when I get through with them."

For a while, I was not even sure that I could speak decent English. I began school feeling out of place, full of doubt, intimidated by the city giants of superior preparation and academic reputation. I know I looked out of place. Befitting the school's prominence, the girls' standard dress included heels and silk stockings. The boys wore suits, white shirts, and ties. One who was there recalls that I came to the first algebra class dressed in Bug Tussle fashion: overalls, a work shirt, and brogans. I honestly did not mind that. What I dreaded was my inability to compete intellectually with what I feared were superior people, city people from city schools, their homes filled with books.

My first effort in class multiplied those fears. Our English teacher, Maureen Watson, called on me to explain a very simple paragraph in our composition text. I arose and started—started stammering, stuttering, and searching for a way to give up unnoticed. The classroom erupted with laughter as I shrank into my seat in the middle of my muttering.

It was two weeks before I said another word in any class. It was in the same English class. We were reviewing grammar. The teacher was calling upon students to identify parts of speech. Students clamored for her recognition to answer questions. Then Miss Watson wrote on the blackboard a simple sentence, something like "There was a beautiful house on the hill."

"What," she asked, "is the word *there?*"

Many tried. Several guessed. No one knew.

"Does anyone have any idea?" she asked.

There was silence until I bashfully raised my hand. I said quietly but confidently, "It is an expletive." Not one of the city kids even knew the term.

That happened more than sixty years ago, now, but I still remember that day. I remember it because I knew then that I had arrived. In a place that treasured competition, I could compete with anybody, and I would. I vowed that I would not make a single grade under ninety on a single assignment, and I knew that I could do it. I knew, too, what stature that could bring me. After our first report cards came out—I was in the nineties in every subject—my algebra teacher told the class that the faculty had singled out Carl Albert for setting an extraordinary standard for work. In that same class, one of the students congratulated me for having solved a problem that no one else had. She did not know that I considered it a triumph just to speak with her. Her name was Shirley Buell.

Just after we got our first report cards, Papa rented a house in town and we moved. It was to the northwest part of town, near the state penitentiary. We did not improve our situation much. We were in an old frame house. Our utilities were a two-hole chick sale (outdoor toilet) and a single hydrant, in the yard, too. It was our first painted house. Our new home was walking distance (just two miles) from the high school.

Our part of town was called formally Talawanda Heights. It was otherwise known as Guard Town. My father mined coal on the state prison grounds, and we boys fooled around the penitentiary. On Sundays, we would buy cigarettes for the women prisoners— our fee was a nickel—and then watch the women's warden take the smokes away. Next door to us lived a more successful entre- preneur: he was a bootlegger. Our neighbor to the north was old man Ritchie, who for some time had been the prison's blood- hound man. He was known for an occasion on which three con- victs attempted to escape by taking a prison secretary hostage. Mr. Ritchie shot and killed all three without harm to himself or the terrified secretary.

Next to him lived that prison's most renowned employee, Richard Owens. Mr. Owens had built the state's electric chair back in 1915. For thirty-three years, he was its sole operator. He also got quite a bit of work in surrounding states. Wardens agreed that he was the perfect executioner. He got neither pleasure nor pain out of pulling the switch. It was just a job. I used to run into him as he walked casually home in the morning, his cowboy boots moving briskly as he came down the street after having used his trade one, two, even three times the night before.

Mr. Owens was a large, tall man who had been a local boxing champion in his youth. The story is that he killed his first man when he was fifteen when somebody stole his father's horse. He found the horse and a man on it. When he challenged the man about the horse, the fellow jumped on him. Rich Owens got his knife out and cut the guy's head off before he could get loose. He had been killing men ever since.

He had started with the prison as a regular guard. Not long after, two convicts grabbed him. One put a knife at his throat; the other led him through the prison yard as their hostage. Rich told them, "Now, you all better make this good. If you don't, I'll make good on you." Then he shouted at the tower guard, "Shoot 'em! Kill 'em both!" The guard did shoot and kill the one leading him. The other dropped his knife in terror and ran into a coal house. Richard Owens followed him in, took up a long-handled shovel, and knocked him down. "Please don't, Mr. Owens," the convict cried, "don't kill me." Richard Owens cut him off. "I told you you'd better make it good, 'cause it was either you or me." Then, with his big cowboy boots, Richard Owens literally stomped the inmate's brains out. The story was all over the front page of the *Daily Oklahoman,* and Owens's picture was in every newspaper. It was the heyday of his life.

For all his notoriety, there was something about Mr. Owens that sometimes made him seem apprehensive. When I would talk with him, he could not look me in the eye for ten seconds. His own eyes darted about, never resting anywhere. That was the way they were moving when I ran into him one time later on, after I had been away from home for some time. I asked about his health. He said it was fine. Then he asked about mine. His eyes flicked aside as he added quietly, "I have been praying for you."

At school, I threw myself headlong into every subject. I threw head, feet, body, and soul into the one I had not intended to take: public speaking. When Perrill Munch got through with me, I could speak very good English indeed.

Miss Munch was a young graduate of the University of Oklahoma. She also had studied speech and drama at a private school in Martha's Vineyard, Massachusetts, where she earned more than the equivalent of a master's degree. Her dark hair lay in the tight waves that were fashionable at the time. Her dress was always professional and always immaculate.

She was everything a teacher should be. She knew her material, and she had it organized to the most minute detail. She delivered it with a clarity and a force that made her the finest classroom lecturer I would ever hear. To this day I keep a little black looseleaf notebook in which I set down my lessons as Perrill Munch dictated them to our fourth-hour class in 1923. I still find use of it.

Miss Munch lived her work and put her whole life into it. She taught five or six classes during school hours, and at night she coached debate and directed plays. In between and afterwards, she made time for any student who needed her. That is why her first-floor classroom attracted practically every outstanding student in the school. Had I taken Latin, I would have learned Caesar's *Veni, vidi, vici* (I came, I saw, I conquered); in public speaking, I came to see what conquering was all about.

Before the common use of microphones, amplifiers, and other mechanical aides, public speaking was a form of oratory lost to a modern age of gadgetry and conversational address. Merely to be heard required training in breathing, diction, and inflection. Miss Munch worked us tirelessly on those now-lost skills.

She emphasized that one method of learning good oratory was to read and recite good oratory. I memorized that first year in high school orations that I can still recite, classics like Demosthenes's "Oration on the Crown," Patrick Henry's liberty-or-death speech, and Abraham Lincoln's immortal trinity, the "Gettysburg Address" and first and second inaugurals. She urged us to recite poetry, for it encouraged one to speak with feeling and passion. I memorized some great poems (and some not-so-great ones), and I recited them on every possible occasion. Frank Sittle, one of my classmates, still remembers crying at my version of Lord Tennyson's "Crossing the Bar." Even Budge was moved to tears with my rendition of Senator Graham Vest's "Eulogy on the Dog."

It was my newfound interest in public speaking that first introduced me to the world of politics. Slick advertisements and thirty-second television spots were innovations not yet inflicted upon the electorate. Politicians still earned votes the hard way: on the stump. Candidates for governor, senator, and congressman spoke every election year at the county courthouse. Aspirants for local office flowered each biennial fall at every country school and crossroads store. For the office seekers, stump speaking was the only way to reach a large audience. For the voters, it was a rare opportunity for entertainment and excitement. For me, it was a chance to see and to hear oratory at its most practical level.

In rural Oklahoma, stump speaking was an art form. I still recall my parents' taking me into McAlester in 1922 to hear Jack Walton campaign at the courthouse. Walton was Oklahoma City's mayor. He was also the gubernatorial candidate of Socialists, debt-ridden farmers, and hard-up union men, all allied into the Farmer-Labor Reconstruction League. Finally, Walton was a born stump speaker, a man capable of moving crowds to laughter, to rage, to praise, to bitterness—and to the polls. He won the Democratic nomination and election to the governorship that year by record margins. Walton served only eight months before the legislature impeached and removed him. His fatal mistake was crossing the Ku Klux Klan. Oklahoma counted many Klansmen in the early 1920s, including a majority of the state's legislators.

The object of my oratory was different from Walton's. It was in the year that I entered McAlester High School that newspaper publishers began the nationwide competition that offered the winners a trip to Washington, an ocean crossing, and a summer in Europe. It was the only contest in America that afforded such opportunities. It surely was the only way that a country kid from Bug Tussle could hope to go. Our entry, Cecil Peters (Cecil placed second in the state contest), was my idol that year. By my sophomore year, the contest was my obsession.

I began that year a serious study of the Constitution of the United States. Knowing that a speaker could not express a thought he did not have, I read everything I could find on it in the McAlester library. I wrote and rewrote my speech a dozen times, always finding it difficult to purge its most ringing lines. I eventually shaped it to my satisfaction and won the McAlester High School contest.

Finally, the day came to catch that worst of trains, the one that took all day to run across 130 miles of rough track to Ardmore, site of the Third Congressional District contest. I thought enough of my speech that I offered to show it to a fellow passenger and competitor, Earl Hirschmidt from Wilburton, but he was so proud of his own that he would not let me see it. Some of his pride was deserved, for he won second place at Ardmore; a local boy took first. I rode the train back carrying my speech and wearing the bronze medal for third place. I wore the medal until my fellow students learned that there had been only three entries.

I knew it, though; and I was pretty blue when I got back home. I went to see Miss Munch. She told me not to be discouraged; she would not give up on me if I would not give up on myself. I could win that contest, but the only way to do it was to outwork every single student in the district, state, and region. She believed I could do that because she believed in me.

Years later—after I had won it and after I had gone to the House of Representatives—some of Perrill Munch's friends and former students gave her a testimonial dinner. I spoke there, saying that "this is the first time I have ever traveled halfway across a continent to attend a banquet. I would have gone halfway around the world if it had been necessary." Then I told about that trip to Ardmore so long ago. I told about my failure, about my talk with Miss Munch, about what she had said. I told them the truth: "It was that little talk that put me in Congress twenty years later. That expression of faith was one of the highlights of my life, not simply because it encouraged me to go on, but mainly because of the confidence it gave me in the dignity and the power and the importance of honest labor."

For the next eleven months, I gave that contest nearly every spare minute I had. I read everything I could find on the Constitution. I wrote my speech. I rewrote it. I threw it away. And I wrote it again. When I was finally satisfied, I started working on the delivery. I worked on the first sentence for more than a month. I said it over and over on my way to school, in my back yard, wherever I could. I worked on making it as direct and natural as possible. I saw my audience before me, and I worked on projecting my voice to that person standing at the back wall. I took parts in school plays to help me deliver the oration in an unaffected manner. One of the best speech teachers in the country kept her promise and stayed right with me.

When the time arrived for the district contest, I was ready. A young journalist named Tom Steed reported the event for a local newspaper. We later served together in Congress for twenty-eight years. Tom Steed always remembered when I was a little freckle-faced, redheaded kid in a borrowed, ill-fitting suit. Then I started talking, and I "damn near blasted the paint off the walls." What did it was the sentence that I had worked on for an entire month:

> In the year 1787 a group of earnest men, representatives of the American states, met in the city of Philadelphia to formulate a Constitution which would provide for a more perfect union of these states and guarantee the individual rights of men to themselves and their posterity.

This time, the train ride home was a triumph. I carried twenty-five dollars, and I wore the gold medal.

In April, I took the oration to two contests on the same day. At Norman in the morning, I entered it in the state interscholastic contest. An OU speech professor named Josh Lee was the judge. When he heard me speak, he wrote "100 percent" by my name and waited to see if any of the twenty-four other contestants would cause him to change it. None did. He gave me first place. My real interest, though, was that evening's finals of the state contest on the Constitution. After we finished, the results were read, starting with the lowest-ranking entry. All the names except mine had been read before the announcement, "Carl Albert of McAlester won first!" My response was odd for someone who had worked eleven months on one speech: I could not say a word.

I went to Kansas City for the regional finals with Mr. McPheron, the principal whose concern for my inferior preparation had put me in public speaking. The finest orators of five states were there. I was the last speaker. Only the one who spoke immediately before impressed me. He was Joseph Mullarky from a well-known private academy in Augusta, Georgia. When he finished, Mr. McPheron turned to me and said, "You have a real opponent there."

I surely did. The first four judges split their votes evenly. Two ranked me first with Mullarky second; the other two reversed the order. The fifth judge decided the contest by ranking another contestant first with Mullarky second and me third. The Georgian won first place and the coveted prizes by a single point. After all that work, I had finished one point short. But I had another year, and the confidence in hard work, to make it up.

I returned to McAlester and news that devastated my happiness. My mother was going to leave us. During my sophomore year, she had contracted tuberculosis, one of the most fearful and deadly diseases of the day. Her spells of suffering had worsened steadily during the previous two years. She had spent more and more time in bed, growing weak and worn. Papa had taken her to almost every doctor in the area, but none could help her. They finally told him that her best chance to survive was to go out west; it was the last, desperate hope for remedy. Just after I returned from Kansas City, she and some of the other kin took the younger children in an old Buick out to Albuquerque, New Mexico, to be under the care of a respected TB specialist. Papa and I took the train out to join them later that summer. The warm, dry climate and the physician's care seemed to be doing Mama a lot of good. Our arrival helped, too, for the family was together for the summer.

We lived in a tourist court, the forerunner of a modern motel. Mama talked with me, laughed with Papa, and played with the kids. She showed us off to her neighbors, a Mr. and Mrs. Bellknap. Mr. Bellknap was especially kind. He helped Mama look after things and got Budge and me jobs with a building contractor that he worked for.

When the summer ended, we had to get back to Oklahoma for school. My brother and I asked the contractor for our summer's wages. He put us off and kept putting us off. I told Mr. Bellknap, who promised to bring either our wages or the contractor back in a sack. He brought the money, and we left Mama in fine spirits under her doctor's and good neighbor's care.

Imagine my surprise when I received a letter from Mama about two weeks later. She wrote that the Bellknaps had left their tourist cabin late one night. They were in an Amarillo jail. They were not married, and their name was not Bellknap. She had heard that they were wanted somewhere for bank robbery. I soon found out where.

The next spring, the prison warden needed some free entertainment for the inmates. Miss Munch took a group of us speech students out to the penitentiary, where we put on a show for the convicts. I recited an Edgar Guest poem, "It Can Be Done." My performance was put quite deeply in the shade by our girl debaters, particularly those who upheld the affirmative on the proposition "Resolved: that capital punishment should be abolished." The girls made the most of their entirely captive audience.

While I sat on the platform enjoying the girls' success, I happened to look down to the very front row. I noticed a big, tall, bug-eyed prisoner. He gave me a smile and a wink that covered the entire side of his face. I suddenly realized who the inmate was: Mr. Bellknap from Albuquerque.

As we were breaking up, I yelled at him, "Are you Bellknap?

"Yeah," he answered. "Remember that old heifer I was keeping out there?"

I said that I did.

"She pulled the rug out from under me, and here I am." He walked off with the other convicts and I never saw him again.

Bellknap was a prisoner, a thief, and an adulterer, but he had been my friend. He got me a job. He got my wages and brought them to me. He looked after my sick mother and her helpless little children. I have seen church deacons who were not his equal.

Everyone's senior year was a time of recognition and achievement. Boys who had sat on the bench put on the black and gold uniforms of McAlester High and became local celebrities. Girls blossomed in musical performances. Students like Shirley Buell continued to compile impressive academic records. It was a year for us all to stand as giants.

I had changed a lot by then. I had not grown much taller—I stood five feet, two inches when I graduated—but I was not the same timid, insecure boy who had arrived from Bug Tussle three years earlier. I had come just short of winning a European tour, I was keeping my vow of academic achievement, and I had made lasting friends of nearly every student in the school. At the start of classes, they elected me president of the student body. I also was president of my homeroom and two school organizations, the Poetry Club and the Golden M Club. The latter was particularly rewarding.

The Golden M Club was Miss Munch's creation of the previous year. Because it required outstanding speech or dramatic performance for membership, it was a small but prestigious organization. Eleven of us were charter members. It was a remarkable group. With me, its original members went on to include a federal judge, a New York attorney, a successful surgeon, a law-school professor, an executive of the American Bankers Association, and three corporation executives. All of us later would point to our high school speech training as indispensable to our lives. The lesson that we each had learned there involved the highly competitive character of things worthwhile.

Our Class of 1927 was outstanding. We swept the interscholastic academic contest held at the teachers college in Durant, taking ten first-place medals in contests on fifteen subjects. I won three of the firsts: in government, physics, and declamation. Our debate teams crisscrossed the state and won the state championship on the topic "Resolved: that the United States should enter into an agreement for the cancellation of the interallied war debts." Taking the negative, my partner and I were undefeated. I wrote a new oration on the Constitution—one probably not as good as the previous year's—and won the district, state, and regional rounds of competition. A week before graduation, I went east, saw the U.S. Capitol, met President Coolidge, and spoke before justices of the Supreme Court. I did not win there, but being there was victory enough.

My grades in class improved. At the year's end, I was named class valedictorian. My four-year average was the highest of any student yet to graduate from the school. It was just a few hundredths of a point above Shirley Buell's.

Just before graduation, we all received our copies of the *Dancing Rabbit,* the McAlester High School yearbook. Beside my senior picture was a list of my activities and awards. There was no men-

SENIORS

Carl Albert

Valedictorian; Student Body Pres. '27;
Home Room President '27; Golden M
Club President '27; Poetry Club President '27; Debate '26, '27; Constitutional
Oration Contest '25, '26, '27; Original Oration Contest '26; Dramatic Reading Contest '26, '27; Declamation Contest '27;
Golden M Club '26, '27; Poetry Club '26,
'27; Romani Novi '25, '26; Dramatic Club
'25, '26, '27; Honor Society.
A little giant.

I only wish my mother could have seen it. Carl Albert's page in the
McAlester High School yearbook, 1927.

tion of my initial insecurities, but at the bottom was an epigram of which I was mighty proud: "A little giant." I only wish that my mother could have seen it.

Just before Christmas, we learned that Mama was worsening. We immediately caught the train to Albuquerque, where others of her relatives met us. Our presence seemed to give her new hope and new life, and we had a joyous Christmas. Her gift to us was her assurance that she was going to get well and live to raise her children. She faded almost immediately afterwards. The TB specialist gave us no hope. On the last day of 1926, her family gathered around Mama's bed. Little Earl, just barely five years old, could hardly see over the edge. Homer stood beside him, crying. Mama took my hand and said, "Son, take care of my little boys." She breathed deeply, shuddered, and she left us.

Papa went to the local undertaker and arranged to send her body back to Oklahoma for the funeral. He and Homer and Earl rode the train back with her. The rest of us set out in the old Buick for home across hundreds of miles of desolate, snow-covered plains. We traveled silently, lost in our sorrow, across the frozen roads until the car slid off into a ditch. We could not move it. As we sat there, the long train carrying my mother passed us, and we saw my father and brothers through the windows. Finally, another motorist arrived and tried to push us out. He could not. He said he had to leave and wished us luck. I explained the situation, that my mother had just died, that her train had passed us, that we had to get home for her funeral, and that the old car had no heater. I offered him twenty dollars, all we had, to get us out somehow. After several hours, he did. In all that time, not one other car had come by.

We left the snow behind in the Texas Panhandle and drove through mud across western Oklahoma. The next morning, we came through Seminole, then the center of Oklahoma's legendary oil boom. The streets of Seminole were part of that legend. Tons of oilfield equipment had turned the narrow pathways into either ruts or mud. On that day, they were mud, mud to our axles, as we inched our way toward McAlester and Mama's funeral.

When we finally pulled in, Papa had made the final arrangements. My mother had a country funeral, the only kind Papa had ever seen or would allow. Her friends and relatives stayed up all night with her body, which was kept in our house. The services were the next day, in the yard. Brother Alexander (he had baptized Mama in Coal Creek) preached the service. Her father, Grandpa Scott, was there and could have done a better job, had he been able to do it at all. Mama's many other relatives were there, too, along with her neighbors from Bug Tussle and most of my schoolmates at McAlester. We buried her in the first of our family plots in the local cemetery. She was forty years old.

The next summer took me away from my grief. Miss Munch may have been right. I must have outworked every other student around. I was going to Europe as a champion orator.

Even the train ride to New York was an adventure. Some of my fellow passengers were from Oklahoma and recognized me from the pictures in the *Daily Oklahoman*. One man recalled reading that my father was a coal miner and cotton farmer. He was determined to take me out of my dismal background. The one way to do that, he was sure, was to get me an appointment to West Point. He wanted to call his senator (Senator Thomas) about it right away. He was absolutely sure that a boy of my record and ability could rise to be a general. As such, he predicted, I would meet "presidents, senators, cabinet officers, and big-city bankers." I thanked him for his concern but explained that I had my own plans.

Another passenger who recognized me was Lorraine Gensman, wife of a former Oklahoma congressman, L. M. Gensman. Old enough to be my grandmother, she decided to take me under her wing. She knew New York City as well as she did Lawton, Oklahoma, her hometown. After we reached New York, she took me down to Coney Island. I must have ridden every ride there, and there were a lot more than there were at the Pittsburg County Fair. Coney Island was also where, for the first time, I heard the ocean's roar.

The next day, I was on that ocean. I boarded the largest pas-

The reward for my faith, the realization of things hoped for, the substance of things finally seen. Carl Albert, in the back row on the left, in Cannes, France, in 1927, touring Europe as a champion orator.

senger ship of the time, the *Leviathan*. I had never seen anything so spectacular or so beautiful. It had been built by the Germans before World War I and seized by the United States during the war. It was one of the most luxurious vessels crossing the Atlantic during the Roaring Twenties. Only Lindbergh had made the trip by air yet, but each summer the *Leviathan* carried thousands of Americans to European vacations. Surely, none had one more spectacular than mine.

I do not know how many times the adults with us claimed that I was going to run out of superlatives before I reached our next stop. They all remarked on the joy that I never thought to conceal.

I suspected that I was amusing some of them, but the boy seeing these things had never before seen two hundred dollars in one place in his life. My father crawled miles under the earth to dig us a living from black rock, or he chopped it out of a cotton patch. But I had found a way to do what I had wanted to do. I had found the reward for my faith, the realization of things hoped for, the substance of things finally seen.

In England, I marveled at Big Ben, the sturdy watchman over the world's oldest deliberative body, the British Parliament. I visited the House of Commons, where I heard David Lloyd George, Winston Churchill, and Ramsay MacDonald. I saw *Hamlet* performed in Stratford-on-Avon, William Shakespeare's birthplace. I visited the Poets' Corner of Westminster Abbey and saw the tombs of some of the greatest figures in the history of the English-speaking people. I saw the spires at Oxford. I remembered that one of my teachers back at McAlester had told us about Cecil Rhodes, that he had left money to send some of America's best college men (women were not then eligible) to study at Oxford as something called Rhodes scholars. I decided then and there that that would be my next goal. I guess I was not the only one. Three of the six male finalists in the 1927 high school contest—Max Lancaster, Jim Tunnel, and myself—did become Rhodes scholars.

In France, I saw the world's most beautiful city: Paris. I stood beneath the Arc de Triomphe, where General Pershing supposedly had saluted and declared, "*Lafayette, nous sommes ici.*" I saw, too, living reminders of the horror of war. At the edge of a French battlefield, there was a young man selling cheap mementos. Along the whole right side of his face and across both eyes, nothing showed but silver. His face literally had been shot off at Verdun. I saw, too, Versailles, where Woodrow Wilson's dreams of a world of order backed by American might had crumbled.

Across the Pyrenees into the Spanish Basque country, down the Mediterranean coast along the Riviera, through Florence and Venice into Rome, I saw the art and architecture of our civilization. In Rome, our group met privately with the Pope. Alone, I walked all over the Colosseum, sat in its seats, hugged its stones, lay on its floor. I walked alone over the Appian Way, a boy from Bug Tussle feeling the same ground beneath his feet that Caesar's legions had felt.

From Rome, we went to Geneva before returning to Paris. We sailed from Cherbourg on the SS *United States*. I had to get to Norman, Oklahoma, to start college.

When I went to the University of Oklahoma in the fall of 1927, the school was rather new, somewhat small, and hardly prestigious. Norman promoters had wanted the capitol but had accepted the university from the 1890 legislature. Four to five thousand students attended its classes, mostly in a few buildings clustered around an oval north of the library. The university had few nationally recognized scholars. That year's football team placed sixth in the conference but did hold Central State Normal School to a 14-14 tie.

For me, however, it was the perfect place. My mother's sister lived in Norman, and I could hold down my living expenses by staying with Aunt Myrtle. The tuition was reasonable. There was no government aid available to college students, no matter how deserving or how needy, but Mr. McPheron believed that he could help me get a student job with the school. He did. With his introduction, I landed a job in the registrar's office. It paid the going wage for college students: thirty cents an hour. It was not much, but it would have been a whole lot had I not gotten it.

My father had little enough that he could give me. The day after I had returned home from Europe, I packed my things and got ready to leave. Papa came into the room. He handed me a twenty-dollar bill. I knew how much he needed it, but I knew that he needed even more to give it to me. It was the last money I ever got from home in my life. I hitchhiked from McAlester to Oklahoma City, where I spent my first fifty cents on college. That was the fare for riding the interurban down to Norman and the University of Oklahoma.

I walked on campus knowing what I wanted to take from there; I would work for the highest possible grades. There was a

I walked on the campus knowing what I wanted to take from there. Carl Albert enrolling at the University of Oklahoma, 1927.

collegiate-level contest for oratory on the U.S. Constitution, and I would compete in it. I wanted the grand prize: the Rhodes scholarship. I knew I had the desire, I had the drive, I had the self-discipline, and I had the will to work. And I knew by then that such goals, the deliberate work toward them, and their realization—all of these were what made me Carl Albert.

I also decided that Carl Albert would enjoy life in the process.

My most important class in my first semester was a step toward each of those purposes. Josh Lee was the head of the speech department, author of an excellent text, and a speaker of considerable renown himself, good enough to talk his way into a House seat in 1934 and into the Senate two years later. He was also the judge who had received my high school oration so favorably. He insisted that I take his advanced class in oratory, and he promised that he would work with me for the intercollegiate contest on the Constitution.

Throughout the school year, I polished my oratory by entering two campus contests. I won both and picked up some two hundred dollars in prize money. The money gave me some breathing room. I was living on a close budget of thirty dollars a month. Every male student had to enroll in Reserve Officers' Training Corps during his first two years, so I cut costs by wearing my ROTC uniform to class when my one suit was at the cleaners.

At my freshman year's end, I became one of seven finalists in the intercollegiate oratorical contest. We met in Los Angeles because of the sponsorship by the Better America Federation of California, a group that included publisher Harry Chandler. Chandler's *Los Angeles Times* gave the contest and the finalists steady publicity. As I looked over the *Times*'s issue for the day of the finals, it seemed that the writers sensed the intensity of the competition that I faced. Amid outstanding scholars from America's greatest schools, I was listed last, the only student from a state college and the only freshman to reach the finals. Because I lacked the others' achievements, they identified me as "the son of a coal miner and proud of it."

I was a freshman from an unhonored college, but I beat the best there was. The next day's *Los Angeles Times* could not resist the drama of my victory, nor could it resist the impulse to exaggerate it into even more of a Horatio Alger tale. According to the news account, I had begun my forensic career "while attending classes, more or less iregularly, in a ramshackle two-room schoolhouse." One of the things that the story got exactly right was my reward: a check for fifteen hundred dollars. It was enough to finance my remaining college education.

That turned out to be only the start of the publicity. Harry Chandler's *Los Angeles Times* kept stories running daily, reporting my appearances before area civic groups. Nearly thirty years later I came to appreciate just how extensive that publicity had been; it was in 1947 on my first day as a new congressman from Oklahoma. Another freshman member came up to me and asked if I was the same Carl Albert who had won the college oratorical contest back in 1928. He remembered reading about it in the papers. He added that he later had entered the same contest, too, but he had been eliminated early. His name was Richard Nixon.

With the appearances came additional money and rewards. I spoke before several clubs and groups for a few weeks, usually picking up a hundred dollars or so as an honorarium. Harry Chandler himself presented me to the sponsoring Better America Foundation. After hearing my speech, he and some other Los Angeles businessmen offered to get me into Stanford and pay all of my expenses through college and law school. I thanked them but told them that I wanted to go back to Oklahoma. My home was there. I wanted to go to Congress, and I figured that Oklahoma was the place I could best represent. Besides, I was and always wanted to be an Oklahoman.

My appearance before the Elks Club did pay a big dividend. A group of Elks was sailing to Honolulu for a few weeks' vacation and invited me to join them. I jumped at the chance. We sailed, the jet-setters of that day and I, out of Los Angeles on *The City of Honolulu.* When I reached Hawaii's capital, I came to appreciate just how important the Elks were there. The Elks Club of Honolulu owned one of only two large buildings that sat at the water's

I never felt myself such a big shot before or since. In Hawaii, 1928.

edge on Waikiki Beach; the other was the newly opened Royal Hawaiian Hotel. The Elks put me there in an elegant ground-floor suite. The mayor made me an official guest and furnished me with a Cadillac limousine and full-time chauffeur. I never felt myself such a big shot before or since.

With a cute native girl that I had met on the ship, I saw every sight Hawaii had to offer. My Elks friends also arranged for me to give my oration before several civic groups. One audience included the president of the Dole Pineapple Company, Hawaii's corporate colossus. My speech so impressed him that he offered me two thousand dollars if I would give it four more times over the next few weeks. I took the offer and the money and stayed over. Upon my return to the mainland by way of San Francisco, one of the Los Angeles Elks called me. He had three more speeches and three more honoraria awaiting me. I took the train, made my speeches, drew down my bank deposits, and bought a railroad ticket back home.

The oratory contest and everything that came from it lasted almost the entire summer. The money I earned, well over four thousand dollars, lasted for the rest of my college years. The memories of that time will last forever.

At OU, my speech activities gave me my first introduction to campus life. Because of press reports, I may have entered the university as the best-known freshman on campus. It certainly did not take long before I was asked to join just about every club there.

In my first semester, some older students from McAlester invited me over for dinner with their fraternity, Kappa Alpha. Only a year old, the house at the corner of College and Cruce was impressive with its Georgian-Southern architecture. In fact, I found everything about the chapter impressive. I pledged Kappa Alpha, thereby making friends who would stand with me for decades.

My grades were good. Most of my early classes were introductory required subjects, and except for Spanish, which I began my first semester, few were intrinsically exciting. Nonetheless, I kept up the study habits that I had developed back at Bug Tussle with the same reward. I finished my first semester as one of only two freshmen to earn all A's.

That record qualified me for membership in the freshman academic honorary society, Phi Eta Sigma. William B. Bizzell was OU's president at the time, and Phi Eta Sigma was one of his principal interests. After I spoke at the society's initiation ceremonies, Dr. Bizzell became a close friend. In time, he had me accompany him on speaking and fund-raising tours, where he introduced me to some of Oklahoma's most prominent and powerful citizens. One was Lloyd Noble, a millionaire oilman from Ardmore. Another was Lew Wentz, a similarly situated Ponca Citian and for decades the state's No. 1 Republican. Despite Mr. Wentz's party beliefs, both became my lifelong friends and supporters, politics included.

My speaking also introduced me to less-prominent men, one of whom was Daredevil Dick Mormon. Daredevil Dick had thought up a great promotion for selling cars. He would chain himself to a steering wheel and drive continuously, without stop and without rest, for a week. He talked some Chevrolet dealers in Oklahoma City into sponsoring him. Still, he needed a speaker to drum up a crowd as he passed by the Chevy agencies. That was my part.

For that week, I spoke at Chevrolet dealerships. Daredevil Dick would come by, chained to the wheel but beaming as I embellished his steadily lengthening exploits. I was speaking when he finished the ordeal. As he pulled into a Chevrolet agency, he collapsed. His chains were removed, and Daredevil Dick was carried, asleep, to a bed in the dealer's show window. He lay sleeping in public view for twenty hours.

Easily the most interesting figure that I met through my speech activities was Thomas Pryor Gore. A Populist during his youth in Texas, Gore had moved to Oklahoma during territorial days. At statehood he was elected, along with Robert L. Owen, as one of Oklahoma's original United States senators. By this time a Democrat, Senator Gore kept something of his Populist past alive. Washington knew him as a fierce foe of trusts, of bankers, and of warlords. It was the last quality that seemed to have ended his career. Gore had resisted stoutly Woodrow Wilson's preparedness measures before our 1917 declaration of war. Once it came, he remained a steadfast critic. What many voters saw as his lack of patriotism cost him his Senate seat in 1920.

Ten years later, the old senator was poised for a comeback. By many his opposition to the war was forgotten; by others it now was applauded. The onset of the Great Depression, nowhere more disastrous than in Oklahoma, transformed this champion of the common people into a prophet. But this one cried in no wilderness; rather, crowds gathered whenever and wherever he campaigned to reclaim a Senate seat.

I had heard him speak before, and I had been awed. In fact, I still consider Thomas Gore the finest American political speaker that I have ever heard. In 1930, he had lost none of his eloquence. However, he did need someone to introduce him at his campaign talks. Since I was just a college student, I bore no political scars, and my appearance would antagonize no local faction. He asked me to speak briefly, introducing him at his rallies. Besides, he needed someone to drive for him. Since childhood, Senator Gore had been blind.

Through the long, hot summer of 1930, I drove the old senator over the roads of Oklahoma to crowds of dispossessed farmers, frightened merchants, and unemployed oil-field workers. My remarks were brief; the old senator's were masterpieces of political oratory. One thing that made them masterpieces was Gore's never-failing wit. He was an expert humorist, one capable of moving the most desperate crowds to laughter, but he used his humor well. He never felt compelled to start a speech with a wisecrack. Rather, he wove his wit into the warp and weft of his addresses.

He also was capable of the perfect spontaneous quip. I remember his campaign back home in McAlester that summer. Gore was to speak from a platform set up on one end of Choctaw Avenue. As the crowd was gathering, the assistant county attorney started speaking from the street's other end. His name was Bob Bell, and he was managing the campaign of Gore's Democratic primary opponent. Bob Bell was a feisty little man, an able speaker himself, though when excited he spoke in a high-pitched voice. On this occasion, his voice got higher and higher as he proceeded to give the old senator quite a bit of Pittsburg County hell.

When Gore got ready to speak, several of us offered to get Bob Bell to stop. But Gore waited for him to finish. Bell finally ran down, and Senator Gore stepped on the platform. He always looked upward, his eyes almost pure white, as he spoke. He did this time as he slowly said: "I seldom refer to my affliction. I cannot see. But it seems that somewhere in the far, far distance I hear the tingling and the jingling of a tiny little Bell." Bob Bell told that story on himself for years. Even he got a laugh out of it. "Boy, he set me down," he would say.

Thomas Gore had a way of setting just about anybody down. The story was already told—and is still told in the Senate—of Senator Gore's dressing down another senator. One of his target's friends rose to say that the senator from Oklahoma was taking advantage of his colleague. If the senator from Oklahoma could see, the other senator would not take it. Gore roared back, "Well, blindfold the senator and send him this way."

The old senator's wit was always devastating and always on the mark. But he was no mere crowd pleaser. His eloquence approached the poetic on issues about which he cared deeply. One involved my old high school debate topic: Should America cancel the war debt owed us by Britain and France? Gore had not changed. He was against canceling the debt. He believed that we had given enough to the British and the French when we gave them our boys. His sightless eyes looked toward heaven as he spontaneously uttered the words that I recall more than a half-century later:

> I see the soldier
> Over there
> Who will never again,
> Even in death,
> Feel the warm soil of Oklahoma.
>
> There he lies,
> With no sentinel

Save the distant star,
With no mourner
But the winds of night.

And I sometimes wonder
If the moaning winds
That play among the tuft above his grave
Do not disturb the slumber of those
For whom he died to save.

He was the best. He was also the winner, in both the primary and the general elections.

In my years at the University of Oklahoma, I developed friendships that have lasted throughout my life. The university remained relatively small and thoroughly friendly. *Howdy* was the byword on campus. One heard it dozens of times while going to classes, attending student meetings, or just hanging out.

Many of the students that I met there would be active in politics in my early career. Aubrey and Bill Kerr, whom I first encountered as leaders of a rival student political party, I would see again as allies in Oklahoma's "real" political party. They became and long remained major figures in the Democratic party, their voices magnified by that of their older brother, a young graduate of the teachers college at Ada. He was Robert S. Kerr, Oklahoma's wartime governor and subsequently the fabled uncrowned king of the United States Senate. Just a year or so ahead of me were several men whom I met as a student and would often see again. One was Luther Bohanon, a leader of the bar and Senator Kerr's choice for the federal judgeship in Oklahoma City. Mike Monroney was another. Mike served four years with me in the House before moving to the Senate for three terms. Such friendships have been among the things that have caused me never to regret turning down Harry Chandler's offer of a free Stanford education.

For all of Stanford's exalted reputation, I doubt that I would have encountered better students—or stiffer academic competition—than I met at OU. I know that I never, anywhere, saw any student the equal of Dean Woolridge. Dean was an OU legend, and properly so. He had entered the university at age fifteen, and he became the first of its graduates to finish with a perfect four-point grade average.

I remember that Dean and I shared nine and eleven o'clock classes. During the hour's break, we always headed for the student union, where we played pool. We would put our French texts on the window ledge and study our lessons during the games. At eleven, we would head for French class. I averaged about 97 percent for the course; Dean Woolridge averaged a perfect 100. At semester's end, the teacher said she did not know which made her angrier: was it Dean for never making a single error in vocabulary, grammar, spelling, or punctuation, or herself for being unable to think of anything that he did not know in French? We chose not to increase her frustration with the knowledge that he had learned his French in a pool hall between shots.

Maybe not as efficiently as Dean, I also managed to find time for play among my studies. I took up the college man's game, bridge, and became a pretty good player in nightly games over at the Varsity Shop, our local hangout. I never could beat Paul Hodge, who took his before-dinner games with deadly passion. Paul's eventual reward was twice to represent the United States in world championship matches. I became a decent chess player and one of OU's very best checker players. I took my reward while campaigning over cracker barrels in the country stores of rural southeastern Oklahoma.

We also had our student celebrities. One, George Milburn, had a national reputation, even as a student. George wrote books, people bought them, and he made money out of them. George Milburn was one of OU's most talented students—and one of its nastiest.

I discovered both qualities when he gave me a copy of one of his books. It was a collection of stories, some poignant, many hilarious, loosely based upon George's experiences in a little town near Tulsa. One of the best was about the town's big shot, a merchant who installed its first indoor toilet. The local folks thought it terribly unsanitary to have human waste right in his house, but he went ahead and put it in and covered his old outdoor pit with boards. Thinking he heard a prowler, the fellow went outside one night and crashed through the boards, into the pit. He began screaming, "Fire! Fire! Fire!" Rescuers finally came and pulled him out. When they found no fire, they asked him why he had shouted "Fire!" He answered, "Because you sons of bitches wouldn't have come if I yelled 'Shit! Shit! Shit!'"

I read the book the day he gave it to me. The next day, George called up and accused me of stealing his book. He yelled that I was a kleptomaniac, that a thief was the lowest creature that crawled the earth, and that a book thief was the lowest form of that species. He threatened me with violence and a lawyer. I yelled back, but I agreed to return the book. When he received it, he called me again. He said I could have the book back if I wanted it. Then he started raving at me again! I hung up just after I screamed back: "Fire! Fire! Fire!"

For organized fun, there was the university's principal pep club, the Ruf Neks. Members shared the privilege of running onto the football field armed with white paddles to complement their bright red shirts. My brief membership was more organized than fun. The Ruf Neks' hazing reputation was unbelievable; the reality was far worse than the reputation.

On initiation night, we pledges were ordered to take a truckload of barrel staves down to a spot on the Canadian River. We knew what that meant: paddles were not merely members' trademarks but gruesome reminders of initiation. To prepare ourselves, several of us sewed big stakes into our shorts. They were little help. During the hazing, I thought once or twice that I was being beaten to death.

I awoke the next morning, crawled out of bed, and limped to class. I expected at least to share our rewards with my fellow sufferers. I reached campus only to discover that we were members of a nonexistent group; sometime after midnight, the university's disciplinary authorities had abolished the club. The cause was our initiation. So I did not run out onto the football field and carry a white paddle to match my red shirt, not until the club was reorganized and invited the old members back. By then, I was a member of Congress.

Far better disciplined was a student group that I came to enjoy: the Reserve Officers' Training Corps. After the required two years' military training, I signed up for the advanced program in my junior year. I had gone to Fort Sill with my brother for a National Guard camp the previous summer and genuinely enjoyed it. Besides, advanced ROTC paid a little money: about thirty cents a day plus six weeks' summer-camp pay. Plus, I got to keep my uniform to wear to class.

Our summer training was also at Fort Sill. We trained with other college units, but we were the most fortunate tenants. Most of the others were infantry units, but the OU corps was in field artillery, and the Lawton military post was one of the world's foremost artillery training grounds. Our equipment was the army's best, though it was of World War I vintage. We used French 75 artillery pieces and wooden caissons, all horse drawn.

Daily, we harnessed our horses, hitched them to the caissons, and drove our big guns out to the firing ranges. We took our training seriously and competed fiercely to bracket our salvos before zeroing in on the exact targets. It was good that we did so, for our officers from the university accompanied us. There to greet us were the old-time Regular Army sergeants. They took everything military seriously. By summer's end, we could have performed creditably on the battlefield. Thus, my decision to take advanced ROTC was a good one.

An even better one arose literally from luck. Paul Hodge came by on one semester's last day. This time he had found a better game than bridge: a big poker game drawing upon the players' last college money. Except for my savings, my last was fifty dollars. I decided that I could lose that and still hitchhike home. By 2:00 A.M., I was down to my last ten. I borrowed twenty-five from a friend and stayed in the game. In the next hand, I drew four queens, paid the money back, and kept going. When the game broke up at four o'clock, I counted my pile: $255. With my bag already packed, I went over to the intersection of U.S. 77 and Main Street, the favored spot for college hitchhikers. I decided to take the first ride I got to anywhere it went.

It went to San Antonio, Texas, and I decided to keep on heading south. I hitched a ride to Laredo, got a permit, and crossed the Rio Grande. For eight dollars, I bought a third-class railroad ticket to Mexico City.

I had been interested in Mexico since my high school trip to Europe. Accompanying us was Arturo García Formentí. He had won a similar contest on Mexico's government and would compete in Europe against other national champions. Arturo became my closest companion in Europe, though neither of us knew more than a few words in the other's tongue. At OU, I had taken two years of Spanish, no doubt because of Arturo's influence. Now I would try it out on the natives.

I was lucky to catch Arturo just before he left the capital for a month's speaking tour on behalf of the president. He found me a rooming house for the *muy pobre* (very poor). It was economical, though not poor. For ten dollars a week, I got a small but attractive room and two meals a day. I probably never had a better bargain in my life. The regular paying guests were all intelligent, and several were well educated. One was a distinguished Castilian Spaniard from Madrid, a true member of the gentry. Another was a Russian émigré who longed for the czar's return. The natives included an educated and cultured civil servant with a keen interest in Mexican history and the guitar, which he played as he sang lovely Mexican ballads. Another made a prosperous business of cutting old automobile tires into strips, punching holes and running straps through them, and selling the product as shoes. Many wore them in the Mexico City of 1929. Most native of all was a very dark, full-blooded Aztec. Tall, straight, and proud, he could have descended from Montezuma.

Our times in the rooming house were a continuous classroom for me. We lingered for hours over the dinner table, discussing politics, art, literature—everything Mexican. My fellow boarders seemed to be pleased, maybe even surprised, at my interest in and love for things Mexican. Gringos were hardly known for their appreciation for the country, but sometimes it would be the natives who had to curb my obvious enthusiasm.

I remember one evening in which I was declaring my affection for their country when the civil servant stopped me. "But, Señor Albert," he said, "we don't complete many things. We start them, but we do not finish them." He told me of taking a visiting Spaniard to the opera house. The Spaniard noted that the building was not finished. They heard an opera. The visitor's judgment was that it was fine, but it was not finished. Later, they went to a speech by Mexico's dynamic one-armed president, Alvaro Obregon. My friend enthused, "Wasn't he great?" The Spaniard answered, "Yes, but he is not finished."

During most days and many nights, I tried to follow the counsel of my OU Spanish professor: "Learn your Spanish from a walking dictionary with a dress on. That is the best kind."

I visited Mexico City's theaters, operas, and cabarets with several dictionaries. With others, I visited the shrine to the heroic Mexican cadets who had stood and died at Chapultepec against Winfield Scott's army. With an attractive student from the University of Mexico, I explored one of the world's most beautiful campuses and one of its largest cathedrals. Alone, I crawled all over the enchanting ruins of San Juan Teotihuacan, just as I had those of Rome. This time, however, my enthrallment cost me: our rickety tourist bus left during my private explorations. Stranded, I spent the night in a hut of some local *peóns*. My fellow boarders in the adjoining room were a loud and smelly group of pigs.

My summer in Mexico may have lacked the glamour and the prestige of my European summer two years earlier, but altogether it was just as thrilling and just as important. My skill in and appreciation for the Spanish language grew immensely and has remained a lifelong affection. As a student, as a congressman, and as a citizen, I have always believed that there are no better people on God's earth than our own neighbors. If the people of this country only could see them as equals and treat them as our friends, both countries—but especially the United States—would be better off.

I believe that it was a wiser person that left Mexico City with a third-class ticket to Laredo. I know that it was a happy and tired one that hitchhiked back to Oklahoma to finish college.

At the university, my academic interests depended somewhat on the professors' abilities. I suppose that is always so; I know that it had been the case with me since my days in the schoolhouse at Bug Tussle. At OU, I had several outstanding professors, among the best I would ever know.

Quite by accident I first met the professor who would serve as my teacher, my mentor, and my friend. In my sophomore year, some of us were preparing for a debate on democratic institutions. I went by to talk with OU's principal authority on political theory, Cortez A. M. Ewing. I had that day a long session with the greatest teacher I yet had met, a man at once knowledgeable, articulate, and warm. I decided then to make his office my intellectual headquarters as long as I was at OU. I followed his counsel in working out my remaining academic curriculum: a government major with a strong history minor.

I started in Dr. Ewing's own classes almost immediately. They were always filled with the university's very best students, for each one seemed to be a model class. My first, ancient political theory, opened up the ancient world to me. Professor Ewing traced the origins of politics, permanently impressing me with the centrality of ethics in politics and government. The same theme reappeared in his subsequent courses on comparative political theory, modern European political theory, and American political theory. More than a half-century later, I still can think of no better preparation for a career in public service.

With other students, I would often visit Dr. Ewing's home in the evenings. He and Mrs. Ewing were delightful hosts. Most of the entertainment was the spontaneous exchange of reasoned and informed opinion on issues of the day, and it was a day of weighty issues. Russians were still talking of global revolution, Italians bowed beneath Mussolini's fascist dagger, Germans were discussing an odd book titled *Mein Kampf*. In America, the spasms of depression were shaking loose Republican control of government and awakening a somnolent nation. Those were heady days, made more momentous by Professor Ewing's incisive observations. He and his wife seemed genuinely to enjoy my frequent visits. Mrs. Ewing probably explained their pleasure much later when she commented upon the tenacity of my student days. "You had to be tenacious," she added, "when you had nothing but a dream to go on."

Professor Ewing helped that dream along immeasurably. With his encouragement, I applied for the coveted Rhodes scholarship during my junior year. The odds against me were long; had I won, I would have gone to Oxford without an undergraduate degree. Nonetheless, I was runner-up in the state finals to select Oklahoma's recipient. Just as I had after placing second in the high school speech contest, I vowed to redouble my efforts and go all the way the next year.

My senior year was rich with honors. It began with my selection as president of the men's council. Later, there followed election as most popular student, a Phi Beta Kappa key, and the Dads' Day Cup as outstanding male student. The year ended with the competition for a Rhodes scholarship. Five hundred thirty-nine of the very best American students competed for the world's most prestigious academic prize. Mine was one of thirty-three awarded.

Winning a Rhodes scholarship was a big part of what Mrs. Ewing had sensed as the dream that I went on. It was a dream born in a cotton patch, nurtured in a country schoolhouse and a special high school, fed by some exceptional men and women. The prize was mine, but the goals that I had set and the achievement of them—for these I was indebted to very many.

The scholarship could not have come at a better time. The Great Depression was fully upon us in 1931. Cotton prices had collapsed. Mines had closed. My fellow graduates often had little hope for a job. Hungry men were rioting in Oklahoma City. Tens of thousands of my fellow citizens were fleeing to California. John Steinbeck and others would call them Okies. I called some of them my friends and neighbors. Cecil Rhodes's trust granted me a different fate: three years of Oxford University schooling and an

. . . The Dads' Day cup as outstanding male student. Velma Jones and Carl Albert, the outstanding female student and the outstanding male student in 1931 at the University of Oklahoma.

annual stipend of four hundred pounds, or roughly two thousand dollars.

My first money would come only when I arrived in Oxford. Knowing that I did not have the money to get there, Lew Wentz, Oklahoma's richest man and chief Republican, lent me five hundred dollars. I got my steamship ticket from an Italian agent in McAlester. I hitchhiked to Saint Louis, where I took a bus to New York City and boarded an Atlantic liner sailing for Southampton. This Okie was going to Oxford.

CHAPTER THREE

Up to Oxford, Down to Oklahoma

I came from a community founded on Indian lands. I carried a degree from a university younger than my parents. I represented a state not even a year older than myself. I was bound for Oxford, England.

Life there was different. The city of Oxford had eighty thousand residents, making it the largest place in which I yet had lived. Lying at the confluence of the Cherwell and the Isis rivers, it surely was the oldest. The Romans knew the place as Oxonia. The earliest bridges across the rivers were built by its first Norman ruler. It was nothing to walk along streets and see buildings that were thriving with commerce when Christopher Columbus pointed his ships westward across the Atlantic. Some of the merchants in those buildings were investors in John Smith's enterprise, the Virginia Company of London.

Oxford's university, chartered in 1571, was the oldest and most prestigious in the English-speaking world. Its origins dissolve into medieval mists, but three of its colleges (University, Balliol, and Merton) date to the thirteenth century. Its earliest scholars included men like Roger Bacon, John Duns Scotus, John Wycliffe, Erasmus, and Sir Thomas More. Richard Hakluyt, whose writings sparked England's earliest interest in colonizing America, had been a geographer there. One of his students, Sir Walter Raleigh, led the first body of English settlers to the New World. Centuries later, another Oxford man, Cecil Rhodes, took Britain's flag across another continent. At his death, the six million pounds that he took out of Africa provided the scholarships that brought talented colonials back to Oxford. What they found there was a system of higher education unequaled in the world and unlike any in the United States. It did not take long to see just how different it was.

Even the language was different. To begin, the English sharply distinguish between a college and a university. A college is a place of residence and of higher learning. Though largely self-governing, their colleges have no authority to hold examinations or award degrees; only universities have those rights. Thus, one could be a student at any of Oxford's twenty-seven colleges of the time, but his examinations and degree came not from his college but from the university. These exclusive privileges of the universities were guarded jealously. In fact, for more than 250 years, Oxford and Cambridge (chartered in 1573) had granted the only degrees in all of England.

Even after that monopoly was broken, the two retained their towering influence and prestige. Theirs were ancient traditions, sizable endowments, honored presses, and massive stocks of books, for by law their libraries received copies of every book printed in England. They also maintained their status as the aristocracy's preferred path into political, ecclesiastical, or academic power. The relative democracy of American higher education was still somewhat foreign to Oxford. The international competition for the Rhodes scholarships likely was its most democratic single feature. It certainly was the only way that a boy from Bug Tussle, Oklahoma, could have gotten there with England's elite.

The language differences carried over into one's studies. I learned that one does not enter Oxford; rather, one comes up to Oxford and thereby becomes an Oxonian. Upon graduation, one does not leave; the Oxonian goes down. In between, one does not study a subject, one reads. Thus, I came up in 1931, read law for three years, and went down in 1934.

Though I was a graduate of the University of Oklahoma, I was called an undergraduate at Oxford. For most Oxonians, the first degree is the bachelor of arts. In law, the B.A. in jurisprudence was awarded after two years. After my third year, I earned Oxford's graduate degree in law, the bachelor of civil law.

One thing that I learned quickly was that each of Oxford's colleges holds over its students a disciplinary authority unknown to American schools. Parliament had made them courts unto themselves, having jurisdiction that the civil courts could not overrule. My college, St. Peter's, was Oxford's newest. Founded only two years before my arrival, its disciplinary code was fashionably light. Other colleges, though, had rules so hoary and so strict that their walls reminded me of the McAlester penitentiary's.

Disciplinary authority beyond the college's walls was the university's. Included in that was the demand that undergraduates wear half-gowns extending to the waist. So clad and identifiable, they could not drink in the city's pubs, sit in the front sections of its cinemas, or date girls from the town.

Enforcing these rules were the university's proctors. Attired in full cap and gown, they roamed the streets, eager to pounce upon the errant undergraduate. Finding one, they would approach him, tip their caps, and say, "Sir, are you a member of the university?" The offender was in a situation similar to that of an automobile driver caught speeding in a small Amish community of Pennsylvania. His misdeed suddenly loomed disproportionately large before him. I was told that it was not a pleasant experience, but I cannot offer personal testimony. My own minor infractions always eluded the proctors.

We lived in housing provided by the separate colleges. Mine was quite modern and impressive. At OU's Kappa Alpha house, two of us had shared a single room. At St. Peter's, each student's quarters consisted of two rooms: a living or study room and a bedroom. Both were well furnished.

Twelve of us students had rooms on a single stairway. Each stairway had its own maid and its own scout. The latter was a high-class servant, a combination valet and army sergeant whose mission was to look after the new recruits. Our scout was a distinguished gentleman whom we knew only as Hamilton. He began my every day from the first with a loud knock at the door. With the broadest *a* in the English language, he would shout, "Five and twenty past eight, sir." At its sound, I always jumped from bed, threw on my trousers, shirt, jacket, and half-gown and hurried over to the chapel. In my college, morning services were the required opening of our every day.

After our classes, we usually gathered in one of our quarters for an afternoon tea. This was an English tradition that I learned to love. The drink itself was secondary. What was important was the pleasant conversation, sometimes fun, sometimes serious, always with some of the brightest young men in the Western world.

I still remember my very first Oxford tea. I had taken the railroad from London through fifty-seven miles of English countryside to Oxford. A taxi brought me to St. Peter's gate, where I met my first fellow Oxford student, an Englishman named George Done. He introduced me to some of his friends, including another American Rhodes scholar, Gordon Siefkin. Some British students met us for tea in Siefkin's quarters. One of them asked where I was from.

"Oklahoma," I answered.

"Oklahoma? Oklahoma?" he puzzled in a perfect Oxford accent. "Is that near Hollywood, or would it be up Chicago way?"

I realized how far I was from Oklahoma, and that it was very different, indeed.

Compared with that offered in most American law schools, an Oxford legal education was a true education, not a form of vocational training. Oxford stressed the institutional basis of the law's growth, not the practical skills of a lawyer's daily work. Of course, a student grappled with knotty problems of contracts and torts, but even more important were the principles of jurisprudence that he followed back to their Roman and oldest English origins.

The instructional method was no less different from the American style. Each Oxford scholar is assigned a single tutor, a don, who guides the student to his degree. When I went there, St. Peter's was still too new and small to have its own law don. For that reason, the college assigned me to work with C. H. S. Fifoot of Hertford College.

When I got Fifoot, I got the finest law tutor in the entire university. He had graduated with distinction from Oxford, where he had read law under G. C. Cheshire, one of Britain's great legal scholars. It was Fifoot's generation that fought the World War, and he had been badly wounded in France. Afterwards, he remained self-conscious of the scars along his neck and lower face. But he was a witty conversationalist, a warm and gentle man, a first-rate scholar. His lectures were among the university's most popular, his scholarly treatises among its most esteemed. Of all the great teachers that I ever had, none topped C. H. S. Fifoot for a depth of knowledge matched with an ability to teach it.

Normally, we had one tutorial session a week. Each usually lasted an hour. To prepare for the tutorial, Mr. Fifoot would give me a reading assignment from standard texts and leading court decisions. He also gave me a specific question to research.

The first course that I read with my tutor was torts. On the day I first met him, he assigned me the text for the course, showed me the law library, and introduced me to the most pertinent cases. He then gave me the topic for our first tutorial session: "How far is a master liable for the torts of his servant?"

A week later, I returned with a ten-page, handwritten essay on the topic. Alone with my tutor, I read it aloud. Over tea, we then discussed my essay, the topic, and the issues involved. Everything was fair game. If I had misread or overlooked a case, I heard about it. If I wanted to pursue a line of reasoning, I did. And so it continued, through torts, contracts, trusts, equity, Roman law, constitutional law, personal property, real property—most of the curriculum.

The tutorial system was at once Oxford's most distinctive quality and its greatest strength. To an American always comfortably harnessed to structured classwork, it might look like chaos, no system at all, but I swiftly learned that its freedom could be either a license to fail or a license to learn. I was there to learn, and the intense sessions, each directed to my needs rather than a general average, made it easier. Neither Mr. Fifoot nor I was interested in wasting my time.

Lectures often supplemented the tutorials, but they only supplemented them. Formal lectures were being held all around Oxford every weekday morning, and they were given by the very top men in the various subjects. Unlike American lectures, however, these were totally unrestricted. Students attended any lecture they wanted to, but only if they wanted to. Moreover, the general understanding was that attendance was not to be indiscriminate. Overdone, it could even be disreputable. No one took roll, neither did anyone dare interrupt the lecturer with a question. A lecturer might be speaking before a handful or a hundred. Some did not seem to care. Others did not seem to notice.

The lectures did allow students to hear some of the world's most respected scholars. One that I heard was Sir William Searle Holdsworth. His specialties were constitutional law and equities, but all of English law was his domain. He was a tireless worker who published nine volumes of his *History of English Law* while holding the demanding rank of tutor. Upon that basis, he was elected, in 1922, Vinerian Professor of English Law. His magisterial *History* continued to grow, eventually stretching to fifteen volumes, each covering the totality of the law's growth and work.

Professor Holdsworth was a large man, large in achievement, large in appetite (before writing each evening, he drank three glasses of port), and large in appearance. He looked like nothing but an Oxford professor, and when he lectured on England's legal history, I felt as though I were hearing the Gospel from the lips of Luke. So complete was his knowledge and so thorough was his presentation that I hardly noticed how poor was his delivery. Determined to impart his knowledge fully, Holdsworth would repeat each sentence three times in three different ways.

The uniform intellectual brilliance of the lecturers covered a diverse range of their personalities, a range running from the staid to the strange. Of course, Oxford insisted that its professors were free to run their lectures as they pleased. In one case, that of a notorious history professor, the consequence was quite memorable. The man simply and utterly hated women, and at each term's beginning, students would flock to his initial lecture to see what would happen. Among the all-male colleges, Oxford had four women's colleges at the time. Their mischievous tutors often suggested that new students attend the old fellow's lectures. The repeated result was an Oxford legend.

One term, I accompanied a friend who was reading history to see if the legend were true. It was. Entering the lecture hall was an old buzzard who looked as disheveled as any tramp. His eyes maliciously searched the audience until he spotted the ladies. "Get those women out of my lecture," he roared.

Stunned, the unsuspecting women sat frozen.

This only made the professor angrier.

"Go! Go!" he screamed.

The women filed out, the professor breathed deeply, and muttered, "When are those bloody tutors going to quit sending those idiots to me?"

Apparently, his rhetorical question calmed him. The old fellow smiled, reached his hands into his pockets, and offered his final judgment. "It's getting around this bloody university to where a man won't be able to use his own bloody vulgarity to emphasize the points of his own bloody lectures." He had no need to say that three times—if any at all.

Considerably tamer were seminars. Although they were common to legal education in America, Oxford began offering seminars only after 1903, making them a contemporary innovation by its standards. As in an American classroom, a teacher and his students gathered around a table to dissect legal doctrines as if in a science laboratory, the seminar's original inspiration. Not surprisingly, some of the best were directed by visiting Americans. One of the finest that I had was under Felix Frankfurter, then a Harvard law professor and later a Supreme Court justice.

A final component of Oxford's legal education was the student's own reading, deep and heavy reading from lists prescribed by his tutor. It was usually done during the long intervals between terms.

In some measure, each student's final education consisted of an individualized mix. Some subjects would be covered almost exclusively in tutorials. Others would involve more lectures. For some, seminars were essential. Some, such as international law, I did largely by reading. One way or another, all the elements of a broad and sound legal education were there. I was blessed to be there, too.

That system's greatest source of strength was its incredible range of opportunity. Its greatest source of potential anxiety was that the student never knew exactly where he stood. There were occasional simulated tests, but grades were never taken. In fact, the student received no grades at all until the very end. Then Oxford University exercised the power that none of its colleges held. Oxford gave the examinations, and Oxford awarded the degrees. A scholar's whole record rested entirely upon two examinations. The more important was a long and gruesome written test that stretched over several days. Morning and afternoon sessions covered each of the subjects in the curriculum. That was when all the tutorials, all the lectures, all the seminars, all the reading—everything—came together. And everything depended on the outcome of those precious few hours.

After the university's three examiners graded the written examinations, they called each student before them for a second ordeal, his oral examination, called the viva. They could, and sometimes did, quiz the student on any aspect of any subject. Their purpose, however, was not to uncover specific lapses of fact or of memory. Rather, it was to judge the candidate's general ability.

Only at that point did the student receive any grades, an alpha, beta, gamma, or delta (corresponding to our A, B, C, or D) for each subject. Upon that basis, he received his degree, known as an honors degree and divided into four classes: first, second, third, fourth.

Altogether, that was the Oxford system. I had never encountered anything like it before. Most Americans never would. But as I think of it now, most of my schooling had prepared me for just that. What kept one moving through the system was a love of learning. My Bug Tussle teachers had given me that; those at

The lovely times we spent together. With Max Lancaster in Spain, 1932, during the Rhode scholarship years.

McAlester had nourished it; the OU faculty had cultivated it. Amid the spires of Oxford, it bloomed.

It bloomed for all of us. And for all of us, our lives would be altered by our experiences as Rhodes scholars. Fifty years after that experience, one of us, Morris Shaffer, spoke for all of us when he judged that the most enduring legacies of our experience were "the lovely times we spent together" and what we learned from one another "regarding alternate ways of looking at life." I know that I treasure those memories of times spent together. I know, too, that I learned much from the brilliant young men who became my friends.

One was already my friend, and knowing him rightly prepared me for the intellectual company that I was entering. Max Lancaster had been a finalist with me in the 1927 high school oratory contest, and we had traveled through Europe together that summer. Now we were meeting again. I knew enough about Max Lancaster to know that he had the kind of mind that Cecil Rhodes had wanted to find and train.

Max read modern languages at Balliol. It was said of the Oxford colleges that it was Brasenose for brawn, Christ Church for blood, and Balliol for brains. Max only added to his college's reputation. He had been teaching French at Indiana University when he won his Rhodes. He also knew German well. He read Latin better than any English Etonian I ever met. Ahead of him was an outstanding academic career teaching Italian at Vanderbilt. While there, he would win Chile's order of merit, the Bernardo O'Higgins Award, for his stirring English translation from Spanish of the national epic *Arauciad*.

For all of Max's abilities, he was in no way unusual as a Rhodes scholar. It was a class—my class, designated by the year that we all went up as the Class of '31—that met Cecil Rhodes's expectations of scholarship. If there was anything special about that class, it was the record of achievement that lay ahead of us and was so indebted to our Oxford years. Many stayed in academics to build distinguished and varied careers. James Pettegrove became an internationally recognized scholar of German drama as well as the collaborator of the celebrated philosopher Ernst Cassirer. Byron Trippet would hold the presidencies of distinguished colleges in both the United States and Mexico. Austin Faricy became both an outstanding professor of the humanities and an honored harpsichordist. Ferdinand Stone taught law in America and in France, Italy, and England, where the monarch named him to the Honorary Order of the British Empire. Others, like John Pirie, later the general counsel of America's leading airline, built businesses and careers upon their brains.

One unique quality of my class was the number of us, almost a third, who went on to justify Cecil Rhodes's faith with careers in public service. In time, Oxford's Rhodes scholars of 1931 provided America with a naval scientist (Francis Coleman), a leader in public education (Robert Jackson), two senior diplomats (William Koren and Alexander Daspit), a special assistant to the president (John Martin), the first head of the Agency for International Development (Fowler Hamilton), a chairman of the Federal Reserve Bank of New York (Alfred Hayes), a judge of the United States Circuit Court of Appeals (Benjamin Duniway), and a four-star general (Charles Bonesteel). Two of us, Secretary of State Dean Rusk and I, rose to the two highest positions of government service ever occupied by beneficiaries of Cecil Rhodes's trust. At the time, though, none of us knew that was in our futures. But we did know that in the future we would hold dear those lovely times that we were spending together.

It was the warden of Rhodes House who, after consulting with the various colleges, assigned me to St. Peter's. Oxford's newest college may have been its least prestigious, but it did have one big benefit: the Rhodes stipend completely covered its smaller costs and left me the money to travel. Oxford's schedule gave me the time. The university ran three terms, each about two months long. Thus, nearly half my time was free to see as much of Europe as I wanted. I wanted to see it all, and seeing it with some of my classmates gave me the loveliest times of all.

Our favored spot was along Spain's Mediterranean shore. The area is now known as the Costa del Sol. Fully developed, it rivals the French Riviera for expensive tourism. In the early 1930s, the coast was quite primitive and hardly a lure for the jet set. What brought us there was the favorable exchange rate, the best in Europe for impecunious college students. Because the Spanish peseta was so cheap, I was able to sleep and have two meals a day for as little as ninety cents.

Spring was our favorite time to visit. The coastal climate is always spectacular but never more so than in the spring. Oxford's climate is never worse than in the winter. The contrast made us appreciate Spain all the more. So spring usually called my very

Spring usually called my very closest friends and me. With Spanish students and two gypsies at Granada.

closest friends and me to the Spanish coast. From there, we would travel forth to places like Cadiz, Seville, Cordova, and Grenada.

Travel was cheap, the weather was perfect, and the country was free. There was talk of a leftist uprising against the republic, but we saw nothing of one. We certainly saw no sign of the fascist revolt to come. We traveled freely through the country, mixing with peasants and workers and students and Gypsies. Sometimes, though, the times were not so lovely.

Our first Oxford term ended in early December, and Max Lancaster and I decided to spend Christmas in Paris. The family of one of Max's Balliol friends, Vala Zetlin, lived there. They agreed to put us up near their apartment at 11, rue Nicolo, just off the Champs-Elysées. We had been to Paris four years earlier. The city was still as lovely, but we could sense a difference. Maybe it was the depression. Maybe it was the unease over a fitful Germany. Whatever it was, the city seemed to be nervous, caught between a world of gentility destroyed and another of horror unborn.

Crime seemed to be rampant. It was nothing to read in the paper of a public guillotining drawing hundreds of curiosity seekers. One took place during the few days we were there. It involved a rapist. His victims were twenty teenage girls. We did not join the crowd, for we were not among the curious. We did join the Zetlin family for a holiday dinner.

The Zetlins were a family of victims, victims of those dangerous times. They were all well educated and highly cultured. Each spoke French, Russian, German, and English and spoke them well. The Zetlins were Russian Jews. Mrs. Zetlin's first husband had been prominent in the provisional government that replaced the czar. When the Bolsheviks overthrew that regime, the Zetlins fled, bribing their way to Paris. Now they were giving us our holiday dinner. Joining us on Christmas Day 1931 was their neighbor and fellow exile Alexander Kerensky.

Here was the man who had headed the ill-fated provisional government. His regime was no match for the Bolsheviks, and his graciousness was no match for Lenin's ruthlessness. His government had collapsed in the October Revolution, which gave birth to the world's first Communist state. Kerensky had barely managed to escape Red firing squads. Over dinner, he told us of fleeing the Soviet state, crossing its frozen border on a motorcycle. We listened enthralled, two American students sitting with a man who had made history and was now, like our hosts, its victim.

The next Christmas I saw another man who would make history—and millions of victims. I wanted to visit Central Europe that year and I made sure to go to Munich. There, I ran into one of St. Peter's dons, an excellent German historian and linguist. We talked briefly before he happened to ask, "I say, Albert, did you know Hitler is going to speak here on Thursday?" After that, there was nothing that could have pulled me out of Munich before Thursday. When Thursday came, we went—with fifty thousand Germans—to hear the man they called "*der Führer.*" It was a spectacle. A huge band blasted out martial tunes in front of a platform alive with waving Nazi flags and banners. The songs became ever more martial, the brass section louder, the beat stronger and faster, as the time for Hitler's speech approached.

He was not there, but we had no doubt of his whereabouts. Every few minutes, one of his Brown Shirts stepped to the microphone. His clothes pressed to a saber's edge, his posture as rigid as a rifle, he would notify the crowd of Hitler's movements.

"Heil Hitler! *Der Führer* is on his train approaching Munich."

Hands clapped, voices shouted, "Heil Hitler!"

After a few minutes, "*Der Führer* has reached the station."

More applause, more voices, "Heil Hitler!"

Another, interchangeable Brown Shirt: "*Der Führer* is traveling in his motorcar."

Much applause, many shouting "Heil Hitler!"

Now, the first Brown Shirt: "*Der Führer* is in sight!"

Caps sailed through the air. Nazi salutes shot up in unison. Spontaneous applause bunched into a rhythmic, pulsating beat of flesh upon flesh.

Just as the noise was passing its crescendo, a Brown Shirt shot to the microphone. "*Der Führer,*" he screamed, "has arrived."

The place came alive with a quickening, throbbing sound. It

continued, driving toward a final spasm as *Der Führer* came across the stage.

He looked like anything but the object of such hysteria. To me, he just looked tired, maybe sleepy, mostly bored. Facing fifty thousand erect, straining arms, he reached his right hand into his pocket and returned their salute with a casual, limp left arm.

As my friend translated for me, Hitler began to speak. His words dragged forth slowly at first. His sentences stopped in mid-thought, then began again somewhere else. Until he lit upon an emotional point. Suddenly and steadily, his voice grew stronger. Then he started to move. His rambling gave way to pacing and that to marching as he stomped back and forth across the platform. The words came faster and faster, louder and louder. Each time he paused for breath, that breath was heated by screams from thousands of throats.

Then, just as suddenly, Hitler's voice softened. For a few moments, the crowd sat silent, ears cocked to hear slow, soft, rhythmic streams of Hitler's words. Until one word became a shout, followed by another and another, each louder than the one before. At the top of his voice, he continued through his peroration. He ended with the crowd afire, a mad pentecost of hysteria.

It was the most remarkable performance I had ever seen. I left the place and I left Munich with the belief that this pathetic little creature had but one talent: he could incite an entire nation to madness. On that particular evening, it was his personal madness. Within a few weeks, the feeble hands of Baron Paul von Hindenburg handed Hitler the chancellorship of Germany, and *der Führer*'s personal madness became national policy.

Back in Oxford, Hitler's madness was no more than an odd curiosity. The concerns of an American seemingly were unshared by Britain's elite. Unlike us, the British had fought four years of bloody war against one German army and were in no mood to face another. Maybe they were in no mood to think about it.

Much more pleasant was the safe world of Oxford in its spring.

Then and there the weather is always perfect, the flowers always beautiful, the countryside always enchanting. When not studying, I joined the other students in the gentlemanly ritual of punting on the Cherwell. We rented boats and with long poles pushed them up and down the river, pausing for box lunches on its graceful banks.

Sports were another diversion. I had not been there long before I realized that competitive athletics were at least as important to Oxford as to any American university. The games were different—the major sports were cricket, rugby, hockey, and rowing—but the intensity of competition was just as fierce. Equal, too, was the athlete's status: a member of the rowing team that faced Cambridge was as honored as an All-American football player for OU.

The Oxford Union was another diversion, though a more substantial one. It sat a few paces from St. Peter's, and I joined it early and attended its debates. They were full-dress affairs held every Tuesday night and featured outstanding student debaters, as well as political leaders. Among the latter, David Lloyd George and Winston Churchill were spectacular. I could have listened to either for hours.

Lloyd George spoke in a beautiful, lilting Welsh manner. Like Churchill, his grammatical constructions were perfect. Perfect, too, was their sense of metaphor and timing. Churchill in particular had an absolutely devastating wit. But it was passion, not wit, that he invoked to warn the union repeatedly and vainly of Hitler's menace.

Academically, my second year was nearly consumed by Roman law. It was Oxford's way to make the law of ancient Rome nearly central to the curriculum. It also was Oxford's way to ground its study in the original *Institutes* of Gaius. Written in the second century A.D., the *Institutes* recorded the earliest development of legal interpretation and did it entirely in Latin. Most English scholars, schooled since childhood for an Oxford degree, read Latin as a second language. I had exactly two years at McAlester High School and knew only the simplest words. For that reason, I spent most of a term in battle with the *Institutes,* the text open before me, a Latin dictionary beside it. I could call in Max Lancaster to help with some of the more obscure constructions, but most of the struggle was word-to-word combat. I slugged my way through it so slowly that I could not help but learn it thoroughly.

At the second year's end came our examinations. I spent a good part of the last term systematically reviewing all of my earlier work. The real push came, though, when the ordeal began. I slept well the night before the first day's exam. I did not sleep again for three nights. As soon as one day's test finished, I began studying for the next. The resulting written examinations thereby tested one's endurance as much as his intelligence.

Compared to that, the vivas (oral examinations) were no challenge at all. In fact, a group of us got ready for them by relaxing on a trip through Scotland. In an old car we drove through the countryside and slept every night in pup tents pitched in farmers' fields.

We spent our first night in the borderlands of Scotland, sleeping in the territory made famous as Sir Walter Scott's setting for his "Lady of the Lake." Our tents sat right where

> The stag at eve had drunk his fill,
> Where danced the moon on Monan's rill,
> And deep his midnight lair had made
> In lone Glenartney's hazel shade.

We left Glenartney's shade for Edinburgh. We had our lunch on the second floor of a Princess Street restaurant overlooking the great gorge that separated us from the beautiful castle of Edinburgh. We then made it a point to go much farther north by Loch Ness. The famous monster, Nessie, had been getting a lot of press coverage and we wondered how she was doing. We did not find her, so we dropped down south, toward Oxford. Before getting there, we made sure to camp "by the bonnie, bonnie banks of Loch Lomond."

When we reached Oxford, we were all fresher and better for our vivas. Mine went very well. I satisfied Oxford's examiners and received Oxford's initial degree. To celebrate, I planned a summer in

We slept every night in pup tents pitched in farmers' fields . . . in the territory made famous as Sir Walter Scott's setting. In Scotland, 1933; above, with Gordon Siefkin and George Done.

Europe. My destination was Germany. I wanted to see how a different monster was doing.

I went to Germany expecting to spend much of the summer there. As was often true on these trips, I had no elaborate itinerary. All I knew for sure was that I would sail to Hamburg and travel the country until I could see if Hitler was making much difference. Otherwise, I did not even know where I would stay in Hamburg. A fellow passenger helped me out there. He was a student, too, attending the University of London. A German native, he was quite familiar with Hamburg. He also was Jewish.

We reached Hamburg and registered at a small hotel. After dinner, we decided to take a walk through the city. It was lovely, if a bit quiet for a couple of vacationing students, so we resolved to visit some of the beer gardens. In our third one, we met two local girls. Both had taken English in school, and they seemed delighted to have an American to use it on. We four had a great time over steins of good German beer.

I remember well one of the girl's pride because she had traveled quite a bit. She reached into her purse and pulled out a heavily stamped passport and visas that recorded her travels. As I was looking them over, some of Hitler's Brown Shirts stepped up to our table.

My German was far too poor to make out what they were saying, but I could not mistake their attitude. Gruff, boisterous, and arrogant, they were badgering the other fellow. His initial politeness in the face of it gave way to anger, then to fear, as the brown-shirted hooligans grabbed him and pulled him away. I was too stunned to move, but I did not have to. The gang seized me and threw me into the street, where my fellow student was. Shaking with rage and alarm, he explained our transgression: we had been talking with two Aryan women, he a Jew, and I a foreigner. That answered the question that had brought me to Germany.

I left the next day. At Lübeck, I bought a ticket for a Swedish boat bound for Copenhagen. Policemen crowded the boarding area, carefully inspecting every person getting out of Germany. I expected no trouble and I had none—until I handed over my

passport. It was not mine. It was the one the girl had been showing me in the beer garden.

Instantly, German officers surrounded me. They threw questions at me. The Swedish captain quickly stepped in to act as my
interpreter. The German officials scrutinized my own passport before they finally accepted my story and let me board the vessel.
They took the young girl's passport with them. I never learned
what happened to it or to the little German girl who was so proud
of her English and her freedom to travel.

My third and final year at Oxford was a bittersweet one. There
were undeniable advantages to that year. Because I now held an
Oxford degree, I shed my half-gown and the restrictions that went
along with it. I could visit pubs, and I did. I could occupy a front
seat in a cinema, and I did. I could date local girls, and I did that,
too. Of course, I now wore the long gown that denoted an Oxford
graduate, and I was proud to be one.

No longer an undergraduate, I had to find my own housing
(digs was the Oxford term), and I was extraordinarily lucky. One
of the dons at Oriel College was taking a year's leave. With George
Carlson, a Rhodes scholar from Colorado, and Wilmore Kendall, a
Rhodes scholar from my home county, I rented his apartment. It
was in a perfect location: No. 4, Oriel Street, just opposite the
college.

We easily had the most lavish digs of any of the Rhodes students. The apartment required three floors for its four bedrooms,
four bathrooms, kitchen, den, and living room. All were hand-
somely furnished; the last held a grand piano.

The place swiftly became something of a social center for the
Rhodes scholars and many of our English friends. People came
and went, sometimes staying so long that I had to lock myself in
the uppermost floor's bedroom; it was the only place quiet enough
to afford a little study time. Still, the apartment and the enlarged
privileges accounted for much of the year's sweetness.

The bitterness came from the realization that I would not have
such opportunities much longer. My legal studies continued,

steadily becoming less academic and more practical. They were preparing me less as a scholar, more as a lawyer. That, too, was a reminder that my years in Oxford were ending. They had been years of great challenge and of great opportunity.

They also had been years removed from much of the real world. I could listen to Hitler, but I need not be governed by him. I knew that America, Britain, and the entire world struggled in a deep, global depression, but I did not feel it. Beneath the fairy castle spires of Oxford, we held quiet tutorials. We cheered our rowing crew, we debated at the union, we punted the Cherwell. All along we knew there would be life after Oxford, and we knew that it would be something very different.

At the end of the spring term, I got ready to join that life. I passed Oxford's examinations and took Oxford's advanced law degree, the bachelor of civil laws. I celebrated and reminisced with my English friends and the Americans who expectantly had crossed the Atlantic as I had three years earlier. Then we left, sailing from Southampton, not knowing this time what to expect. We went our separate ways; mine was back to McAlester, Pittsburgh County, Oklahoma. Life there was different.

I returned to an America still held tight in the Great Depression's jaws. The bite was especially severe in rural Oklahoma. In no time, I felt it myself. I got home only to learn that there was not a single job opening in the county that was not some form of government work relief. Every lawyer in McAlester agreed that the local legal business was all but nonexistent. Some confessed that the only reason they had any at all was because they took chickens and eggs for fees.

I could not even get that until I passed the state bar exam. Through the fall of 1934, I stayed at the university's law library, studying for the test. I also scouted out future employment, only to learn that things were not much better anywhere else in the state. I took and passed the bar exam with no job prospects at all; by then it was winter. I was far from Oxford and close to desperate.

A break finally came with an article in the *Daily Oklahoman*.

President Franklin D. Roosevelt's New Deal had created a Federal Housing Administration in 1933. According to the paper, the FHA soon would be opening an Oklahoma City office. The office would need a few administrators, a handful of secretaries, and one other employee: a legal assistant.

I ran to the nearest telephone and called Washington. Senator Elmer Thomas remembered his high school visitor; Senator Thomas Gore remembered his college driver. They gave me their recommendations and put me in touch with the local administrator. He hired me on the spot to my first real job. The pay was $150 a month, exactly $16.67 less than I had been paid for going to school at Oxford. I was mighty glad to get it.

Working with the FHA gave me an education as well as a check. I had not worked there long before I understood that I was right at the center of some major national problems.

The housing industry had been unhealthy long before the 1929 stock-market crash. Indeed, its deterioration had been one source of the economic erosion that led to the overall collapse. With the Depression, the housing industry and the general economy began a mad dance leading to total exhaustion. Swelling unemployment rolls left fewer and fewer Americans able to build, buy, or repair homes. Home construction, sale, and repair slowed, swelling those unemployment totals. The resulting spiral could never reverse itself.

Moreover, the housing industry was tied directly to the banking industry. Unemployed men could not meet their mortgage obligations. Lenders could not collect on their loans. The only available recourse, mortgage foreclosures, benefited no one. Homeowners lost their homes. Creditors accumulated buyerless properties. Families took to the streets. Banks closed their doors.

Here, too, was a deadly spiral that threatened nothing less than total financial collapse. Already it had doomed much of the country to be that one-third of the nation that FDR knew was ill fed, ill clothed, and ill housed. Unless somebody did something, too many would stay there too long. Buyers needed mortgage money they could use with with monthly payments they could handle.

Lenders needed assurance that they could recover larger loans requiring smaller down payments and stretched over longer periods. Everyone needed protection against shoddy and hazardous construction methods.

To any but a mossback reactionary, the crisis called for decisive government action to relieve the present misery, to reform the underlying problem, and to recover a large piece of the American Dream. It was the mission of Franklin Roosevelt and his Democratic party to take that action. It was their genius to do it not by reversing American capitalism, but by rescuing it. They helped capitalists save capitalism from itself.

The housing act enlisted the existing private elements—the bankers, the buyers, and the builders—in a systematic attack on national needs. It encouraged financiers to require smaller down payments (twenty percent became standard) and to lengthen repayment schedules, usually to twenty years. For these reasons, monthly payment schedules fell markedly and borrowers had some assurance that they could keep their homes, even if hard times returned again.

In exchange for these liberalizations, the federal government maintained a fund to guarantee the lenders' loans against default. A fee of one-half of 1 percent added to each borrower's monthly payment financed the fund. The guarantee, while virtually painless to the homeowner, assured lenders' participation and cooperation in the entirely voluntary program.

Finally, reasonable but detailed rules prescribed loan standards. Some sought to ensure that borrowers would be capable of repayment; others governed the properties to be financed. These protected the buyer, the lender, and the government from unscrupulous building practices that already had defrauded Americans of billions of dollars.

Altogether, the national housing act was a model of modern statesmanship. I am proud of the president who proposed it, proud of the party that sponsored it, proud of the Congress that adopted it. I am proud, too, to have worked in its administration.

Up in a second-floor office across from the old post office, we worked in Oklahoma City to bring the FHA to Oklahoma. Some called us bureaucrats, but all we were was a very hardworking group of people, about a half-dozen, trying to help other people. Our chief responsibilities were central and western Oklahoma, where we maintained offices in the principal towns. Local people employed by the Works Progress Administration (WPA) regularly staffed these. Local chambers of commerce usually donated the office space.

Much of my work was in those scattered offices. I bought my first car, a Model A costing $475, and drove across much of the state. As the legal assistant, I helped interpret and explain Washington's rules and prepare the paperwork. Most of my work, however, was more personal than legal. In one community after another, I met with loan applicants and helped them fill out their applications. I visited the local bankers and the savings-and-loan directors, explaining the program and urging their cooperation. It was a pretty good use for an Oxford education.

It was also an education in itself. Driving across Oklahoma, I saw things that I can never forget. One was on the MK&T Railroad running north into McAlester. I was driving home one weekend when I passed a long freight train. It had a string of at least fifty coal cars, all empty of coal, each filled with desperate men and boys. They were economic refugees trying to find some kind of work somewhere else.

I got home still shaken. For some reason, I went out to Bug Tussle. I visited one of my old schoolmates. He, his wife, and their nine children were living there in a three-room shack. No one in the family had had a pair of shoes in more than two years. His only income was fifty dollars a month, earned with the WPA.

"How do you get by?" I asked.

He answered, "Oh, I fish in the spring and summer, trap and skin wild animals in the winter."

My friend's lips smiled but his eyes did not when he added, "I have to steal chickens on the side."

You never can forget things like that. All you can do is try to understand them.

My fieldwork with the FHA contributed to my understanding. It gave me my first real experience with western Oklahoma. Up until statehood, there were two distinct and entirely separate territories, Indian Territory and Oklahoma Territory. The first became roughly the eastern half of the state, and it was where my people had settled. Its lands were rolling, forested hills, later cleared for small cotton farms, usually worked by tenants. Its people were migrating southerners, Baptists and Methodists mainly, Democrats almost always.

Oklahoma Territory was considerably different—different enough to have justified a separate statehood. It was flatter, drier, almost treeless. Migrating midwesterners settled there. They plowed up wheat farms, built Church of Christ and Presbyterian churches, and voted Republican.

Despite those historic differences, every corner of the state suffered mightily in the 1930s. Oklahoma's people were proud people and strong people, but they, no less than some of the Europeans I had seen, were victims of a history larger than they. In the old Indian Territory, the tenant system collapsed under the weight of ten-cent cotton. In the old Oklahoma Territory, the hardworking men who had plowed the prairie to grow wheat in the twenties tasted dust in their mouths in the drought-stricken thirties. All over the state, the oil boom that followed Oklahoma's birth ended when crude oil prices hit a dime a barrel.

Cotton, wheat, and oil—everything—had collapsed. The resulting emergency overwhelmed state and local governments. Human needs swelled as public revenues shrank. They did their best, but their best could not even slow the tide of ruin. Neither could it slow the human tide. Abandoned farm cabins and oil-field shacks lined the roads that I drove. After all, Oklahoma lost a fifth of its population in the 1930s.

The photographs of Dorothea Lange and others recorded the faces of many of those migrants, the ones called Okies. There were haunting photographs, too, of the ones who stayed. Some captured the awesome, fearsome majesty of the howling winds and billowing clouds of dust that roared across the western plains, hollowing out the Dust Bowl. Some caught old people without hope, young people without work, small children without promise. To see those pictures is to know something of what it was to go down from Oxford to Oklahoma in the 1930s.

The reality was worse than the photographs. Driving across the state in my model A, carrying federal loan applications, I saw things that remain more vivid than any mere picture. I remember driving right through the heart of the Dust Bowl in the summer of 1936, when the temperature was 120 degrees. A little west of Guymon, I pulled into a tiny filling station that sat upon a sterile plain. A little boy—he could have been no more than thirteen—came out to the car and filled my tank.

"Mister," he said, "this is the first sale I have made today."

I knew then that this little boy was in charge of the station. Then he told me why.

"Sir," he said, "it looks like this country is going to burn up. We can't make it here. My parents have gone to California to look for work, and they left me here to take care of things. 'Doesn't look like there's much left to take care of."

There was not much left. Just a little boy with the oldest eyes I had ever seen.

I climbed back into the car and kept going. Blowing dust howled about me. Before long, I had to pull off the road and wait for the duster to pass. I finally made it to Boise City, the county seat of Cimarron County and epicenter of the Dust Bowl.

If God had not forsaken the place, He was one of the few that had not. Stores, banks, nearly everything seemed abandoned. I did find a resident leaning on a light post. We talked a bit, and I asked him how long the place had been without rain.

"Fella," he answered, "I got a boy three years old that has never seen a drop of rain."

But drought was not really the problem. It was raining elsewhere in Oklahoma, but the people were no better off. Right in the state's capital, where the North Canadian River literally had flowed with oil, a camp had sprung up on the riverbanks. I went through it once with a McAlester doctor, there to attend a dying child. I saw five hundred people living in shacks, most made of cardboard, their only toilet and running water the river itself.

This was man's depression, not God's. It would not help much to wait for rain, any more than it would help to wait for the sinking economy to raise itself. This was government's task. Here was its purpose.

That is what I learned when I went down from Oxford and back to Oklahoma. It added to my resolve to go to Congress. I wanted to be part of a government that accepted that task and met that purpose. In time that happened. What Franklin Roosevelt began, others would extend. I was able to be one of them. I was able to do my part to see that the government of all of us would act in remembrance of these, the least of us.

In the years ahead, I would never once see that happen without seeing, too, a little boy left behind to take care of things.

CHAPTER FOUR

I Think I'll Go Back Home and Run for Congress

By the spring of 1937, I had spent nearly two years with the Federal Housing Administration. It had been a valuable experience in many ways, but money was not one of them. I was still earning Depression wages with no raise in sight. I knew that I was ready to move on for the right opportunity. It came in May.

The Sayre Oil Company was a family-owned business that took its name from the town of Sayre, home of its founder and president, E. L. Martin. Buddy Martin was his son and the company vice president; he also was my Kappa Alpha fraternity brother. It was Buddy who asked me if I would be interested in working as the in-house attorney at the company's Oklahoma City headquarters.

I jumped at the chance. Sayre Oil had wide and diverse holdings that belied its localized name, and I could count on some interesting work. Oil was second only to agriculture in its economic significance to Oklahoma. I knew that I could never really know or serve the state without understanding the industry. Finally, the job paid $250 a month and that was nearly double my FHA salary.

Mr. Martin had built his company on some very profitable leases and wells in the fabulous East Texas field. To them he later added wells and leases in the Permian Basin of West Texas. The

Texas crude that he sold refiners was bringing in better than $3 million a year at the time. The company also had oil properties in Oklahoma and Kansas, and Mr. Martin owned extensive tracts of land in western Oklahoma and the Texas Panhandle. All in all, there was plenty of work for the company's legal department: me.

Much of the work—easily the most interesting work—was out in the field. Oil had just been discovered in southern Illinois, and Mr. Martin and some wildcatters were busy buying up leases and drilling wells in America's latest pool. It made for a lot of legal business. It also gave me my first close-up view of some of the world's biggest gamblers and smoothest operators. Few of the oil men were well educated; some had no education at all. Mr. Martin certainly had no Oxford degree, but I came to believe very quickly that none of my Oxford dons could have outsmarted him on a business deal.

There was a banker up in southern Illinois who learned the same thing, and his education cost him more than mine. Mr. Martin was buying leases and entrusting them to a small-town banker in the new oil patch. In no time the lease prices shot upward. I went over to the county courthouse, looked in the land records, and found out why. Our banker friend had taken advantage of our trust to start buying royalties in his own name. That was what was running the prices up on us. He should not have done that.

When I told him what was going on, Mr. Martin sent me out to buy up leases in two different parts of the county. The leases in one, the one where our geologists told us we could expect oil, I kept with me. The other, in a place of no promise at all, I recorded with the clerk at the courthouse. Sure enough, the banker started frantic buying in the new area. He was taking everything he had made off our trust and pouring it into the new leases, jacking the prices up, and buying still more at the inflated prices. Meanwhile, we kept buying quietly and cheaply in the other area without recording the leases.

After a few weeks, Mr. Martin had me spring the trap. I recorded every one of the leases that covered nearly an entire field—Sayre Oil had it all. Our competitor ended up with a trunk full of worthless paper. Too late, he learned that he had paid a fortune for leases to a field as dry as a banker's eye.

One of the best things about my new boss was his politics. Mr. Martin was a Democrat, a down-the-line, Franklin Roosevelt, New Deal Democrat. Of course, I was, too. I had seen too many of Oklahoma's neediest people to be anything else. In a place like Oklahoma, at a time like the Great Depression, I did not know how one *could* be anything else.

It appeared that not many Oklahomans were anything else. Although Republican nominees carried the state in two of the three presidential races of the 1920s, the popular identification of the Depression with the GOP decimated the party. In 1932, Franklin Roosevelt became the first presidential candidate to carry every one of Oklahoma's seventy-seven counties. In 1936, he got two out of every three Sooner votes. One of his record total was my first presidential ballot.

Oklahoma's voters had every reason to support the president so faithfully. The relief and recovery projects of the New Deal were chipping away at some of their towering economic troubles. The Federal Housing Administration saved homes that would have been lost. The Federal Deposit Insurance Corporation saved banks that would have failed. The Works Progress Administration created jobs for people who would have stayed idle. The National Youth Administration kept youngsters in school who would have withdrawn. The Agricultural Adjustment Administration got government checks to farmers who faced doom without them. The National Recovery Administration kept small-town merchants in business. A dozen relief projects kept families eating.

One thing that Roosevelt and the New Deal could not do was give shape to the state Democratic party. Oklahoma Democrats have always been a fractious crowd. In the 1930s, they were something of a mob, and the party tended toward catch-as-catch-can chaos. One symptom of that attracted considerable national attention, attention that was either bemused or hostile. It was my state's penchant for famous-nameism.

It began in 1932 when an obscure schoolteacher filed for election as a representative at large. His name was William C. Rogers, and his few friends had always known him as Bill. But when he filed for office, this Mr. Rogers instructed the election board to enter him on the ballot as Will Rogers. So identified, he ran all over twenty opponents to capture the Democratic nomination. He went on to lead the entire ticket in the general election. He drew even more votes than Franklin Roosevelt.

Two years later, this Will Rogers sought a second term. I returned from Oxford to discover his name among those of the 241 candidates who sought 31 offices on a Democratic ballot that measured 531 square inches. He won that year, too. In fact, Will Rogers won five consecutive terms. He served until the office was abolished after the state lost a House seat following the 1940 census.

It is said that this particular Will Rogers contributed little humor to national affairs—little humor apart, that is, from his own elections. Over the years, he kept returning to Washington after beating back challenges from men named William Cullen Bryant, Brigham Young, Sam Houston, Robert E. Lee, and Wilbur Wright.

Congressman Rogers's success encouraged others to try their hands and famous names at winning steady employment through the Democratic primary. In 1938 alone, thousands of Oklahoma's Democrats marked their ballots for Oliver Cromwell, Daniel Boone, Huey Long, and Patrick Henry. Sixty-seven thousand Democrats voted that year for an Oklahoma City housewife named Mae West. All lost—all except Will Rogers—but all contributed mightily to my state's reputation for political buffoonery.

Far more serious was the inability of the state party to work with the national administration. Few politicians dared criticize the president or his policies openly; FDR and the New Deal were far too popular with far too many for that. But at the same time, some of the congressional delegation feuded openly with the White House and their party's leadership in Congress. In Oklahoma City, William H. Murray, known as Alfalfa Bill, who was the state's governor from 1931 to 1935, stubbornly refused to cooperate with New Deal agencies. After Murray's term, much of the legislative leadership stayed in open and permanent rebellion against its party's policies in Washington.

None of this was unique to Oklahoma. America's federal structure never has promoted the party loyalty and party discipline sustained by Britain's unitary system. During the 1930s, this became steadily graver. A growing number of conservative Democrats, especially southern conservative Democrats, were deserting the New Deal. In Congress, they were moving toward an informal alliance with the bitterly anti-Roosevelt Republican minority, an alliance that threatened to bury FDR's program on Capitol Hill.

Of course, many southerners in Congress were steadfastly loyal to the administration. It was my early friend Elmer Thomas who pieced together much of FDR's farm program in the Senate Agriculture Committee. Josh Lee, my speech professor at the University of Oklahoma, joined Thomas in the Senate in 1936. He proved to be an even firmer friend of the New Deal, a dependable vote for FDR and an eloquent champion of his policies.

It was while I was working for Sayre Oil in 1938 that Senator Thomas faced a tough reelection fight. E. W. Marland, the legendary oilman who had built and lost an empire, was closing out a frustrating term as governor and seeking solace in the Senate seat. Gomer Smith, who had served very briefly in the House of Representatives, had run awfully well against Senator Thomas six years earlier. Smith subsequently had risen to the vice-presidency of the Townsend Clubs, the group agitating for generous pensions for the elderly. Fortified by the old folks' votes, he was running again.

Both of these were formidable contenders, and neither was as dependably for FDR as Senator Thomas. I wanted to help the old senator, and I asked Mr. Martin one day if I could take a month's unpaid leave to campaign for him. Mr. Martin would hear nothing of it; he insisted that I take as long as I wanted at full pay. That would be his contribution to the Thomas campaign and to the New Deal.

I spent most of the summer campaigning for Senator Thomas. I must have given a hundred speeches or more, speaking at every crossroads in southern Oklahoma, all the way from the Arkansas line to the Texas Panhandle. In July, I got some mighty powerful help: President Roosevelt came to Oklahoma.

That summer, the president took a decided and singular gamble. His program was stalled in Congress, so, in order to move it, he resolved to throw himself into the Democratic congressional primaries. In a few carefully selected races, he would campaign personally and directly for the renomination of his most loyal supporters who were facing strong challenges. More important, he would actively enter other races to call for the defeat of powerful Democratic apostates. Never before had a president so directly intervened in his party's congressional nomination process.

That is what brought FDR to Oklahoma. Three days before the July primary, his train roared into the state, stopping at towns along the Santa Fe line before pulling into Oklahoma City for a climactic address at the state fairgrounds. Estimates are that a fifth of Oklahoma's electorate came to one or another of the stops to hear the nation's most popular public man. Seventy-five thousand of us heard his address at the fairgrounds. It was the finest stump speech I ever heard. The president really laid the lash to the Republicans. Then he moved on to what he called the "yes, but . . ." Democrats. Yes, they wanted prosperity, but not to underwrite it. Yes, they wanted reform, but not this one. Yes, they called themselves Democrats, but they voted like Republicans. The crowd went right along, shouting its agreement. There was an explosion when the president urged them to give him in Washington the strong right arm of "my old friend, Senator Thomas."

Our old friend did return to Washington, where he continued to support the president in peace and in war. Others of FDR's friends—Hattie Carraway in Arkansas and Alben Barkley in Kentucky—fended off strong conservative challengers with Roosevelt's assistance that year. In these cases, the president could persuade voters to return his friends. He almost never could convince them to defeat his foes. Not even FDR's earnest and public pleadings could defeat senators like Ellison D. ("Cotton Ed") Smith in South Carolina, Millard Tydings in Maryland, or Walter George in

Georgia. Each of them returned to Washington, too. They returned to positions of power and authority. Unchastened and unafraid, their influence actually grew, for they had withstood the assault of a politician heretofore believed to be invincible. Their survival and success only emboldened other conservative Democrats to break with the White House and the national party.

FDR's gamble had failed. Worse, it had backfired. After 1938, a conservative coalition of most Republicans and many conservative Democrats emerged as a political phenomenon that would survive for most of my own public life. Not even Franklin Roosevelt could overcome it; no subsequent president could ignore it. I later learned just how much the congressional leadership had to understand it, too.

My legal work in the Illinois field became more and more interesting. I enjoyed the work and my colleagues, too. I was not the only attorney working for the only oil company in the area. In fact, I was not the only one from McAlester, Oklahoma. Tom Ed Grace had been a friend since high school. Like me, he had been valedictorian at McAlester High and had gone on to OU, where we had been bridge partners. I ran into Tom while he was working for Carter Oil, one of the Standard Oil companies. Tom had the original idea, but I thought it a grand one: we both left our salaried jobs to open a new firm, Grace and Albert of Mattoon, Illniois.

Grace and Albert hung its shingle in an excellent location. We occupied the second floor of a building on Main Street in Mattoon. The first floor belonged to a Greek restaurant, the most popular eatery in the whole area. Across the street sat Carter Oil Company, my partner's former employer. It was the chief source of our bread-and-butter business, title examinations that the legal department farmed out to Grace and Albert.

Title examinations remained our specialty. From time to time, we did have litigation. For instance, Tom took on a divorce and child-custody case and won a splendid victory. I also went into court to argue a complicated case regarding land transfer. Most days were spent poring over land records. I must have studied thousands of abstracts, plowing steadily through uncountable records of deeds, conveyances, and covenants. Our clients demanded secure leases. Their landmen got the leases; we saw that they were secure. It was not glamorous work, but it was work, and in the late thirties that still meant a lot more than glamour.

At their start, the 1940s seemed not to offer much more glamour. In the spring of 1940, I accepted a good job with The Ohio Oil Company. The Ohio—*The* was part of its formal name and always capitalized—went back in the oil business to the days of the original Standard Oil and old John D. Rockefeller. Although it never reached the size of Standard or the Texas Company, it was a fine, well-run, fully integrated firm. It refined its own crude oil from its own wells in Illinois, Texas, and other fields. A subsidiary, Illinois Pipeline Company, was a major midwestern shipper. Another subsidiary, Marathon, had filling stations all across Ohio, Indiana, and Illinois. For all its reach, The Ohio proudly bore the image of the founder and his family. James Donnell, a pal of old John D. himself, established the company and passed it down to his son, then President Otto Donnell. Otto's son, James, was steadily moving upward at the time.

The Donnell influence pervaded the company. As a Democrat and a Methodist, I had to notice how many of the other employees were Republican and Presbyterian, as were the Donnells. My own boss later told me that he had been a Methodist when he started with The Ohio, but he had changed. According to him, that was true of nearly every man who wore The Ohio's white collar.

My office was with the company's district headquarters in Marshall, a little town near the Indiana border. In effect, I was in charge of all the company's legal business in Illinois. I chose the work I wanted for myself and farmed out the rest to independent firms. In the first year, I took three cases into the courts, and I sent a lot of abstracts out of the office. It was an excellent job. It paid well—three hundred dollars a month was awfully good money at the time—the work was challenging, and the people were great. I still clung to the dream of one day representing Oklahoma in Congress, and I took every opportunity to keep up with the folks in my home state. Lest I be tempted to quit The Ohio, though, I only had to recall how tough it had been to find any legal work at home. Things there had hardly improved by 1940. In some ways, they had worsened, as the largest waves of Okie migrants were only then leaving. The lingering uncertainty of the Great Depression was no occasion for me to make a sudden career move.

There was one other uncertainty at the time, but its resolution came with frightful dispatch. While I was searching land abstracts in the American midwest, Hitler had been seizing national estates in central Europe. Events showed Britain and France the ugly truth of which Churchill had warned and toward which they had been so stubbornly blind. Adolf Hitler was not just another politician; this mad genius would stop at nothing to build his thousand-year Reich and stretch its influence across the Continent. He would rule in Europe or he would serve it hell. Too late, the democracies had drawn the line at the border of Poland. When Hitler's panzers crashed across the Polish frontier and his Stukas rained death upon Poland's cities, war was again upon the world.

Unlike Americans just a little older than I, I could not say with President Roosevelt, "I have seen war," but I had seen its results (the young man's silvered face at Verdun appeared before me often) and I could say with FDR, "I hate war." Like millions of others, I supported his pursuit of an unprecedented third presidential term, hoping that that personal abhorrence and his great political skills could make a difference. They could not. The neutrality laws hastily and idealistically assembled early in the 1930s crumbled before awesome reality. Just as quickly, America accepted the role of democracy's arsenal, furiously began lending and leasing war matériel to the Allies, and looked toward its own anemic forces. In 1940, after ferocious debate, Congress gave the nation its first peacetime conscription law, the Selective Service Act.

Watching these events rush past, I thought to look into my own military liability. After four years of college ROTC, I had graduated from OU with a commission in the Army Reserve. I hardly had thought about it since. Now I did, and I realized that my commission had expired. I had missed the required annual training while I was at Oxford. I checked with the adjutant general and learned that the army's policy was not to reinstate any expired commission.

Still, the country was not at war and might not be. I was in my thirties, and I saw no reason to volunteer. When the new Selective Service Act set up a lottery to determine the order of induction, I knew enough to know that the odds were that it would be a long time before my number was drawn. Secretary of War Henry Stimson did the drawing, pulling slips of assigned numbers from a revolving drum. Mine was the second number he drew. Early on the morning of June 16, 1941, I boarded a train, as ordered, bound for Camp Grant, Illinois. By noon, I was a private in the army of the United States.

I was not at Camp Grant long. Within two days, all of us new recruits were traveling through the southern darkness, headed for Camp Polk, Louisiana. I suspect that several of the boys wanted to leave even earlier. At least, some said they were thinking about taking off and heading for home—until the officers lined us up and read us the Articles of War. That part about punishment by "shooting to death with musketry" really got our attention.

Our arrival at Camp Polk hardly increased our delight in our new experience. We rode a train for a day and a half and reached the Louisiana post late at night, carrying all of our gear through mud for a mile to our barracks. We had just dropped, exhausted, onto our cots when a tall, skinny, blond corporal busted through the door. In a voice I had thought reserved for the announcement of Armageddon, he welcomed us with the memorable words: "Get off them damn bunks! Who in the hell do you think you are? You had better learn right now that you are not going to lie on your fat asses around here."

After that, we were not inclined to. Neither were we apt to forget the corporal's gratuitous judgment that "I don't like college boys. I want you to know that there ain't gonna be no book reading around here." A tough-looking draftee from Chicago looked around and said, "He's a nice son of a bitch, ain't he?" Some of us smiled. All of us knew we were in the army now.

Actually, basic training was not bad. I was assigned to Battery C of the Fifty-fourth Armored Field Artillery Battalion. Much of our training was exactly what I had already done at Fort Sill with my college ROTC unit. We even used the same weapons: old French 75s. I just polished up the skills that I had acquired in summer camp and really impressed the officers. Before long, our field artillery officer, Colonel Vincent Meyer, had me transferred to his office.

That was a good break, less because it took me out of the field than because it put me in an important place at an important time. I had a desk in the same room as Colonel Meyer. That summer, our entire Third Army was taking part in a massive training exercise, the largest military movement since the Armistice. The 240,000-man Third Army was "invading" Louisiana, which was defended by the 180,000 men of the Second Army. Colonel Meyer's office thereupon became a major headquarters.

I was working there one day when some senior officers came through. At their center was a hawk-nosed general outfitted in riding boots and a brace of ivory-handled pistols. George S. Patton, Jr., needed no introduction; he was already a legendary figure. Nonetheless, he systematically shook the hand of every officer and enlisted man in Colonel Meyer's office. General Patton inspected our operations—he seemed to like what he saw—and stayed to lecture us on his favorite subject: the tank in modern warfare. When Colonel Meyer asked him if he thought our artillery would be more effective at some distance behind advancing tanks, Patton answered him with "Hell, no. I think they should go right up with the tanks."

Colonel Meyer tactfully retreated by telling Patton, "Well, you know more about tank warfare than anyone."

"That is right," the general affirmed instantly.

I was so intrigued with Patton's performance that I barely noticed the men who accompanied him. Later, one of Colonel Meyer's aides told me that another of our visitors had a pretty good reputation among professional soldiers, too. He told me his name: Colonel Dwight Eisenhower. It was the first time that I heard that name.

I enjoyed my work with Colonel Meyer enough that I decided to apply for Officer Candidate School. The colonel told me to forget it; I could apply directly for a commission. With Colonel Meyer's recommendation and encouragement, I started the application through the channels to the adjutant general. The papers were moving somewhere a few days later when Congress passed a bill amending the Selective Service Act. The original statute conscripted men for one year only. The brass who had trained those men did not want to lose them, not when the world picture was worsening. Not in August of 1941. After a bitter struggle, Congress agreed. By a vote of 203 to 202, it extended the draftees' service another eighteen months. At least it did so for those under twenty-eight; those older, it released immediately.

So it seemed that my military service was to be a grand anticlimax. I went back to my job with The Ohio and took up right where I left off. Again, I picked my own cases, often to allow me the chance to travel. I remember one of those, a suit filed by a Marathon distributor, because it took me into Waynesville, Missouri. What made the town so memorable is that I was there on the morning of Sunday, December 7, 1941.

Within days of the Pearl Harbor attack, I went to Washington. Certain to be called into the army again, I had to see how my commission request was proceeding. I knew enough about the military and the government to know how slowly paper could move through it even in the best of times. I had little idea how to hurry the process, for these truly were the worst of times. I was walking up Connecticut Avenue, wondering what to do, when I heard someone say, "Hello, Carl."

The tone was as natural as could be. I looked around to see someone in a major's uniform. That someone was Frank Rogers; I had known him at McAlester High School. I had seen him just once since then: when I learned that Frank was in the army and making it his career. What I had not known is that he had risen so fast, that he was with the very top of the Army Air Corps, that he worked with commanders responsible for commissions and promotions, and that I would walk into him on Connecticut Avenue. Until then, I did not even know how lucky I was.

Once I told him the situation, Frank offered to help. In no time he had the matter worked out with the Air Corps command. I left my civilian work and reported back to the army. In mid-March, I received my commission as a second lieutenant. On March 20, 1942, I reported as ordered to the judge advocate general's office, United States Army Air Corps, Washington, D.C.

I reported to my commander, a Colonel Snodgrass, with the air judge advocate's office. Young attorneys were daily coming into the army, and the colonel was glad to get one who had some military training. For that reason, he appointed me his assistant executive officer.

Our headquarters was in the old Munitions Building. While construction proceeded on the Pentagon, that building housed much of the War Department. General George C. Marshall, the army's chief of staff, had his office there; Eisenhower had moved in to help him on December 14. Just beyond my work station sat a desk in a hallway. I noticed that no one ever sat there, though it was assigned to a Major Doolittle. Apparently, he was on a training mission somewhere else. I learned why Jimmy Doolittle was away when his bombers visited Tokyo.

The office next to mine belonged to a Colonel James Fechet. I soon learned that the colonel had been a great World War I pilot. With his close friend Billy Mitchell, he had helped build the Army Air Corps. For four years, he was its commander. He had worn a general's stars until the great military contraction of the post–World War I years, when his rank was reduced to colonel. At that grade he had retired, but he had volunteered to serve his country in the new emergency. He returned to Washington and the Air Corps, but he returned as a colonel, outranked by dozens of men of considerably fewer years and considerably lesser achievements.

I had an instant liking for old Fechet, and I instinctively

thought his present situation unfair. In my spare time, I started looking into the statutes and military precedents, wondering whether he could be restored to his original rank. Sure enough, after some digging I discovered that such things occasionally had been done in war. I took my information and precedents to my senior officers, and they jumped right on it. In less than a week, Fechet proudly wore again his two stars.

General Fechet's new responsibilities included approval of all Air Corps staff promotions, and one of his first approvals was to raise my rank to first lieutenant. In fact, it came at his own initiative, the general explaining that a man could not live in Washington on a second lieutenant's salary. I was awfully appreciative of the improvement, as I am sure the general had been of his own. I was appreciative again in August 1942 when he approved my rise to captain. Each promotion improved my pay and status. I was glad for the prestige, and I needed the money because I had met someone else in the air judge advocate's office. Her name was Mary Harmon.

Mary was a South Carolina girl, raised in Columbia. After high school, she had attended a business college and worked for the telephone company. She had taken a federal civil service exam for a secretarial job and scored well enough to be called to Washington during the military buildup before Pearl Harbor. She had been a civilian secretary with the Air Corps for about a year when I arrived. Later, we learned that our co-workers had played quiet matchmakers for us. She had been home sick with the measles during my first week in the job, but the other secretaries made sure that I learned her name and one thing else about her: just under five feet, Mary Harmon was my size. They gave her the same information about me.

The next Monday, I was working away when I heard the assured rhythm of heels clicking briskly across our marble floor. I looked up into sparkling blue eyes. I mumbled some pleasantry, and Mary Harmon introduced herself in a gentle Carolina accent that softly sheathed an inordinate poise and confidence. She could

August 20, 1942, we exchanged vows in a little Lutheran church. Carl and Mary Albert.

have been anything from three feet to seven; it made no difference. I knew then and there that Mary Harmon was just the right size for me.

We began to date. I remember that our first was to see the Ringling Brothers Circus. Mary was sharing a room over by the national zoo, and we practically made the zoo a second home for each of us. With some other young couples, we enjoyed the capital's other most scenic and least expensive sites. In early August we even celebrated my new captaincy by taking in New York with some friends.

Pretty soon, the only thing preventing our marriage was Mary's insistence upon her sister's approval. We invited Frances, her sister, up, and she and I hit it off instantly. As I recall, Frances bestowed her blessings on our plans as we were heading for the zoo.

The army gave us four days' leave for a marriage and honeymoon. Most of the first was consumed by a tiring ride on a long and packed train to Columbia. On the second, August 20, 1942, we exchanged vows in a little Lutheran church. On the third, we had our honeymoon, a whole day of it, in Charleston. On the fourth, we rode the train back to Washington, back to work, back to the war.

There is no job that does not allow a person to do something for someone else. Done well, the payment is a satisfaction that transcends any mere salary. To some, work as an army attorney during wartime might seem a battle with boredom, its skirmishes the shuffling of paper across a Washington desk. I quickly learned that the work's object was not paper but people. It was not a safe sinecure, it was an opportunity for service.

One of my first assignments was certainly that. One morning, an officer walked into my office. With him was a staff sergeant. The officer laid out the enlisted man's story. He had joined the army in the late thirties and was assigned to Clark Field in the Philippines; that is where he was when the Japanese attacked the base with a ferociously surprising air raid on the war's second day. Oblivious to his personal safety, the young man had set up a machine gun and had taken on the warplanes singlehandedly. He shot down two and stayed with his machine gun until the attack ended. His commander was so impressed with his courage and resourcefulness that he recommended him for the Distinguished Service Cross, the award that is second only to the Congressional Medal of Honor. He rightly won it.

In the process, however, the army had learned something about the young hero: he was not a citizen. He was not even a legal alien. He had been born in Hungary and had gone to Canada. With no visa, no passport, no identification of any kind, he had tried to enter the United States, but American officials had turned him back at the border. The fellow subsequently had hidden in a freight car and had come into the country illegally.

No one paid attention to that when he enlisted in the peacetime army. No one bothered to look into his papers when he served in the sweltering Philippines. Certainly no one thought his citizenship too important when he grabbed that machine gun at Clark Field. Now, though, it was important. In fact, the young man wanted and needed America's citizenship more than he did its military honors.

I knew that Congress had passed a law providing for accelerated citizenship to servicemen during the war. The problem was that the statute explicitly applied only to legal immigrants. In fact, his application already had been rejected on just that basis. His cause seemed unquestionably hopeless until I dug up an obscure statute from World War I. It empowered the courts to grant citizenship to any serviceman who rendered extraordinary national service in time of war.

I drew up the necessary papers and prepared the petition for a court hearing by our staff attorney, who was most experienced in Washington's federal courts. By this time, however, the young soldier had built up such confidence in my work that he insisted that I argue his case in court. Although I was not a member of the local bar, I got special permission to appear. Of course, the judge had no problem in ordering the boy's award of citizenship. The young soldier was the hero, but his infectious gratitude left me feeling awfully good.

A lot of the rest of my Washington work left me less impressed with mankind's virtues. In the winter of 1942–43, I attended the law courses run by the army's judge advocate general (JAG) at the University of Michigan. My record was such at the JAG school that I returned to Washington as a department head: chief of the military justice division. My section's major responsibilities were in criminal matters.

There was no little of that. Much of it involved the black markets that sprang up as our troops advanced on every front. The black market in currencies was probably the most lucrative for the criminals and the most troublesome for us. Troops were forbidden to change currency in any but official exchanges. Nonetheless, wholesale operations appeared around the globe, their only business the trade in black-market money. We tried to crack down hard, but the job was almost impossible.

In the case of one airman who had made a tidy profit dealing in black-market dollars, our attempt at prosecution failed because most of the witnesses had been dispersed by troop movements. That was a common occurrence, and it thwarted more than this one prosecution. In this case, however, we were able to see some measure of justice. We had an order issued transferring the culprit to the United States. Patiently, we waited until the fellow filed his income taxes, and then we pounced. We had no trouble proving that he had failed to report income that we knew he had—never mind how he got it. He went to prison for a while and paid a fine that wiped out his ill-gotten gains.

Another problem was the scope of operations. Millions of dollars were involved in exchanges weaving through several countries. One notable case, for instance, began with a Frenchman in North Africa. Before the trail ended, it involved immense sums of dollars fed through Turkey into Nazi Germany. The radio reminded us in those days that Lucky Strike green had gone to war.

Working where I was, trying to follow that trail of money, it seemed that the Mafia had gone to war, too.

I knew that my brothers had.

"Son, take care of my little boys" had been Mama's last words, and I had done it as best I could. Only Homer had wanted to go to college, and I had paid all his expenses to Oklahoma A & M (now Oklahoma State University) while he was there. I also had helped my other two brothers and my sister Kathryn from time to time.

When the war began, my two youngest brothers went into the army. Homer was first. He trained at Camp Barclay, Texas, before his assignment to the Ninetieth Division. Earl went into the 457th Parachute Field Artillery and was stationed at Camp McCall, North Carolina. That was close enough to Washington that Mary and I took the train down to see him. We stayed at a dinky, dirty, old hotel. Earl was allowed off the post to stay with us there until we had to go back.

Meanwhile, Homer's unit went out to California for desert training. We expected that that would put him in the 1942 invasion of North Africa, but instead his division got no closer than Indiantown Gap, Pennsylvania, where it sat some time for overseas readiness. During the layover, he took the train down to visit us once in Washington; otherwise, we stayed in touch through the mails. In time, though, both brothers' letters stopped coming. When the mails resumed, Earl's letters came from New Guinea, Homer's from England. Earl's unit was preparing for MacArthur's return to the Philippines. Homer's was ready for the Normandy crossing.

At just about the same time, I got my own overseas orders. Mary moved back to Columbia, and I boarded a Liberty ship in California to sail into the Pacific. None of us knew where we were going until the ship docked. The first solid ground was Oro Bay, New Guinea. I was not there long—just a few days—but I was there long enough to run into one of the last people I expected to see in that place: my youngest brother, Earl. His paratrooper division was already there when our Liberty ship arrived. Running into each other a half-world away from our McAlester home was quite a shock for us both. Earl had another one for me. He was the one who informed me that Homer had been badly wounded at Normandy. I instantly recalled that it was Homer's birth during the First World War that had caused our mother such forebodings.

I only wished that I could have taken better care of him.

My assignment was with General MacArthur's Far East Air Service Command in Brisbane, Australia. I was there as part of the huge army buildup in preparation for the invasion and conquest of the Philippines, Okinawa, and Japan itself. In a C-47, several other officers and I flew from New Guinea to Brisbane.

It was hard to tell there was a war going on. Australia had been MacArthur's refuge since his flight from the Philippines three years earlier. Most of the men with him had never had it so good. They were about as far from Washington and its supervision as one could get and stay on this planet. Japanese forces were only a fading line on a map; they were no military threat to Brisbane. The Australians genuinely welcomed the Americans. Many soldiers took Australian wives; more took Australian girlfriends. Many lieutenant colonels and everyone of higher rank maintained private quarters, usually in fine homes. They made their own rules and had pampered enlisted men for their errands. It was small wonder that officers and men stationed in Australia relished their assignment. They stubbornly resisted transfers, including rotation back to the States.

They resisted, too, the influx of new troops into their pleasant operation. It was a sign that their war party was about to end. And it was. General MacArthur was determined to restore military discipline. For that reason, he wanted a strong JAG branch, one particularly fitted to criminal prosecution. That was the assignment that brought me to Brisbane.

I had not been there long before I realized just how important that task was. Black markets operated openly. Theft—organized, massive theft—was gaining momentum. Both officers and men had grown accustomed to treating government property as their personal possession. The intelligence units that MacArthur had ordered beefed up had no trouble at all locating offenders and gathering evidence. The judge advocate staff had the more difficult mission: winning convictions in an environment that had come to expect such misdeeds as routine, even the soldier's fair reward.

In that regard, one case was particularly critical. A certain lieutenant colonel from Kansas City was charged with numerous criminal offenses, most involving the large-scale misappropriation of government property. As I looked over the documents compiled by the investigating authorities, I was amazed. The scale and the audacity of the man's operations were almost unbelievable.

What I found even more unbelievable was the prevailing belief that we could never win a conviction against him. It was that thinking that made the case so critical. A defeat would doom any hope to restore discipline, and we would lose control of our obligations. A victory for the prosecution would be a victory for military authority. Our duty was to fight for that victory.

The preparation and trial of the case fell to me. Part of my task was to serve the formal charges on the accused. I made sure that he knew when I would be there. I could tell he was ready for me. I met him at his quarters, an excellent, neat private home. The fellow graciously introduced himself and invited me to join him for refreshments in the dining room. He directed me to a seat. As I sat down, I noticed an open letter, laid out ever so casually, before my hand. It was on the stationery of the United States Senate, and the signature at the bottom belonged to a pretty important Missouri politician: Senator Harry Truman. I later learned that my man had known the senator when both were with the Pendergast machine. I was thoroughly underwhelmed by the old boy's connections, if that was his point. I was not sure, since I did not try to read the letter. I just served him my papers. I was pretty sure that he would read them.

The trial was long and complex. Through it, the accused and

his attorneys all but sneered as we assembled and placed our evidence before the court. Slowly but deliberately it grew, until it became a large, heaving volcano of proof. My final speech before the trial officers must have ignited it. We won our conviction.

The lieutenant colonel got five years in a federal prison. Military prosecutors got the feeling that future convictions would be much easier, free-living soldiers got the word that discipline was real, and I got something, too: a Bronze Star for meritorious service.

From Brisbane, Australia, I next moved to Hollandia in northern New Guinea. MacArthur, in fact, moved the entire operation there as the American army began to rush northward through the Pacific toward Japan. The Australian cities had looked like American cities, except that their civilian quiet and calm made them look like a city from earlier in the 1900s. Hollandia looked like nothing that belonged to America or to this century. It was spectacular country with stunning hills, a splendid harbor, and a beautiful lake. Its permanent residents were semicivilized natives who spoke an Indonesian dialect. The army gave us booklets to help us converse with them, and I studied mine carefully. With some practice, I became fairly adept at it, enough so that I could visit with them in their grass houses built on stilts in the lake.

Not too far away was Mount Hagen, which the army used as a rest area. Its native population still lived in the Stone Age. They really did use stone tools, and their only dress was grass skirts. Until the world war and the United States Army reached them, their entire contact with white men or the outside world consisted of two Catholic priests from Pennsylvania. With their senior priest's help, I set out to learn their language, too. I worked up to a functioning vocabulary of around five hundred words. This so impressed the native chief, a man of many wives and forty children, that he got up a dance in my honor. The entire tribe and many of their neighbors gathered for quite a memorable festival.

The army kept up a steady flow of legal work. As MacArthur's forces grew to outnumber a good-sized city, the JAG prosecutors confronted as many criminal cases as an urban district attorney's office. Many were just about the same kind. We tried assault cases, theft cases, murder cases, and rape cases. On one occasion we hanged five men for raping a nurse.

I suppose the only difference between our work and that of civilian district attorneys was that we confronted situations and crimes that rose largely from our military circumstances. One such case involved an army doctor determined to make enough in the service to buy and equip a medical clinic when he returned home. His method was to sell alcohol to the enlisted men. In no time he came to run a complete bootlegging network that involved supply officers and other agents. What he sold was government-issue alcohol, requisitioned in massive quantities for claimed medicinal uses and peddled through his dispensary. When we caught up with him, he already had socked away forty thousand dollars from the racket. We got it all back in fines—and another five years of his life in prison.

When General MacArthur kept his promise to return to the Philippines, we went, too. We built our camp just outside Manila. This time, there was no doubt that there was a war going on. There were still pockets of Japanese resistance within a few miles of our office. We saw its victims—Americans, Japanese, and Filipinos—almost daily. I remember interviewing one of them. She was an old American lady whom the Japanese had imprisoned when they overran Luzon. She had spent nearly three and a half years in the prisoner-of-war camp that the Japanese had made of the honored religious site Santa Tomas. She described her confinement as the most forlorn experience a human could have. Rotten food, lousy clothing, inadequate medicine—all of these were a part of a day's physical tribulations. Worse, though, was the psychological strain. In particular, she never had any news of the outside world except for what the Japanese told her. That was always bad and rarely true. One day it might be that the emperor's forces had besieged San Francisco. The next might be that they had overrun California. So many times had she heard of the eminent surrender of the United States that she quit believing anything. She resigned herself to dying a prisoner of the Japanese.

And then one morning she was awakened by a lot of noise in the prison yard. Before she could get to her window, she heard an American-accented shout: "Get them damn trucks out of here!" She described it as the sweetest music she had ever heard. In the person of a salty-tongued U.S. Army sergeant, her liberator had arrived. The American army had taken the prison during the night and had killed all of the Japanese guards.

Our command outpost was almost as much of a rumor factory as the POW camp had been. Of course, most of the rumors had to do with the long-awaited and much-dreaded invasion of the Japanese homeland. The favored topic was what American unit would spearhead the assault. It was an honor that few combat veterans wanted, for whichever it was, it was sure to suffer horrendous causalities. The odds-on favorite was the Eleventh Airborne Division, the one in which my brother Earl served. After what had happened to Homer at Normandy, I did not want to see Earl part of an even bloodier invasion of Japan.

That is why the radio news one morning was such music to us. A military announcer told us that a single powerful new weapon had leveled an entire city, Hiroshima. A few days later, we heard that a second such bomb had destroyed a second city, Nagasaki. The next news—by then it was no surprise—was that Japan had given General MacArthur its complete and unconditional surrender. Unlike Hiroshima, we had expected the end to come a full year later, and we thought it would come on a tide of American blood, the blood of a million paratroopers, soldiers, marines, and sailors. Instead, it came in a dignified ceremony on the calm waters of Tokyo Bay.

I am told that President Harry Truman never once regretted his decision to spare all those lives by dropping those two bombs. I know that Earl never regretted it. Neither did I.

My brother and I both got to Japan after all, but it was as part of an occupation army, not an invasion. My unit moved into Haneda Airstrip, about halfway between Tokyo and Yokohama. It was quite a place. There was not one flyable Japanese plane in the vicinity. The whole area was a blackened desert, its landscape of bomb craters littered with twisted cactuslike steel beams, yet the airstrip itself was untouched. It looked for all the world like a civilian runway in Kansas. The contrast was a testimonial to our flyers' skills. They had destroyed the field's military value to the enemy while preserving the airstrip for their own use after the certain conquest.

Haneda was an appropriate introduction to the whole country. Everywhere it was a land of contrasts. There was the contrast between Japan's beauty and its devastation. Even amid the greatest destruction in the history of warfare, carefully nurtured trees and shrubs still bloomed. Every morning, Japan's industrious people scurried about like a huge team of ants steadily clearing away the rubble. And yet they always found unlimited time to be gracious to their conquerors, particularly those like me who bothered to learn some of their language. It seemed strange to think that such beauty-loving, hard-working, and gentle-living people had only recently made war upon my own country. Until a few weeks earlier, they were my mortal enemy. But that was true, and I saw the consequence of that truth. As soon as possible, I visited Hiroshima. It was an awesome sight, one forever seared into my memory. Looking at it, I saw what man could do and what man must avoid.

Otherwise, my chief interest in Japan was that of nearly every other serviceman there: to get out, to get back home, and to get on with my life. The American army was demobilizing fast, but barely fast enough for me. My turn finally came in February 1946. With twelve thousand other homesick boys, I boarded the USS *West Point*. In ten days, we crossed the Pacific, passed through the Panama Canal, and docked at New York City.

My feet had barely touched American soil when I ran into a McAlester boy who was returning from the European theater. It was Frank Rogers, the same Frank Rogers whom I had encountered on Connecticut Avenue in Washington four years earlier. We talked briefly about our war assignments. Frank had been in

Vienna and said he intended to go back with the service. He asked me what I was going to do.

"Why, Frank," I answered, "I think I'll go back home and run for Congress."

When I told Frank that I might run for Congress, it was not the first time that I had thought about it. That had happened in a country schoolhouse more than thirty years earlier. But 1946 was a rare opportunity. I feared as much as I hoped that it might be a once-in-a-lifetime opportunity.

I had been watching the politics of Oklahoma's Third Congressional District since I was a boy. If there was one dependable fact about its Democratic politics, it was the tremendous power of incumbency. The district had had only three congressmen since statehood. Once elected, each tended to stay in Washington about as long as he wanted. Twice incumbents had lost reelection campaigns, but both of those had been very close contests involving very prominent challengers in very unusual circumstances. Only the last of those elements seemed to involve me in 1946. This would be the first election after the greatest war in American history. Anybody could reckon that a returning veteran would have a rare opportunity against a sitting politician.

The problem was just that; anybody could calculate it. And one already had. His name was Bill Steger, and he came from a prominent Bryan County family. His father was a director of the First National Bank of Durant, the county seat. Bill had gone to Harvard and held a law degree from OU. He had begun his political career before the war when he was elected Bryan county attorney. After Pearl Harbor, he had resigned his office and enlisted in the navy. He had been discharged in October 1945 and had started running for Congress the day he got back to Oklahoma. By the time I got there, you could not drive down a highway in the Third District without seeing one of Steger's signs on some farmer's fence post, and his cards and pamphlets were in every café and crossroads store. His friends were talking up his candidacy all

I think I'll go back home and run for Congress. Back row, Earl, Ernest, Kathryn, and Noal Albert; front row, Homer and Carl Albert.

over the place. Part of the talk was that he was prepared to spend an unheard-of sum—fifty to sixty thousand dollars—on the race.

The incumbent was Paul Stewart, the Old Man from the Mountain. He may have been a sitting politician, but he was no sitting duck, not for Bill Steger or anyone else. Stewart published a newspaper over in the county-seat town of Antlers. For years he had been a major figure in the state senate, and in 1942 he had pulled off the feat of himself beating an incumbent congressman, Wilburn

Cartwright. Two years later, he beat him again in a campaign that left bitter enmity between the two. Paul Stewart was not going to be easy to beat. Beating him and Bill Steger both looked pretty formidable.

There were a few ready to try, however. State Senator Bayless Irby was already running, and state senators had quite a few friends in that day's courthouses. The word was that one or two others were ready to try their hands, too. Any other entries would not make much difference, though. The Democratic primary would decide the winner (not for nothing was the Third District called Little Dixie), and the primary was almost sure to be a two-stage affair. No one was likely to get a majority of the votes in a large field; thus, a runoff election would be necessary for the top two contenders. Paul Stewart and Bill Steger seemed to have those slots in their sights, maybe in their grasp.

Through the spring months, however, I went over the district. In a rickety old public bus, I rode around to the various county seats. Anybody who knew politics—anybody who knew me—could tell what I was doing. I was testing the waters. I found them muddy.

Everywhere I went I found encouraging signs. I had friends and potential supporters all over the district. The contest was still a race, yet I knew that the other horses were out of the gate ahead of me and moving on down the track. Realistically, I had no money beyond the wartime savings that Mary had hoarded carefully. Not only had I never held a public office, I had never even campaigned on my own behalf. Because of OU, Oxford, law practice, and the war, I had been away from home and the district pretty steadily since leaving high school in 1927, nearly twenty years earlier.

I talked it over with men I trusted. I counseled with my McAlester friends. I even discussed it with Congressman Stewart, whom I found to be open, honest, and respectful. Then I made my decision just two weeks before the filing period opened. I would not run for Congress. It turned out to be the best decision I ever made.

At 7:00 A.M. on Monday, April 22, the state election board in

Oklahoma City began accepting filings for public office. Bill Steger was there early on Monday. Paul Stewart filed on Tuesday, Bayless Irby on Wednesday. Two more Democrats and a lone Republican filed on Wednesday. Friday ended the week and, at five o'clock, the filing period. That afternoon, I was pretty depressed. A chance had come to realize the boyhood dream that literally had carried me around the globe. In missing this one, I might well be missing the only one I would ever have. Bill Steger was five years younger than I, and if he took that seat from Paul Stewart, he might keep it for an awfully long time. Even if he did not do it in 1946, he would be set to move upon any opportune vacancy.

That is why I was pretty miserable on that Friday afternoon in 1946. I walked up and down the McAlester streets most of the day. Only occasionally did I stop by the apartment or my law office. At one of those stops, the phone rang. It was Truman Bennet, our county superintendent of schools and one of my best friends. I had never heard him so excited. Paul Stewart had been trying to get hold of me, Truman said. Unable to find me, the congressman finally had called him. He wanted me to know that he had come down with some worsening heart pains—no one even knew he had a problem—and had decided to withdraw from the race. He was so appreciative that I had chosen not to run against him that he wanted me to know.

The next sound I remember was Truman Bennet's car horn on the street outside. I ran through the door, jumped in the car, and we took off for Oklahoma City. If there was a bump, we did not notice it. If there was a speed limit, we did not heed it. At twenty-five minutes past four o'clock, we ran into the office of the state election board and I filled out some papers. I handed them to a weary clerk, one too tired to notice my face. Surely no one had ever worn a bigger smile at the exact moment that he officially became a candidate for the United States House of Representatives. I would not have traded that filing form for any oil well, ranch, farm, or bank in the whole state of Oklahoma.

I was in the race but I was still far behind, and it was only two months until the primary election. Instinctively, I decided to spend the first of those organizing. In the second, I would take the stump.

Folks have always taken their politics seriously in Oklahoma's Third District. The saying was, even then, that everything was political in the district, everything except politics. That was personal.

My organization was certainly personal. Like every other Oklahoma candidate, I had no regular party mechanism to turn to. What I did have was a network of friends, most dating to my high school or college days. Once I announced my candidacy, it seemed that they came out of every valley and from behind every hill in the district. This one thought he could help over in Latimer County. That one had a lot of kin down in Pushmataha County. Here was one who had some influence back in LeFlore County.

Money? That was personal, too. Mary cashed in our $9,000 worth of War Bonds and thereby became my major contributor. Some of my Bug Tussle playmates threw in. Bill Anderson, my best friend since before I had shoes, came up with $500. J. G. Puterbaugh, one of the coal industry's prestatehood pioneers, pitched in $1,500. Julian Rothbaum, whose father had been a merchant among the miners at Hartshorne, put in $1,000—the first of many generous contributions during my career. Norman Futor, a friend from OU and still a soldier in the army, added another $500. That was about it. Any other support we hoped to get by passing a hat at my speakings.

By June, I was doing those speakings at the rate of five to ten a day. Wherever two or three were gathered, there I tried to be also. At first, I did it alone. Driving over the district, I made every political rally my organizers could get up. In between, my eyes searched for groups to address. I remember one morning, about seven o'clock, driving through the little hamlet of Clayton on my way to a county rally. Nine old men were hunkered down on the sidewalk, whittling and spitting. I pulled up, hopped out, and handed them my cards with my solemn picture and slogan: "From a Cabin in the Cotton to Congress." I stayed to make a little talk.

For ten minutes, I laid some fiery championship oratory before that audience on a sidewalk in a village.

Pretty soon, I got some campaign help in the form of a three-piece string band and a seventeen-year-old redheaded girl singer. In the hot, early days of summer, we would pull into some village like Howe or Fox or Tom and set up under a shade tree. The little girl blasted out something like "Sioux City Sue" or "Tumbling Tumbleweeds." After her singing attracted a crowd, I would make my speech, work the crowd with handshakes and cards, and move on to the next stop.

If we passed a farmer out in his fields, I always tried to stop. I would talk a bit about his crops and a lot about his price supports and rural electricity. I promised to help him keep the first and get the second. I would always mention, too, that I was from a cabin in the cotton. Usually, I left a friend ready to help send me to Congress.

When we hit a good-sized town, I would walk up and down every street, go in and out of every store, and shake every hand I found. Back in the car, back on the road, all over the district, I met the voters where I found them.

I recall driving over those back roads down by the Red River, not quite sure where I was. Finally, I came across a little store and saw three or four men standing around outside. I rolled up, handed them my cards, and asked for their support. One of them looked at the card, looked at me, and asked, "Congress? Is that for the state?"

"No, sir," I said. "It's for the United States House of Representatives. In Washington," I thought to add.

He put my card down, looked me over again, then said to his friends, "I don't think he can beat Sam Rayburn, do you?"

Sure enough, I had wandered across the river into Texas—just one of the places where no one could beat the great Mr. Sam.

But Sam Rayburn I did not have to beat. My friends and I figured all along that we could not overtake Bill Steger. Our hope was to place second, force a runoff, and use the extra time to catch him. To do that, my greatest asset was my energy, a passionate, driving energy fueled by a life's ambition. My greatest weapon was my speaking.

All the skills that I had worked to acquire and sharpen from McAlester High School to the Oxford Union went into stump speeches delivered all over southeastern Oklahoma. In most of them, I was careful to tie myself to the New Deal's record, a record of changing "soup lines into production lines and relief rolls into payrolls." Usually, too, I would talk about the world war, about what I had seen in the Pacific graveyards and at Hiroshima, about America's new and awesome responsibilities.

A supporter later told me about one of those speakings. He had brought along a full-blooded Choctaw, a poorly educated but quite respected fellow, one whose judgment influenced a lot of votes in the Indian community. The story was that when I stood up to speak, the Indian noted my slight stature and mumbled, "Don't know. Congress takes a *big* man." But he listened to my speech and smiled broadly when I finished. "What do you think now?" my man asked him. "I think the little owl has a big hoot."

I may have never gotten a better evaluation in my life; certainly I got no more important one. By July 2, Election Day, I had given enough speeches, met enough voters, passed out enough cards, and shaken enough hands to pass every Democratic contender save one. Bill Steger, as predicted, led the pack. Carl Albert, as I had dared to hope, was second, twenty-seven hundred votes back, headed for a runoff, and coming up fast.

Three terribly hot weeks separated the first and second primaries. Looking over the results of the first, it seemed to me that one county, Carter, was the key to the election. It was the district's most populous county, and Steger had run up a big total there. If I could cut into that significantly while making lesser gains elsewhere, I could catch and pass him. So I concentrated everything I had left on Carter County and its seat, Ardmore. I found there an unexpected but important ally: Lloyd Noble, the Republican millionaire whom I had met when I was at the university. Mr. Noble offered to pay the cost of all of my newspaper and radio advertising in the county. The total was only seven hundred dollars, but it was seven hundred dollars that I did not have and could not afford to miss.

The runoff results were close enough that the difference could be credited to that seven hundred dollars, or, for that matter, almost anything. The earliest counts gave me a 95-vote lead. The official tabulation put the margin at 259. Steger, of course demanded a recount, but that only drove the margin up to the final official figure: 27,574 to 27,244—a 330-vote majority. I was as happy as if it had been by a million.

The general election was but a formality. John Fuller had been the lone Republican to want the hopeless honor of carrying the GOP banner through Little Dixie. John was a longtime friend of mine. In fact, his wife was my distant cousin. When I won the Democratic nomination, John gave me a one-hundred-dollar campaign contribution and withdrew from the race. The Republican Central Committee found a willing substitute, Eleanor Watson. She and they knew how hopeless was the cause. Like most Democratic nominees, I carried the district by a lopsided margin of six to one. Winning every single precinct, though, was pretty special. To tell the truth, I would have been as happy if it had been by one.

Just after the general election, Mary and I got ready to move to Washington. We bought a new car (the one new car available in town) and put nearly everything we had in the trunk and back seat of the two-door Pontiac. Then we pointed the car east and started driving.

In 1946 there was not one mile of four-lane highway between Oklahoma and Washington. So we drove on narrow, two-lane pavement except in parts of Tennessee and West Virginia, where the route was a gravel pathway through the mountains. In 1946 there was not a single bypass along the way, so we drove through every city, town, and village. In 1946 it took me three hard days' driving to get to Washington and the Congress.

Or thirty-eight years, depending on how you look at it.

CHAPTER FIVE

The House Habit

After such a long time driving, I was in a hurry to get to Congress. I was in so much of a hurry, in fact, that when Mary and I drove that road-weary Pontiac into the capital we did not as yet even have a place to live. Luckily, a Washington friend from our World War II days arranged for us to sublet a suite at the Jefferson Hotel. With some awfully cheap furniture that we got from a manufacturer in Guthrie, Oklahoma— he asked no down payment and gave us unlimited time to pay— we set up housekeeping.

The new Congress had not even convened, but I could not wait to get to the Capitol. As quickly as we could, Mary and I inspected the office that I would occupy as the United States representative from the Third Congressional District of Oklahoma. It was a letdown.

The Republican victory of November, the first since the start of the Depression, made me a freshman congressman of the minority party. As such, I was about at the bottom of the list for office assignments. So I started in Room 452 of the Old House Office Building in a space vacated when Albert Cole, a Kansas Republican, moved to better quarters. It would not have taken much to have been better than what he left for me. Every chair needed new upholstery. The carpet was threadbare. The blinds did not work. There was no desk adequate for a congressman, even a freshman minority congressman. In fact, there was no usable desk or file cabinets for his secretary. For a time, I would have to operate the office out of cardboard boxes and manila envelopes. Still, I was a congressman and I did have a place to hang my hat. Besides, as Mary said, I might someday be able to do better.

That day looked to be pretty far off, though. I might have been a freshman, but I knew that a congressman's entire career was launched down the path of his committee assignments. It was in the committee rooms that a congressman's work was done and measured. It was his assignment to the right committee that led most directly to a member's influence within the House and tangible rewards for his grateful district. Knowing that, I had aimed high. The ink was barely dry on my election certificate when I wrote the Democrats' committee on committees with my preferences. Each newcomer was allowed to list three choices. My three, in order, were rules, appropriations, and ways and means. These were the big three, the most powerful, the most prestigious committees in the House of Representatives. They were also the most difficult to land. Seasoned congressmen of several terms' outstanding service always sought assignment to each. Even they were not often successful.

I did not have a chance. Even when I lowered my sights appreciably (by offering to serve on the Public Works Committee), my case was hopeless. Years of accumulated grievances against the New Deal and the Democratic party had festered through the world war. President Roosevelt's death had removed the most articulate champion we had. Harry Truman, as yet unappreciated, had assumed FDR's office but neither his popularity nor his leadership. His first rocky months in office were bedeviled by labor strikes, consumer frustration, and business hostility. All of this the Republican party had played upon with its 1946 slogan of artful simplicity. "Had enough?" the GOP had asked. And the voters had answered, sending fifty-five veteran Democratic congressmen (and twelve senators) packing and giving the Republicans control of both houses of Congress.

The unaccustomed Republican majority took over every committee, leaving few slots for even veteran Democrats. A newcomer had some pretty poor pickings left, and mine were about the poorest of all. Despite the GOP's national landslide, Oklahoma sent three other freshmen Democrats (Glen Johnson, Toby Morris, and Preston Peden) with me to Washington. Each represented a district less securely Democratic than mine. For that reason, our party's leadership was more interested in bolstering their reelection chances with attractive assignments. By the time they got to

The Oklahoma congressional delegation of 1947–49: Toby Morris, Glen Johnson, Mike Monroney, Bill Stigler, Preston Peden, George Schwabe, Ross Rizley, and Carl Albert.

me, all the leaders could offer was the unrequested House Committee on the Post Office and Civil Service. In all the later years when I would have a voice in committee assignments for hundreds of freshmen members, not once did I know of one who sought post office and civil service.

Still, I accepted my assignment: maybe someday I might do better there, too. In fact, I was grateful enough that I was ready to thank our party's House spokesman, the great Sam Rayburn. Speaker after 1940, Mr. Rayburn would have to serve as minority leader in the Republican-controlled House. I visited his office, only to encounter his secretary since 1919, the formidable Alla Clary. Miss Clary glanced over my youthful appearance and slight stature. Coolly she informed me that Mr. Rayburn did not have time to talk with pages.

However inauspicious those first few days may have been, I was thrilled beyond words on January 3, 1947. It was my first official day as a congressman. There was another first on that day, too. Through the new medium of television, millions of Americans were watching the House convene. With befitting solemnity, the clerk of the House began calling the alphabetical roll of members. The first called, Thomas Abernathy of Mississippi, did not respond. The second was Carl Albert of Oklahoma. "Here," I answered. It was the sweetest word in the English language.

Behind that response was my entire life's experience. Sitting on the House floor, looking up at the massive Speaker's dais, I remembered one that went all the way back to Bug Tussle, back to the eighth grade and Mr. Craighead's little talks about a man who had once stood right there. Speaker Champ Clark, my teacher had told us, loved the House of Representatives. It was from that very spot that Champ Clark had rejected the Missouri governor's offer of an appointment to fill the unexpired term of a dead United States senator. That was where Champ Clark had read his telegraphed answer. "There is a House habit and a Senate habit," he had said, "and I have got the House habit so bad that I can never get out of it."

I wanted to have the House habit, and another of Mr. Craig-

Carl Albert as a freshman congressman.

head's little talks told me how to get it. He had told us of Champ Clark's observation that a man has to learn to be a congressman, just as he must learn to be a farmer or a carpenter or a lawyer or anything else. If his constituents were "to select a man of good sense, good habits, and perfect integrity, young enough to learn," and keep returning him to the House, he and they would both profit. For as he learns his job, as a congressman acquires the House habit, "such a man grows into power and high position as surely as the sparks fly upward." For myself, I was ready to keep my end of that bargain. The spark glowed within me to learn the House habit. Maybe someday, that spark would carry me upward, too.

For many days, though, it carried me only between Capitol Hill and the little apartment at the Jefferson Hotel. After just a few of them, I wrote myself a letter dated February 2, 1947, the last day of my first month in Congress.

Looking over that letter now, I see it as the testament of another dream. Just as I had earlier dreamed of winning oratorical contests, traveling to Europe, capturing a Rhodes scholarship, or going to Congress, I dreamed again, this time of what I hoped to accomplish there. It had to be a long letter, for, as always, I dreamed big, but then I had never known a little dream to carry anyone anywhere.

Only months before I wrote, my country and the world had been at war. I had stood in the black deserts that that war had made of Japan's cities. And so I prayed earnestly that "God give me the power and the resolution to work daily as long as I am in Congress for world peace." For me, that path was illumined by the blunders that I saw following the First World War. I believed that the path to peace lay in an active international organization, the new United Nations, which must not be allowed to go the way of Woodrow Wilson's old League of Nations. America could not afford to ignore its responsibilities once more, nor must it ever again lack "military preparedness equal to that of any potential hostile power on earth." The old idea of a Fortress America had died at Pearl Harbor; its tombstone was a mushroom cloud. In a dangerous world of armed might, "we must unite with other free nations to insure the continuation of both their freedom and ours."

The freedom that we were defending also had to be enlarged. Already I believed that "no baby should be born into this land to drag a chain only because of the race or color which God gave it." At the time, I could only hope that "my career in Congress is long and that I will have the ability and political and personal courage to make a contribution to the civil rights of all people."

One right that I wanted all people to share was the right to a quality education. My own life bore witness to its power, and it left me persuaded that "this tommy rot about the education of our children being the sole responsibility of local communities, however poor, is disgraceful. There is nothing so sinister about educating our children that would tarnish our national government by getting into it."

Because my state was poor and my district poorer, federal aid was no demon; it was a deliverer. Directed to their schools, Washington's dollars could deliver my people from ignorance. Federal dams could save their farms from floods, reclaim their soils from erosion, and ease their toil with electricity. Sensible farm programs could bring prosperity to the poor children of pioneer parents, the rural folk who were both my neighbors and my constituents. Those townsfolk who made their living from oil and gas production needed a watchdog for their interests. Those with special needs—Indians with unsettled claims, veterans with ruined lives, employees of my hometown's naval ammunition depot, and all the rest—deserved an attentive champion in Washington.

There was pride in that letter of February 1947. "After all," I wrote, I was living "the fulfillment of a life-long dream." But there was humility, too. I closed it with these earnest words: "As much as I like my job I would not want it unless I could help my people. I hope, when I am through, it will be said that I represented them well and that I served my country as a congressman in my day and generation to the best of my ability."

In 1947, I was just a freshman congressman of the minority

party, the lowest-ranking member of the most obscure committee in the entire Congress. Never again would I find the time or the compulsion to write out my dreams. I was too busy making them come true.

It is unfortunate that Americans who know next to nothing about any other congressional session can recognize readily the Congress that I entered in 1947. It was the famous Do-Nothing Eigh-

Truman had a special place for me. President Truman and Democratic congressional leaders: Senator Mike Mansfield, Congressman Carl Albert, Speaker Sam Rayburn, Senator Carl Hayden, and House Majority Leader John W. McCormack.

I do remember first knowing the two future presidents. John Kennedy is in the third row from the back on the right side, five seats in from the center aisle; Carl Albert, two seats to his left; Richard Nixon, second row from the back in the fifth seat in from the center, on the opposite side of the aisle. The photograph, taken in 1947, is of military veterans serving in Congress.

tieth Congress. Harry Truman appended the nickname when he made the Republican-controlled legislature his election foil in 1948, and the name stuck. The tactic certainly served Truman well: his presidential campaign in '48 remains the miracle election. The memorable adjective, however, obscures the fact that this was a Congress of remarkable figures and remarkable achievements.

First elected with me to the House side of the Do-Nothing Congress was a group of ninety-two men and women who remained my friends for years. They included two future presidents, John F. Kennedy and Richard M. Nixon. The latter would also serve as vice-president under Dwight Eisenhower. In addition, nine would serve in the United States Senate, and five went on to become state governors. Outside elective politics, another five became judges, seven became high officials in the executive branch, and two became American ambassadors. In 1971, when I was first elected Speaker, eight of the original members of the Class of the Eightieth Congress still served with me in the House. No longer green freshmen, five then were chairmen of House committees or major subcommittees.

I cannot claim to have been able to foretell their futures at the time, but I do remember first knowing the two future presidents. I met them both on my very first day in the House. I was standing on the floor when Richard Nixon came up, introduced himself as Dick Nixon, and asked me about that college oratorical contest on the Constitution of nearly twenty years earlier. He grinned when he told me of his own quick elimination in a later contest. While we both served in the House until Nixon went to the Senate in 1950, we got along quite well, often finding ourselves in agreement on bipartisan matters of foreign policy.

Later that same day, John Kennedy (he called himself Jack) introduced himself to me. He asked if I was the new Oklahoma congressman who had been a Rhodes scholar in the 1930s. He seemed pleased to know me, and he mentioned that he had often visited Oxford while his father was our ambassador to Great Britain. Before Kennedy, too, moved on to the Senate on his way to the

White House, we often conferred as House members, particularly about the knotty issue of labor-law reform.

On that same day, I met another future president, though not a freshman congressman. Lyndon Johnson had come to the House in the mid-1930s as a supporter of Franklin Roosevelt and had become a protégé of Sam Rayburn. Mike Monroney, Oklahoma City's veteran congressman, introduced us in the Democratic cloakroom. I soon learned that it was Johnson's favorite habitat. I never spoke with him there without being impressed by his burning political ambitions. Never did I sense that he had, or wanted to have, a House habit. I already sensed that the Senate's much different habit was more fitted to Lyndon Johnson's ways.

Because the Republicans were the majority, they provided the formal House leadership of the Eightieth Congress. Joe Martin, a Massachusetts representative since 1924 and the Republican floor leader since 1939, won pro forma election as Speaker over our Sam Rayburn, who thereupon became the minority leader. Quite conservative by temperament—Martin had opposed most of Roosevelt's New Deal and would marshal his Republican forces to bury much of Truman's Fair Deal—the new Speaker proved to be both affable and effective. In the Speaker's role, he put aside most of his partisanship to work well with the Democratic leaders. His oft-repeated observation that "you've got to follow in order to lead" testified to his awareness that there were many political facts that transcended partisan maneuverings.

Never was that clearer, or more important, than in the critical field of foreign policy. Hitler's defeat had removed the basis of our alliance with Soviet Russia. Stalin's brutal installation of puppet regimes in Central and Eastern Europe had removed hope for a postwar partnership. Even as we freshmen congressmen were learning our way around Washington, events were transpiring overseas that would permanently alter America's way in the world. In February 1947, the nearly bankrupt British told our government that they could no longer afford to support the Greek government's civil war against Red insurgents. The British were leaving Greece, Turkey—the entire eastern Mediterranean—a vacuum, a vacuum that seemed doomed to be filled by the Soviets. In that same grim winter, the second after World War II, 125 million Europeans remained malnourished. National Communist parties in France and elsewhere were ready to feast on their misery. All that blocked their way was Harry Truman, the leaders of Congress, and the members who had learned too well the costs of isolation and appeasement.

In a breathtakingly short period, Harry Truman and the Eightieth Congress checked the threat of Stalinist advance and laid the foundation for a generation of American diplomacy. First was the Greek-Turk loan, $350 million that preserved the independence of Greece and Turkey and kept the Mediterranean from becoming a Russian lake. Next was the European Recovery Program (the Marshall Plan), $13.5 billion that honored Secretary of State George C. Marshall and drowned the Communist threat in a flood of new prosperity. In between was the epoch-making Truman Doctrine. Its declaration that it would be "the policy of the United States to support free peoples who are resisting attempted subjugation by armed minorities or outside pressure" reversed sixteen decades of American isolation and defined our mission as protector of the Free World.

Thus, in the spring of 1947, in my first months of Congress, America shouldered the burdens of global leadership that it had shunned after the First World War. President Truman pointed the way. Speaker Martin and Sam Rayburn led the Congress. Jack Kennedy, Lyndon Johnson, Dick Nixon, two-thirds of both houses, and I marched along. I did because the Second World War had taught me that those commitments represented our best chance for peace in a hostile world. Every president since Truman has extended those commitments and believed in that policy. Not one thing has happened since to cause me to doubt it, either.

Ours was, then, a do-something Congress. Off the stump, Harry Truman agreed. Whatever his campaign protestations, President Truman appreciated the remarkably bipartisan statesmanship of our foreign policy. I certainly appreciated him. Of the six presidents with whom I served, Truman has a special place for me. Of unexceptional looks, his was an exceptional character. Everyone, Joe Stalin included, could measure it when he announced the Truman Doctrine and won from Congress Greek-Turk and Marshall Plan aid. Stalin and the world saw it, too, when Harry Truman later preserved Berlin's independence by airlift, fortified the United Nations in Korea, and served our Constitution by dismissing General Douglas MacArthur. The man had steel in his blood.

I recall the first time that I met him. Early in my first year in Congress, George Smathers got up a group of us new congressmen and went down to the White House. It was George's idea, so he laid out some issues that he thought would help the president with the next election. When George finished, Harry Truman pointed to a globe that he had sitting on his desk and said, "I'm not interested in forty-eight. I'm interested in that little globe. I'm going to do what I can to preserve it." I barely held back the tears to choke out, "Mr. President, I will do what I can to help you."

A very little thing that I could do happened in 1948. Harry Truman was running what everyone knew was a hopeless race to keep his job. The Republican nominee, Tom Dewey, was ready to preside over his funeral. Two renegade Democrats, Strom Thurmond of the Dixiecrat right wing and Henry Wallace of the Progressive left wing, were going to be the pallbearers. Begrudgingly nominated by a demoralized party, Truman did not have much going for him.

Not much except courage, tenacity, conviction, and a plainspokenness that just made sense. That is all he had to offer, and offer it he did in his famous whistle-stop campaign tour of 1948. I joined the tour in Bonham, Texas, Sam Rayburn's hometown. Oklahoma's governor, Roy Turner; our Senate nominee, Robert S. Kerr; and I were the ones who rode with the president into Oklahoma. We each made a little talk at every stop on the line, but Harry Truman always had the last—and the best—words. The crowds got steadily larger and steadily warmer, and it began to dawn on us that the news of Mr. Truman's death (like Mark

Twain's) was greatly exaggerated. If Harry Truman could keep getting his message out, he could win this thing.

At least he could win it if he could get his train out of the station. It ran out of money in Oklahoma City. We each got on the phone and found Sooners who threw in enough to get the train out of Oklahoma City and down into Little Dixie, my part of the state. There, the crowds got even more enthusiastic. Fortified, Truman carried the tour across the nation. Tom Dewey ended up going to a funeral, all right, and Harry Truman went back to the White House.

My initial assignment to the Post Office Committee had one great virtue. The committee's workload was so light and my other duties were so inconsequential that I had plenty of time to educate myself. My school was the House chamber. It is where I learned how to be a congressman.

In my first term, I do not believe that I missed a single day of the House's proceedings. I was there when the chaplain opened the day's work with prayer. I was there when the Speaker's gavel sounded adjournment. In between, I stayed on the floor, because that is where I had wanted to be all my life.

Of course, every day hundreds of tourists pass through the House galleries, there to watch their representatives work for them. My initial impression was not much different from those of tourists: the chamber is a lovely sight. Measuring 139 feet by 92, the room seems to enclose much of the majesty of American history. I never entered it (not on my first day, nor on my last, nor in the thirty years in between) without feeling slightly awed. It is part of the House habit that I acquired instantly and never lost.

Sitting on the floor of that magnificent chamber gave me a daily education in the incredibly complex proceedings of the House. Because of its larger size and subsequent greater need for organizational formality than the Senate's, the House of Representatives works with a unique sense of tradition and incredibly complex rules. Codified, the rules of the House run to well over ten thousand, seemingly to match any past situation or imaginable future circumstance with a formal rule. Like the tourists, I was dumbfounded early on by the arcane exchanges between the members and the presiding officer. "I have an amendment on the desk." "Third reading. A motion to recommit is laid upon the table." "Without objection, it is so ordered." The tourists were not alone: to a freshman member, too, it sometimes seemed like a foreign language.

But I was in the House to learn its habit and I came swiftly to love its traditions, its procedures, and its language. It took me a while to master them—after about two years I had a firm working knowledge—but it did not take even a day to fall in love with them. They are the living, breathing anatomy of the House as an institution. Like the English common law, the House rules have grown from the soil of tradition.

Because of my speech training, I expected to hear some great oratory in the House. I quickly learned, though, that speech making was a much overrated part of a congressman's job. Men of great reputation sometimes never spoke on the floor. Illinois' Tom O'Brien was one. Representative of Chicago's massive Democratic machine, O'Brien always sat languidly on the floor or leaned against the back rail. I do not recall once hearing him address the House, and yet every member knew that Tom O'Brien's judgment could pass or could doom virtually any bill. That I learned from talking with my new colleagues. They could tell you which were the eagles and which were the sparrows.

I learned something else from them, too: how very impressive the membership was. Denigrating Congress long has been one of America's favorite sports. I learned that there were some bigots and fakers among the members and a few show horses, too, but most congressmen were truly workhorses. Quiet, unassuming, dedicated members who were unsung by the press and unknown to the average citizen—these were the great majority. To my awe of the House's chamber and my love for its traditions, I quickly added respect for its membership.

However, the most important thing that I learned in those early days of sitting attentively on the floor was that House members were individuals. I heard every speech delivered. I watched every vote cast. I talked with every group and every member I met. Within three months, I knew the name and face of every one of the 435 members. I knew that this one came from a district that usually elected the opposition and feared losing his seat. I knew that that one followed his committee chairman's every lead. I knew that this one needed union votes to keep his job. I knew that that one was so secure that he could vote his convictions on anything, and I knew what those convictions were. My first session was not halfway through before I could tell how 80 percent of them were going to vote on any question.

And I knew that the Democratic leadership needed to know just that.

Nothing could have prepared me for the great legislators I found serving as the Democratic leadership. For my first fifteen years (half of my total service), John McCormack and Sam Rayburn directed the House Democrats. Except for the brief interlude of Republican majorities after 1946 and Dwight Eisenhower's 1952 landslide, they directed the House of Representatives as well, John McCormack as majority leader and Sam Rayburn as Speaker. Neither I nor the Democrats nor the nation had ever seen such a team.

Chosen by the members of the majority party, the majority leader technically is not an officer of the House but of his political party. Nonetheless, it is inconceivable that the House could function without him. Working closely with committee chairmen, he helps define each session's legislative program. Through the year, he directs the House calendar. Chief spokesman for his party, he often closes debates on major bills. As his party's leader, he also works to assemble winning majorities behind those bills deemed important to the party. John McCormack did all those things, all for a long time, all with distinction.

Born in 1891 to a builder in Boston's Irish ghetto, John left school in 1904 to support the family when his father died. Working long hours at unskilled jobs, he went to school at night until he entered the Massachusetts bar when he was only twenty-one. A born politician, he served in the state constitutional convention in 1917 and went to the state legislature in 1920 as a Democrat, a progressive Democrat. For another fifty years, he championed liberal reforms for state and nation, though he shunned the term *liberal* in favor of the more old-fashioned term *progressive.*

In 1928, John went to Congress, where he made friends with Sam Rayburn and impressed Speaker John Nance Garner. A diligent worker in committees, John won a seat on the Ways and Means Committee in 1933 and served to bring FDR's New Deal alive. Three years later, he delivered vital New England votes for Sam Rayburn's successful bid for the majority leadership. In 1940, when Sam Rayburn became Speaker, John McCormack became majority leader.

Of formidable intellect and equipped with sharp analytical skills, he was long our party's best debater in Congress. Sam Rayburn told me more than once that he would rank John second only to Alben Barkley as a debater in the fifty years of his own service. In one session alone I saw him debate powerfully, knowledgeably, and effectively more than two hundred separate bills. His tall, gaunt figure striding the floor, his long finger jamming out his points, he was for decades the Democrats' most forceful champion and the Republicans' most feared foe.

As a statesman, John had a remarkably national orientation. Representing an urban district, he cared deeply about rural America. Time after time, he cast New England's only affirmative vote for farm legislation. Thoroughly northern and thoroughly unprejudiced, he earned the respect of southerners for his fairness and willingness to compromise. In 1944, 1952, and 1956, the Democratic party put him in charge of writing the platform of the national convention. Each time, he engineered civil-rights planks that kept the party's northern and southern wings united. Only in 1948, when he was not in that position, did the party split open in the Dixiecrat revolt.

As a man, John was a true gentleman. Seldom was he ever heard to speak critically of a colleague. He once said of Claire Hoffman, *llvi*

a most contemptible member, that he held him in minimal high regard. As a boy, John McCormack had sworn an oath of abstinence to his mother, and he not once tasted liquor in his life. His devotion to his beloved wife was legendary. Whatever else he was doing, John had dinner with her every night of their long married life. When Harriet McCormack finally died in a hospital room, John McCormack occupied the bed next to hers.

As a freshman congressman, I first met John McCormack as my party's whip. Thereafter, I was proud to call him my friend. Sam Rayburn became my friend, too, but Mr. Rayburn (no one of my generation called him anything but that or Mr. Sam) became far more than my friend. In my last letter to him, written after he had gone home to Bonham, Texas, to die, I wrote the only words that can express my feelings for him. "I love the Speaker as I have loved no man in my lifetime except my own father. He is the greatest man I ever knew."

I still remember the first time I ever saw him. He was giving a rousing Democratic campaign speech from a railroad car over in Denison, Texas, back in the 1920s. Elected to the House in 1912, he was already a famous congressman, and his fame and contributions grew steadily. His fingerprints were on the legislation that transformed American life; some of it had transformed my own. Until I was fifteen, I studied by a coal-oil lamp. More than any other man, it was Sam Rayburn who put electric lights and running water in the homes of Americans like me with the bills he pushed through Congress in the thirties.

He represented Texas's Fourth Congressional District, the one lying just across the Red River from Oklahoma's Third. I almost regarded him as my own congressman. My mother and her father were born in that district, and I had dozens of relatives still living there. One of Mr. Rayburn's brothers lived for a while in my own district. His home in Bonham was only six miles from the Oklahoma border.

I had made it a point to visit Mr. Rayburn in Bonham as soon as I had won my first primary. During the next few years, I returned often. We took to fishing together once in a while—Mr. Rayburn

I first met John McCormack as my party's whip.

I love the Speaker as I have loved no man in my lifetime except my own father.
Carl Albert with Sam Rayburn.

used to say that he would rather catch a two-inch fish than spend two days playing golf—in Lake Texoma, which lapped across our districts' lines. He bought his alfalfa down in Yuba, in my district, and we would talk for hours, leaning against a truck.

Physically, he reminded me very much of my father. Both men were about the same height, though Mr. Rayburn was a bit stockier. Like my father, he tended to look you straight in the eye; like him, too, he tended to talk very straight as well. Both men could joke, but both took the world seriously.

Mr. Rayburn's entire life was the House of Representatives. Most people did not know that he had been married for a few months in the 1920s. His real wife was the House, his family its members. In just under fifty years of congressional service, he left the United States only once: to inspect the Panama Canal. Otherwise, his years revolved around Washington and Bonham, the twin foci of his life as a complete congressman.

No one who met him could escape the force of his character. Many disputed his politics; none doubted his integrity. He absolutely could not tolerate lying, even of the little white variety. For decades he was known as Mr. Democrat, yet his fairness toward the Republicans and his respect for their leaders was legendary. Hardly a single member of either party could not recount at least one kindness from his hands. The veterans could count dozens. We junior Democrats quickly learned of his kindness, indeed, his fondness. Particularly as he aged (he celebrated his sixty-third birthday on my fourth day in Congress), Sam Rayburn kept his eye out for promising junior Democrats. He once explained that young men kept him young watching their growth, and he was always looking for young Democrats who had the capacity to love the institution of the House of Representatives. He was especially interested in finding promising junior congressmen from his own part of the country. Sam Rayburn loved the people with honest dirt under their fingernails. The men and women who toiled in the cotton patches, cornfields, and peanut rows of the southwest and the Red River valley—these were the ones he called the real people. He looked unblinkingly for one who might represent them as well and as powerfully as he did.

I suppose that that is what first drew his attention to me. He knew me from our early talks, and I know that he respected my family's roots in the soil and my education at Oxford, both about equally. I nearly burst my buttons with pride when a friend told me how Mr. Rayburn had bragged on my maiden speech in Congress. It was a short defense of the working folks threatened by the viciously antilabor Hartley bill. People told me that Mr. Rayburn had pronounced it one of the best speeches he had ever heard by a freshman member.

But more than anything else, what drew Mr. Rayburn was my obvious enthrallment with Congress. Sitting on the floor day after day, listening to every speech delivered, watching every vote cast, talking with every member I could corner—these things I did not from ambition but out of love for the House. Sam Rayburn liked me for what I did; he liked me more for why I did it.

After a while, he would sometimes call me to the Speaker's dais and ask me how I expected a vote would come out. I would tell him, and I would usually be right, maybe within a half-dozen votes of the actual count. When he could not identify a particular congressman, he learned that he could ask me. I knew each one. Usually I could tell him what he wanted to know about the member. Generally, I could predict and explain the fellow's position on an upcoming vote.

Growing from my hunger for the House habit, it was these qualities, not the accident of geography, that first gained me entrée into Mr. Rayburn's inner circle. The occasion was the prize most cherished by every member, freshman and veteran alike: an invitation to join him at the Board of Education.

The Board of Education was an unofficial but not invisible institution of the House. At the end of each day's session, Mr. Rayburn liked to invite a select group of friends to join him to talk over politics and "strike a blow for liberty," as he and his friend Harry Truman called the evening's libations. When Sam Rayburn invited me to join the group, I knew that I was on my way.

The board met in Room H-118 in a place small (twelve by twenty feet) by Capitol standards. Once a House committee room, for decades it had been assigned to the Speaker for his own use. Over the years, Mr. Rayburn had furnished it to his personal tastes. An old Persian carpet covered the floor; framed political cartoons, signed photographs, and a few portraits covered the walls. Eight chairs, some straight backed, most overstuffed in leather, were scattered around Mr. Rayburn's big desk. A long black leather couch lined one wall. It was noted as the place where Harry Truman was sitting when the White House summoned him to give him the news that Franklin Roosevelt was dead and he was president.

In my first term, Mr. Rayburn invited me frequently; thereafter, I had a standing invitation. The usual group included Texans (Lyndon Johnson, Homer Thornberry, Frank Ikard, and the like), some of Mr. Rayburn's oldest friends (typically Gene Cox, Clinton Anderson, John McCormack, and Lew Deschler, the House parliamentarian), and a select group of promising youngsters (maybe Hale Boggs, Henry Jackson, Wilbur Mills, and usually Richard Bolling). Over drinks, we would talk some legislative business and listen to Mr. Rayburn's stories of Texas and of Congress. He listened, too, constantly judging men's characters and measuring the shifting moods of the House. Sam Rayburn consumed information, and the information that he gained in those evening sessions kept him in touch with the House. About seven o'clock, we would break up, almost always to Mr. Rayburn's last words, "Let me know if you hear anything."

The knowledge that Mr. Rayburn collected plus the character that he displayed gave him power far beyond a Speaker's institutional authority. Actually, the revolt against czar Joe Cannon's rules back in 1910 had stripped the Speakership of most of its formal authority. The power that Sam Rayburn exercised over the House was the power of his being Sam Rayburn. No Speaker of this century had had such respect. None had known better the mood of the chamber, and none had accumulated such a bankroll of personal favors granted and intimate kindnesses extended. It was a blessing to know him. It was a privilege to serve with him. It was my great good fortune to have him as my friend and my mentor.

I learned very early to trust his judgment. On important votes, I hardly needed it. Representing the same kind of people, we almost always thought alike on major issues. I honestly do not recall a single instance of his asking me to vote a certain way on any bill.

He knew that I would vote my convictions and that they were almost always one with his.

What I did take to heart was his counsel regarding my career in the House. Because of his influence, I won a seat on the Agriculture Committee in 1949. He knew that the assignment was good for me and good for our people. A little while later, a vacancy occurred on ways and means, the most prestigious and powerful committee in the House. Several members urged me to seek the position, but Sam Rayburn advised against it. He told me frankly that I could expect to be in Congress for a long time and that I had a bright career ahead of me. Assignment to a committee as controversial as ways and means, he said, would only complicate the career.

I remember that Lyndon Johnson urged me to ignore Mr. Rayburn's advice: go for the power. I trusted Mr. Rayburn's judgment instead. As usual, it was exactly correct; it always was. Even as a freshman congressman I had learned to appreciate his wisdom. The first time we talked in Washington, he told me what he had told hundreds of newcomers before me. He spoke about the importance of judgment and common sense, "the only kind of sense there is," he said. He told me to ignore the adage about freshmen being seen but not heard. He did, however, stress that any congressman had best be sure he had something worth saying when he took the floor. "There's a whole lot more men have talked themselves out of Congress than have talked themselves into it," he observed. Mostly, he stressed that a congressman should never forget his district. Answer every letter you get, he told me, particularly the ones handwritten in pencil on Big Chief tablet paper. He said when a person like that writes you, he really needs help. If you help him, he will never forget it, and he will be your friend for life.

I never forgot that advice.

I doubt that I even needed Mr. Rayburn's advice about the importance of keeping up with the home folks. I had wanted to go to

Congress so badly and my first election had been so close that I was determined to put Carl Albert's name before every voter in my district and keep it there. Besides, visiting with my friends in the courthouse, talking to school groups, eating campaign barbecue—these gave me as much pleasure as anything that happened in the capital.

In the earliest years, this was relatively easy. Congress usually adjourned in late summer, leaving the fall months free to return to the Third District before a new session convened in January. Through the year, I also made just as many trips home as possible. They were long railroad trips that a congressman paid for out of pocket back then because they were part of his job. Typically, I would pull into McAlester late Saturday, spend the weekend at home (Mary and I kept a residence there), and take out across the district on Monday morning. I would be gone all week before returning home for the weekend and hitting the road again the next Monday.

Typical was one long stay when I made it a point to visit every house on the east side of Ardmore. My poor returns there in 1946 had almost cost me my dream, and I was determined to win those people over. So I printed up some cards with my name and address, saying that I was their United States congressman. I parked my car at each block's end, walked both sides of the street, and then went on to the next block. When no one was home, I left a note: "Sorry I missed you. Please contact me if I can be of service." If someone answered my knock, I would chat a bit, often hearing that I was the only congressman they had ever seen, especially at their front door. I made it a point to get the name, address, and telephone number of anyone who showed interest in me. These started getting periodical letters. No one who got one ever forgot me after that.

I also tried to meet my constituents at their post offices. Cards, posters, and newspaper notices would announce that I would be at the post office in Howe or Tom or Smithville at a certain time. I met and kept in touch with a lot of voters that way. Usually, I would take with me a notebook to record their concerns or their needs. In addition to being a good way to make contact, I found it invaluable for helping with my constituents' problems with the federal bureaucracy. My post-office visits were especially important to the poor folks, who had nowhere to turn for help. It was my job as their congressman to help when I could. Sometimes it was my privilege, for these were times when I truly served them.

One came during the Korean War. One of my campaign helpers called Washington from the little town of LeFlore, Oklahoma. LeFlore is just about the most isolated town in the state, and it is one of the poorest. So small and so isolated is the place that there used to be only four telephones in the entire town. My friend was calling from one of them.

He told me that one of my constituents had come to see him. She had ridden in on a horse. She knew that he knew her congressman and maybe he could help her. She had lost three sons in World War II. Her only remaining boy was in the Marine Corps, stationed in San Francisco but under orders to be shipped to the Korean front. Someone had told her that the government could keep her boy out of the war, since he was her only surviving son. She wanted her boy home. "You gotta remember," the caller told me, "she came in here on a horse."

I was familiar with the sole-surviving-son rule from World War II, so I got on the phone and called the Navy Department. I got quite a runaround before some officer finally told me there was nothing he could do: the rule applied only to World War II. Besides, he added gratuitously, "this is just a police action. It's not important, like a war." I knew—and I told him—that it was a war to that woman and it was awfully important to her.

Dejected, I went over to the office of Congressman Carl Vinson. Mr. Vinson was a Georgia Democrat, the longest-serving member of the House and the unflinching chairman of the Armed Services Committee. Congressmen, presidents, admirals, and generals—all yielded to his authority. I told him the story. "Mr. Chairman," I ended, "the woman came to town on a horse." Carl Vinson raised his right arm. "By God!" he vowed, "the Navy's either got such a rule or they will have one before sundown." When I got back to my office, the secretary of the Navy was waiting on the telephone. He said that he had just held a staff meeting in which it was decided to reinstate the sole-surviving-son rule for the Korean War. Moreover, he had traced this marine's orders. The boy was on a ship off Japan; the moment it docked, the Navy would put him on a plane back home.

The boy came back. In fact, he came to see me and he was furious. His brothers had had the chance to fight for their country, he was a marine, and he wanted that chance, too. In marine-barracks language, he told me that he did not want any congressman to do anything for him.

"Son," I told him, "I didn't do anything for you. I did it for your mother."

Representing the Third District, I welcomed every opportunity to appear there for public occasions. In time, my staff would sometimes chide me for my determination. But to me, that was part of the House habit. On one occasion, I had promised that I would appear at a certain village, only to discover the roads blocked by a flood-swollen river. Luckily, a farmer lent me his plow horse, I forded the stream, and I met my obligation and my constituents. More than once I turned down appearing at a big national fundraiser because I had agreed to give the commencement speech at some tiny high school. Those people of my district knew which was more important to me, and I did, too.

Gradually, I used those personal contacts to build up quite a file, about four thousand names in all. As my duties in Washington grew and became unavoidable, the file and the telephone allowed me to keep in touch. Three afternoons a week I would spend on the telephone to the people of my district. I would call about twenty different people scattered in twenty different towns. That way, I knew the next morning in twenty different coffee shops twenty conversations would begin with someone saying, "I talked to the congressman yesterday . . . ."

In no time I built up a network of listening posts throughout the district. In every community I had at least one dependable friend who could tell me who wanted what and who was mad at whom. Sometimes these were local politicians; sometimes they were just special friends. Probably the best I ever had was a waitress in a little café. In my very first campaign, I learned that she knew absolutely everything about everyone in the surrounding county. Thereafter my staff knew, even when I was majority leader and Speaker, to put Miss Virgie White through immediately when she called me. Years later she was on the Johnny Carson show and she really held her own.

One thing these listening posts helped me with was the treacherous factionalism that divided even the smallest community in Little Dixie. As long as I represented the area in Congress, I became ever more convinced that it really was true that everything down there was political except politics. That was personal. Congressional patronage was just one of the trouble spots, but always a big one. In those days, a congressman named every rural mail carrier and many postmasters in his district. Picking the wrong one was sure to stir up a lot of local enmity.

My allies were usually dependable counselors on how to antagonize the smallest number of people. Sometimes, though, even they could not fathom the depths of local feeling. I well remember one occasion when I appointed a woman the postmistress of some tiny hamlet. Overnight, every man in the community was complaining, declaring that I had passed over many needy men supporting families, men who had veteran's preference at that. I checked and made it a point to announce a visit to that post office. When I got there, I told them that the woman had a veteran's preference, too. She had lost her husband, who was killed in action in World War II, and was supporting a family. She was going to stay the postmistress. She did, and I doubt that I ever named a more conscientious or more deserving one.

However sensitive I believed a congressman had to be to public sentiment, I also believed that he had to be his own man, too. Of course, that involved much more than selecting a postmistress. It went right to the heart of my beliefs about the nature of representation. Just after my first election to Congress, I told a reporter how I looked at it. "There are two theories of how democratic government should operate," I said.

> One theory holds that a public servant should listen closely to his constituents and give 'em what they want. That's the simple old formula of "let the people rule."
>
> The other theory, and the one to which I subscribe, contemplates that a public servant should have a mind of his own. Listen to the people, sure; hear their arguments on all questions and weigh all sides. But have convictions of your own and act on them, even when they don't jibe with the popular wishes. You'll have to stand or fall on that basis.

Back at Oxford, that was called the Burkean theory of representation in honor of the great Edmund Burke's view that what a representative owed his constituents was his independent judgment. I doubt that many voters in Oklahoma's Third District had ever heard of Edmund Burke or his formulation of representative theory, but I know that they had a congressman who was willing to stand or fall on that basis.

For my part, I would not have wanted it under any other circumstance. As much as I loved being a congressman, I did not want to twist and turn with every momentary breeze. My constituents never expected me to. Because the Third District's voters knew and trusted me, they let me build a career of service. They knew that that career was more important than any vote I ever cast because they knew that my service embraced the best of their beliefs and the greatest of their needs.

Philosophically, few things trouble a congressman more than the tension suggested in his formal title. A United States representative must at once recognize the national interest of the entire United States; at the same time, he represents the special interests of his own district. I believe that it can be said of me that I resolved that tension. On nearly every major vote cast over thirty years, I was able to vote what my conscience understood to be the national interest. One reason that I could do that was that I was always very attentive to my district's special needs.

Most of those needs were economic. Oklahoma's Third District is the poorest district of one of the nation's poorest states, yet its people are independent. They do not reach for handouts, but they do deserve a fair shake. My job was to see that they got one. Very early on in my career, I got them one on something mighty important to them. It was peanuts.

Back in the 1930s, the New Deal's Agricultural Adjustment Act had sought to improve farm prices by slashing surplus production. For major cash crops—peanuts were one—national production quotas set in Washington trickled down to establish state and county quotas. Out of the county quotas, individual farm allotments were calculated on the basis of acreage planted to the crop the past five years.

The Second World War completely absorbed any problem of surplus production. Quotas vanished and allotments disappeared. In fact, the government called for vast expansion of production, and Oklahoma's farmers answered by planting worn-out cotton land in peanuts, peanuts planted, cultivated, and harvested with expensive new machinery. Peanut production quadrupled in two years and reached 240,000 acres, most of them in my district.

Then, in 1949, decreased demand at home and abroad met that increased production to upset the economic balance again. Once more, quotas and individual allotments would govern farmers' work and farmers' income. The national peanut quota was set at 1,610,000 acres. Except for Virginia and North Carolina (major peanut states with major power in Congress), every state's allotment would be cut severely. None would suffer like Oklahoma, where the very recent expansion would be lost in the calculation of average plantings over five years. By the law's formula, Oklahoma growers would be held to 60,000 acres, a sudden drop of 75 percent, ensuring sudden ruin for tens of thousands of our small farmers with equipment unsuited to any other crop. That was not peanuts.

As a very junior member of the House Agriculture Committee, I lacked the power that protected Virginia's and North Carolina's farmers. About all I had was the solace of knowing that the same thing was happening with other crops to other states. Cotton was most important. During the war, cotton production had shifted from Oklahoma and the old Confederacy to the irrigated fields of Arizona, New Mexico, and California. By the same calculations, New Mexico, for example, was set to lose about 80 percent of its cotton crop.

Except that New Mexico's new senator, Clinton Anderson, was not about to let it happen. Sitting on the Senate Agriculture Committee, which was headed by my old friend Elmer Thomas, Clinton Anderson pushed through a cotton bill that saved New Mexico's farmers by guaranteeing that each state could plant at least 70 percent of its average cotton acreage of the past *two* years. The Senate quickly passed the bill and sent it over to the House Agriculture Committee.

On a very cold night, I awoke in the middle of my sleep. What awakened me was a simple realization: what Clinton Anderson was doing for New Mexico, Carl Albert could do for Oklahoma. I could amend his cotton bill in the House committee to provide the same guarantee for peanuts. Working with Steve Pace of Georgia, a legislative genius and chairman of the price-support subcommittee, I presented the amendment and won committee approval on the crucial question by two votes. So amended, the bill passed the House and went to a conference committee headed by Senator Thomas. There it faced the inexplicable and unyielding opposition of Clinton Anderson. He was determined to strike that peanut amendment from the final act, and my own senator seemed willing to let him do it.

At that point, I called upon all I had yet learned of the House habit. And I demonstrated to my old friend just how much I had learned about politics since the spring night in 1927 when he had shown me the Capitol.

I got a membership list from the Oklahoma Peanut Growers Association, and I got on the phone to every member. I called every peanut processor and sheller in the state. I called every banker in every peanut-producing county in Oklahoma. I told each of them the same thing. I told them that Senator Thomas needed to be educated about just how important that peanut amendment was to Oklahoma. During the next three days, the senator received five thousand letters, telegrams, and phone calls—a pretty educational experience.

The next thing I knew, Elmer Thomas invited me, a very junior congressman, to meet with his Senate conferees. I told them the plain truth in a politician's language, "I can't get a peanut bill to pass alone, but Senator Anderson has a horse that will ride, and I want this peanut amendment to ride on it." Senator Thomas threw several hundred telegrams on the table and spoke even plainer: "There won't be any cotton bill until Carl Albert is satisfied on peanuts."

There was a cotton bill. Carl Albert was satisfied on peanuts. The little peanut farmers kept most of their acreage, and the people of the Third District could judge whether they had a congressman worth keeping.

Every two years the voters could decide whether to keep me. My good friend and fellow Oklahoma congressman Tom Steed for years told a story about how I approached those election times. One year I drew no opponent at all, but Tom reckoned that I would still find something to worry about. Sure enough, when Tom observed that I was lucky to have no race to run, I answered, "I know it looks that way, but my name won't be on the ballot this time. Did you ever think about what that might do to me two years from now?"

I guess that I did earn my reputation as a worrier, particularly in my early years. That was one reason that I was so determined to work my district year round. In 1952, when I found my most serious challenger, it all paid off.

Nineteen fifty-two was a good year to challenge any Democratic incumbent. The stalemated war in Korea had devastated Harry Truman's popularity and had cast a dark shadow over all office-holders. The 1950 census returns had registered a significant population loss for Oklahoma, enough to cost the state one House seat and require complete redistricting for every incumbent. The state legislature added two new counties, Johnston and Murray, to my district. Both were dependably Democratic (there were no other kind in that part of the state), but neither had ever cast a single vote for Carl Albert in a Democratic primary election.

Those circumstances called forth the challenge of a formidable rival. Kirksey Nix had the euphonic name that voters remembered. His background was deliciously humble. His father had died three months before his birth, leaving the widowed family an estate of one sorghum mill and a pack of hounds.

The old man also left a son who was a natural-born politician. After working his way through law school, Kirksey built up a lucrative practice defending hundreds of poor folks in workmen's-compensation cases. Not one client ever forgot him, and he never forgot one of them. He was legendary for his ability to recall the face, name, nickname, job, and kinfolks of thousands of voters. My hometown, McAlester, had sent him to the state senate and kept him there. By 1952, he was easily the strongest man in the Oklahoma Capitol, maybe the strongest in southeastern Oklahoma. When he launched his long-delayed challenge, I had cause for worry indeed.

His campaign never lacked for money. The story was that sixty thousand dollars stood behind it, every penny donated by a Hollywood fellow who had invested in some of Kirksey's oil interests, a fellow named John Wayne. Whatever the source, the money paid for billboards that plastered the district, unending radio time, and scores of well-orchestrated Nix rallies, the last with the obligatory string band. In stirring tones, my opponent rarely mentioned my name and never my record. Rather, he stuck to the tried-and-true formula of blasting the big shots and fat cats who allegedly stood behind me and between the people and their poor-boy champion, Kirksey Nix.

By that time, after three congressional terms, I had the record to match his rhetoric. My own campaign never mentioned the challenger; I ran for Carl Albert, not against anyone. We updated our original campaign tract to proclaim: "The Man Who Went from the Cotton Patch to Congress Has Made Good." Inside, we detailed the work that I had accomplished for the district and its people: peanut farmers, veterans, schoolchildren, workers, and Indians. My campaign organization (that is, my local friends) tacked up 9,000 posters and passed out 170,000 campaign cards. We also mailed the voters 66,199 letters, 40,000 of them handwritten by me.

When Congress recessed for summer campaigning, I hit the stump full time. Kirksey and I crisscrossed the district a dozen times, never meeting but always providing Little Dixie's electorate with the kind of campaign oratory that they just loved. According to him, that is what made the difference. Years later when he served on the bench of the Oklahoma Court of Criminal Appeals, he smilingly remembered that hot campaign of 1952. "For a while," he told a reporter, "I had Bug Tussle's pride treed up on his own well-worn stump. But in the last two weeks of the campaign, he laid the lash of that Biblical oratory on me. I don't know why folks call that guy 'little.' He's just wound up tight. When he talks, he commences to unwind, and before he shuts up, he's ten feet tall." Maybe so. I know that when the votes came in, I felt ten feet tall. I carried every county, including the new ones, and the district by a margin of two to one.

Thereafter, I never had a serious challenge for my seat. In fact, my friends in Washington came to tell two jokes on me. One was that I was the only congressman who did better in his elections than Nikita Khrushchev did in the Soviet Union's. The other was that I could always find something to worry about at election time.

Tom Steed was the one who most liked telling those jokes on me. In fact, Tom liked to tell almost any joke. Every morning he would greet his Capitol friends with a new joke, and if they did not laugh hard enough, Tom would tell them another and another until he got the volume of laughter he wanted.

That quality would have surprised many voters because Tom

Steed looked just like what he was: a former newspaperman steadily building up a record of quiet public service. We had known
each other since I was in high school and Tom was covering some
of my speech contests for a local paper. When I first ran for Congress, Tom Steed directed my campaign in the northern part of the
Third District. Two years later, in 1948, Tom came to Congress,
too, to start representing the Fourth District for thirty-two years.
Over that time, he was quite a congressman, one who rose up the

He was a first-class congressman, and I never had a better friend, in or out of
Congress. Carl Albert with Tom Steed.

ranks of the Appropriations Committee to direct its treasury, postal service, and general government subcommittee. In that capacity he supervised the appropriation of billions of dollars and did it with absolute integrity and professional expertise.

Of course he could be tough, as anyone who dealt with him knew. When some of his constituents got all riled up over some insignificant vote, Tom flew back to Oklahoma, walked into a protest meeting, stated his position, and walked out. As he left, he told the disgruntled that they would find the state flower (the mistletoe) pinned to the bottom of his coat.

He flew back to Washington as he always flew: first class. When a young reporter for Oklahoma City's *Daily Oklahoman* thought he could win favor with E. K. Gaylord, the paper's reactionary Republican publisher, with a story on Tom Steed's extravagance, Tom's answer was exactly right: "What the hell, I'm a first-class congressman." He *was* a first-class congressman, and I never had a better friend in or out of Congress.

In those early years, I developed other friendships that came to stretch over the years. Tom Steed is dead now, but Bill Natcher of Kentucky's Second District is still going strong, still in Congress, and still a model for any young member to emulate. He came to Congress in 1954 to fill an unexpired term and quickly impressed everyone. Like Tom Steed, he always did his work quietly. Like Tom Steed, he did it professionally. No one I ever served with was his equal as a complete congressman, for whatever the job demanded, Bill Natcher gave it, and gave it with no superior. Certainly no one ever can surpass his attendance: at this writing, Bill Natcher has not missed a single quorum call or a single recorded vote in more than thirty-four years of service. Always a member of the gym group, Bill has stayed fit and vigorous well into his seventies. I am told that he is still as well groomed as when I first saw him and that he still changes his starched white shirts three times daily. I know that no one ever equaled him in presiding over the Committee of the Whole House, the legislative device in which legislation is initially debated and amendments initially voted.

Everyone—every Republican, every Democrat, every northern liberal, every southern conservative—knew that he would preside with absolute fairness.

It is a wonder (maybe it is a comment) that few citizens outside central Kentucky or the United States House of Representatives even have heard Bill Natcher's name. One day they may, for Bill Natcher will leave Congress with a priceless contribution to our republic's history. Two contributions, really. One is a complete daily diary, now bound in forty-eight leather volumes, of Congress's work since 1954. No one in two hundred years of our history has done that. The other contribution is Bill Natcher's service that it records. No one in my lifetime has matched it.

Even as a young congressman I learned that many of my best colleagues—and, it seemed, my best friends—were like Tom Steed and Bill Natcher: hard-working, selfless men devoted to the House and oblivious of national publicity. Another of my very best friends was just that way, though not himself a House member. Lew Deschler was not a congressman, but the Congress could not have functioned without him. He was our parliamentarian and had been since Speaker Nicholas Longworth's day back in the 1920s. I guess that meant he was a Republican (most old-timers said he was), but no one could tell, for he was first and last the Speaker's invaluable right hand, dispensing seasoned advice to Republicans and Democrats alike. I first saw this large (six feet, four inches tall, 275 pounds) but almost painfully shy man do that for Sam Rayburn on parliamentary subjects at the Speaker's dais. In the Board of Education, I saw him do it, too, on political questions. In time, I was lucky enough to have him at my side when I was Speaker. When I was just a young congressman from Oklahoma, I was lucky to have him as a friend.

Steed, Natcher, Deschler—I am almost reluctant to list those names now because I made so many more friends in those days, and any list leaves out too many. Let me say only that these three are not a list but examples. Some of my closest friends in this life I made in the House. Like these, they made public service their career. Like them, they loved the House and did the countless little

I was lucky enough to have him at my side when I was Speaker. Carl Albert with Lew Deschler.

jobs that made it work. Like Tom Steed, Bill Natcher, and Lew Deschler, they blessed me with their friendship and honored me with their loyalty. And their name was legion.

I was just as lucky in the people who worked for me. It was only a few in the early days. In fact, I started as a congressman running an office with a pencil and one secretary. As my career advanced and as my responsibilities grew, I built a real staff. Most came to me from Oklahoma, a place I judged to be of undervalued talent. They were all talented. Charles Ward, for instance, left a small newspaper and started working for me on district problems in the 1950s. In no time he became a master at dealing with federal agencies. After I moved into the leadership, I was able to add bright young people to help with my legislative duties. Back home, I later had an office in the Federal Building in McAlester. I staffed it with Bill Anderson and Sara Lane. Bill is the one I had known as

Mook when we were both boys back in Bug Tussle. All of them shared the qualities that I had known forever in Bill and valued in all others: personal loyalty and a devotion to duty. Most of them stayed with me for years, and during those years they stayed with me from the time I got to the office, about 7:00 A.M., till the time I left it, seven or eight o'clock at night.

Mary sometimes kidded me that the staff and the job were my real family. She added that she had married a soldier and ended up with a politician. Being one put a whole lot of strain on my family, but Mary saw to it that it was an awfully good politician's family. In the early days, she campaigned right beside me. Despite her South Carolina ancestry, she quickly became thoroughly Oklahoman and revealed a priceless gift I had not imagined when she was a War Department secretary: Mary Albert almost never forgot the face or the name of a Third District voter.

Something awfully close to her own face reappeared in my life in the middle of my first term when she gave us a daughter, Mary Frances Albert. From birth, Mary Frances had her mother's perky face. When she learned to walk, it was with her mother's quick, toes-out stride. In no time, too, she displayed her mother's taste for humor and a strong streak of independence. If it had not been for her own mother, I might have thought that Mary Frances Albert was the most willful female on earth.

A son, David, was born in December 1954. He took after the Albert men: small, quick, curious about his world. Like Mary Frances, David turned out to be a fine student, too. In fact, the demands of their education largely defined where Mary and I would live. She and I both wanted those children to know that their father worked in Washington but that Oklahoma was their home. For as long as possible, that meant that we lived in a small Washington apartment (one bedroom, a kitchen with dinette) but kept our house in McAlester. Mary and the children would go there early every summer, and I would join them as soon as Congress adjourned. When fall came, Mary would go down to McAlester's neighborhood school, enroll Mary Frances, and keep house through the fall semester.

Only reluctantly did we have to give that up. Congressional sessions kept running longer each year, keeping me back in Washington, first through the summer and in time through much of the fall. But the turning point came when Mary Frances discovered that she could not take part in Brownie Scouts if she was not in Washington when the school year began and the troops were organized. Thereafter, we stayed in Washington for the entire school year, in time settling in an apartment on Cathedral Avenue so that the children could walk to school, Mary Frances to National Cathedral and David to St. Alban's.

Watching them grow up, I was often struck by how very much different their lives were from what I had known back in Bug Tussle. It was not just that they went to bigger schools and stayed out of the cotton patches, it was the whole atmosphere. Sometimes it was a big improvement. I remember in the 1960s, when civil rights was a major issue and a tough one for my folks in Little Dixie, Mary Frances announced at the dinner table one night that anyone who did not believe in civil rights should drop dead and she was willing to help them! She was as old as I was when the Ku Klux Klan was running rampant in Pittsburgh County.

Sometimes, though, it seemed a more mixed blessing. When I was a boy, every lad had a .22 rifle. With his father and his friends, he freely hunted the meadows and valleys near Bug Tussle. My own son wanted to hunt, and I bought him his own little rifle, which he learned to shoot. But I was a congressman, not a farmer or a coal miner, and I worked day and night at the Capitol, not in a field. What Papa and I could have done almost any day at home required David and me to take the time somewhere else. I remember when we finally could, how excited David was when we went down to Congressman Frank Boykin's big forest and private hunting preserve in Alabama. With the first blast of his shotgun, David brought down a huge tom turkey. When I bagged a goose, David was more impressed than if I had been on network news with the president. He insisted that we take mine back to Washington and have his mother cook it as our dinner. She did, and right in the middle of the preparation the phone rang and Mary stopped to

With Mary and the children there, I always knew that whatever was cooking at home would be well done.

answer it. Somebody at the Capitol was trying to reach me but, being polite, first asked Mary what she was doing. "Why, I'm cooking Carl's goose," she said.

Maybe so. But with Mary and my children there, I always knew that whatever was cooking at home would be well done.

Just as Speaker Champ Clark had said, as my constituents kept returning me, they helped me and them both. For me it granted the freedom to vote my convictions. I could be the only kind of representative that I wanted to be, the kind who gave his people the benefit of his judgment and his appreciation.

That was not the only benefit they got.

After my amendment had saved tens of thousands of peanut farmers, Alabama's Lister Hill had told me that I had just reelected myself to three more terms, that I did not have to do one thing more. But I was not in Congress to be reelected. I was there to serve. And I did. What we told the voters in the Nix campaign was true. I wrote amendments increasing Oklahoma's funds for twelve thousand students in the 4-H programs run by the Agriculture Department's Extension Service. I secured and increased monies for McAlester's naval ammunition depot, the city's largest employer. I wrestled through Congress the appropriations that brought Rural Electrification Administration power lines—and the modern world—to the people of my district's hills and valleys. I took on my constituents' problems with the federal bureaucracy, by our count, on more than thirty-five hundred occasions in the first six years alone. In one long battle, my work literally changed my constituents' lives and the entire face of my district and state.

Even in the 1950s the word *Oklahoma* still conjured up images of billowing dust and echoes of howling winds. The Dust Bowl lingered as an indelible part of the state's image and its collective memory. So dramatic was that disaster of the 1930s that it overshadowed the brutal history of floods during the 1940s, even though the latter caused more damage and drove more of our people off the land.

The droughts and the floods were opposite sides of the same

coin: the state's powerlessness to transform its environment so that it might serve people rather than destroy them. Water was the key to the difference. Stored, it would ease the pain of future droughts. Controlled, it would lessen possible floods. Harnessed, it would provide power for better lives. Channeled, it would provide cheap transportation for Oklahoma's producers and consumers. Altogether, Oklahoma's control of its water could lift the burden of poverty from the state.

As an Oklahoman I knew that. As an Oklahoma politician I learned just how hard the battle over water could be, and I also learned how sweet victory tasted.

My position on the Agriculture Committee put me in close contact with the Agricultural Stabilization and Conservation Service. A little-known federal agency, it did mighty big work building farm ponds throughout the nation. I saw to it that the ASCS built thousands in Oklahoma, thousands of tiny ponds that collectively made possible a prosperous cattle industry on land reclaimed from a miserly despot, King Cotton.

I also worked closely with two other agencies, the Soil Conservation Service and the Bureau of Reclamation. With the SCS, Oklahoma developed a model for upstream flood-control projects. The eleven experimental projects the SCS built on the Washita River inspired nationwide efforts resulting in hundreds of small lakes that gave other states the benefits first seen in my district, particularly in flood control, municipal water supply, and recreation. When the U.S. Army Corps of Engineers refused to recommend a small dam in Murray County, I turned to the Bureau of Reclamation; its regulations supported the project. The House Interior and Insular Affairs Committee authorized it, the House passed the bill, and the president signed it. The appropriation was soon forthcoming, and the lake was built.

My district's geographic location put me in the center of the two largest water basins in Oklahoma. Every drop of water that leaves Oklahoma makes its way out of the state in one of two river systems, the Arkansas or the Red. The Third District is the only Oklahoma congressional district that is part of both basins. The Red

River defines the district's southern border, the Arkansas part of its northern.

Before I entered Congress, the Flood Control Act of 1946 authorized major dam projects all over the nation. Those for the Arkansas River promised real benefits for northeastern Oklahoma. Those authorized for the Red River offered far less to southeastern Oklahoma. The dams to be constructed in Oklahoma were to be built only for the protection of lands in Arkansas and Louisiana. To keep the Red River from flooding in these states, the act called for three dams near the mouths of the Boggy, Kiamichi, and Little rivers just above where each emptied into the Red. The dams were purely for downstream flood control, almost all of it in Arkansas and Louisiana. In Oklahoma, they would back up floodwaters for miles, spreading the floods' damages. When the rains subsided, the waters would be released, leaving behind nothing but mud flats and mud holes. No recreation, hydroelectric power, irrigation, or navigation was ever contemplated.

One reason for those uneven benefits was political: both Arkansas and Louisiana had some awfully powerful men in Congress. Another was bureaucratic: the Soil Conservation Service and the Bureau of Reclamation each had its own methods, its own pet projects, its own constituencies. The U.S. Army Corps of Engineers had its own, too, and the three could rarely cooperate on any united effort, rarer still in a coordinated program for an entire river system or, in this case, a multiriver system. For both the political and the bureaucratic reasons, I knew that I had to find an ally, a man of both strength and vision, the two welded by unbreakable tenacity. Bob Kerr was that ally.

I had known Bob's brothers back at the University of Oklahoma and I had thought them two of the strongest men I had ever known, but Bob was even stronger than the two of them together. When he announced for the Senate in 1948, I knew instantly whom I was going to support.

As soon as he arrived in Washington, I knew that I had been right. The first bill that he introduced (S. 1576) was to create an interagency commission forcing the appropriate departments to coordinate a massive public-works program for the Arkansas, White, and Red basins. Its task was to bring to all three river systems "a comprehensive and coordinated plan or plans for the control, conservation, and utilization of the waters [and] . . . for conservation and development of the land areas of such area; for flood control, navigation, reclamation, agriculture purposes, power, recreation, fish, and wildlife."

I had been in Congress only two years, but the old veterans agreed with me: this was the broadest proposal for a public-works project they had ever seen. Soon those veterans were agreeing with me about Bob Kerr's strength. Kerr rammed the measure through the Senate as an amendment to the Flood Control Act of 1950, lost it in the House-Senate conference, and won it back when President Truman ordered the agencies to cooperate toward Kerr's end. Eighteen months after he reached Washington, Senator Kerr had an official Arkansas-White-Red Basins Interagency Committee. For the rest of his life, he rode that committee to reclaim Oklahoma's land, wood, and water—almost a holy trinity to Bob Kerr.

It solved my problems on the Red River. Emphasizing interagency cooperation and broad public purposes, its stacks of reports and recommendations gave me the ammunition to change the 1946 authorization in favor of a string of multipurpose dams bringing enormous benefit to southeastern Oklahoma. We built multipurpose dams on the Little River, and the Millwood, Pine Creek, Broken Bow, and Glover dams brought clean water and recreation, not mud flats, to the surrounding communities. The same came from new dams on the Kiamichi system at Hugo and Sardis.

Even the transformation of the Red River basin paled before the work done on the Arkansas. It was Kerr's obsession: a vast project for flood control, water use, recreation, hydroelectric power, even ocean-bound navigation. When completed in 1971, it did all that at a cost of $1.2 billion, making it the largest and most expensive project ever built by the Corps of Engineers. At the dedication ceremony, President Richard Nixon unveiled the marker that said it all:

Conceived in Dust
Cradled in Flood
Created by Men

Oklahoma's congressional delegation provided the men who did it. Armed with massive studies of the interagency committee, we fought battle after battle for the project, one of them within our own ranks. Mike Monroney left the House for the Senate in 1950 and took his opposition to the Arkansas project with him. An Oklahoma Citian, Monroney said of the eastern Oklahoma project: "You could pave the Arkansas cheaper than you could navigate it." By 1955, though, Senator Kerr and some eastern Sooner Democrats had sat Mike down and made a Christian out of him.

We still had to deal with President Eisenhower's opposition to new projects—"no new starts" was the slogan—and Chairman Clarence Cannon's tight grip on the House Appropriations Committee's purse strings. The latter was especially tough for me and Ed Edmondson, the Second District's congressman after 1953. We were not the only members having trouble with the smart but eccentric Cannon; dozens of authorized projects went unfinanced because Cannon refused to give them money.

Fortunately, he went too far, far enough to stir up a floor revolt to add money to Cannon's appropriations bills. Ed Edmondson and I were next to each other on the House floor when the revolt erupted, and we could tell it would be successful and that it was our best chance to take a giant first step on the Arkansas project.

"Where do you want to start?" Ed asked. I answered, "Eufaula," the site that lay on the line dividing our two districts. Thereupon, Ed offered a $900,000 amendment for new construction on the Arkansas River with $450,000 earmarked for Eufaula Dam and $450,000 earmarked for Dardanelle in Arkansas. The coalition held together on the floor of the House, and the entire package of new projects won House approval. Immediately after the adoption of the amendment, I ran to a telephone booth in the Democratic cloakroom of the House. I called Bob Kerr and told him what Ed had done. He said, "You don't mean it." I said, "Yes, I do, and it's in the bill and the bill is on its way to the Senate."

When the bill went to the Senate, Ed asked the senator if he was going to add some money to it. Senator Kerr answered, "Absolutely not. I am not going to change one comma. There is no going to be anything in the conference report that will enable the House to come back in disagreement. The amendment will be passed as it came to us from the House. It will never be changed." What the Senator had projected happened. The Senate adopted the amendment exactly as Ed had written it.

Both houses passed the bill, but Eisenhower vetoed it as too expensive. Cutting 2 percent off, we passed it again. Ike vetoed that one, too, but both houses overrode the veto. The president then refused to release the money—nobody said a project like this would be easy—and we turned to our delegation's one Republican, Page Belcher, for help. Page represented the Tulsa district, sat as ranking Republican on agriculture, and was invaluable to the administration in Congress. Page told the president that if he could not get that Arkansas River money released, he would not be in Congress much longer. The money came forth quickly, and the work began. There would be other fights, but none would be so hard and none would stop the progress.

It was going ahead full steam when Bob Kerr and I were out on the final campaign day before the 1962 election. After a round of speeches, all of which predicted the completion of the Arkansas navigation project, Bob Kerr and I drove down U.S. 59 to the Arkansas River. We drove onto the bridge that crossed the river, and Kerr stopped the car. As we both got out, Kerr talked about the river's future and said to me, "If anything should happen to me, I hope you will finish this project for me. You're the one person that I know can do it."

We climbed back in the car and drove on over to Spiro, where Kerr gave a ringing speech about Oklahoma, its rivers, and its future. Closing, he shouted, "Let's all sing 'Shall We Gather at the River?'" We must have sung it a dozen times, each with the fervor of a brush-arbor revival. We liked doing it so much that we did the same thing at Poteau, the stop that finished the day's campaign. The words were ringing in my ears when Bob Kerr and I shook hands and promised to meet in Washington when the 1963 session opened.

I never saw him again.

On January 1, 1963, I had just taken my seat at the Orange Bowl to watch Oklahoma play Alabama when I got the message that

The man who had done the most to create that future. Bob Kerr campaigning with his good friend Lyndon Johnson. Mrs. Kerr is on the left, and Carl Albert is beside her.

Senator Kerr had died unexpectedly at Bethesda Naval Hospital. I flew to Oklahoma City for Bob Kerr's funeral at the First Baptist Church, where he had taught Sunday school for twenty-five years. As his pastor said, a mighty oak tree had fallen, leaving a lonesome place against the sky.

We finished that project, though. With the other water projects, it did indeed transform Oklahoma's environment. It made unbearable dust and uncontrollable floods part of our history, a modern life part of our future.

By then the man who had done the most to create that future was gathered with the saints at the river that flows by the throne of God.

There is no better judge on earth—and no fairer jury—than a congressman's own colleagues. The other members could survey my record on my district's and state's behalf. It testified to the quality of my work, just as successive reelections forecast my long tenure. The flower of both was added respect, the most precious quality a congressman can have in Washington.

The fruit of that flower was my steadily increasing responsibility in the House. After my appointment to the Agriculture Committee, my colleagues later added me to the committee that oversaw the Library of Congress. It was a great assignment, for I came to enjoy its staff people and to love their work with the world's greatest library. In 1950, the Democratic leadership put me on a select committee to investigate lobbying activities. The Buchanan committee, named for its chairman, Frank Buchanan of Pennsylvania, did a thorough job publicizing the work that lobby organizations, particularly extremist groups, were doing to whip up grass-roots hysteria against Congress. Four years later, Mike Kirwan put me in charge of the speakers' bureau for his Democratic congressional committee. That was where I came to respect Mike immensely, for in spite of his second-grade education this son of an Ohio coal miner was a tough and resourceful congressman and campaigner.

Our work in 1954 helped contribute to the Democratic recapture of the Congress that year. Two years after the Republicans had ridden General Eisenhower's coattails to give them only their second control of both chambers since the Great Depression, we picked up seventeen House seats and two in the Senate to restore Democratic majorities on both sides of the Capitol. All of us Democratic congressmen celebrated. Among other things, the victory would increase our share of every House committee and put our senior men into their chairmanships. One of those senior men was Percy Priest of Nashville, Tennessee, due to move up to chairman of the House Committee on Interstate and Foreign Commerce.

That seemingly small fact became the most important single thing that happened during my entire tenure in Congress.

Percy had served four years as the Democrats' House whip. The term was of English origin. It derived from *whipper-in,* the title given the man assigned to keep the dogs close to the pack in hunts. As early as the 1770s, the parties in Parliament were designating their *whips,* charging them to mobilize their memberships on major votes. Both the term and the function reappeared in the American Congress. In the early years, various members served their parties in that role in a more or less haphazard fashion, often for a single floor fight only. In 1900 the position was institutionalized when the Democratic caucus voted to create the office of party whip. Oscar Underwood, the Alabamian who authored the initial resolution, thereupon won the floor leader's appointment to the job. Since then, the position's influence had grown, but one thing remained constant: the whip was appointed by the Democratic floor leader. When the party held the House majority, the whip thus became (with the Speaker and the majority leader) the third member of the leadership team.

Just after the 1954 election returns came in, Percy wrote Sam Rayburn, saying that no one congressman could do both the whip's and a major chairman's jobs. Of the two, he preferred the chairmanship of interstate and foreign commerce. Through December 1954 and January 1955, Washington was abuzz with rumors of whom the Democrats would name to the post. Wilbur

Mills of Arkansas and Hale Boggs of Louisiana, both young, established, and very outstanding members, were the betting favorites. No one mentioned Carl Albert, least of all Carl Albert.

On January 4, 1955, I was working in my Washington office. The Eighty-fourth Congress would convene the next day, but I had plenty of routine work to do. I was answering some mail from the Third District when my secretary stuck her head in the door and said that John McCormack wanted to see me right away. I remember wondering at the time what the Democratic floor leader might want with me, but since I had no idea, I just trotted down the hall, like any other young member summoned by Mr. McCormack.

When I got there, I was surprised to see Sam Rayburn—a very smiling Sam Rayburn—in the office. John McCormack got right to the point. Congress would convene in less than twenty-four hours, and he and Mr. Rayburn needed to name a new Democratic whip. They had been going down the list of Democratic members, John reading the names aloud. When he called off the name *Carl Albert,* Sam Rayburn stopped him. "That's it!" they both cried in unison. I was a champion orator and a Rhodes scholar-graduate of Oxford University, so I responded, "Who, me?" I thought to add: "I didn't even know I was in the running."

Then Sam Rayburn took over. "Son," he said, "you've been in the running since your first day here. Since you sat there on the floor every day and listened to every speech and watched every vote. Since you showed us that you loved the House of Representatives."

I do not even recall my response, but I do remember that Sam Rayburn looked at John McCormack and said, "We believe you have enough sense not to make people think you can drive them anywhere, but we think you have finesse enough to lead them part of the way." Then Sam Rayburn looked straight at me. He smiled and said, "Besides, I like the kind of dirt that grows under your fingernails."

Only minutes later, Mr. Rayburn, John McCormack, and I announced the news. Tall and thin John McCormack made the announcement. Then Sam Rayburn, only a little taller than I, spoke, as always, plainly. He did not say anything about the Red River dirt beneath my nails, but he did say something that made me mighty proud, something he would say again and again: "Carl has tact and energy, intelligence, education, and a sense of responsibility. And mind you, these things don't always come together. I've been watching House members since Woodrow Wilson's administration, and I can tell big timber from small brush."

I can tell big timber from small brush. No metaphor had pleased me so much since the McAlester High School yearbook had called me a little giant.

CHAPTER SIX

You Have to Plow with the Horses You Have

Just as Mr. Craighead had told us back in Bug Tussle, Speaker Champ Clark had known the House of Representatives. I had set out to master "the house habit," and I had done it. The voters kept returning me to Congress, and my career had prospered "as surely as the sparks fly upward." The old Speaker was just as correct when he described the responsibilities of my new job. The parties' whips, he had said, existed to serve as "the right hands of the two party leaders."

In my case, I was becoming the right hand of John McCormack, himself the strong right arm of Sam Rayburn. Hand, arm, and brain—we three were the team that gave our Democratic party its formal leadership in Congress.

That part of the job put me at the highest level of congressional leadership yet achieved by an Oklahoman. Sometimes it seemed that the home folks were even prouder of that than I was. One of them sent me a gift that we put on the wall of my new office. The fellow who sent it thought it a fitting token of my new job. It was a long, braided leather bullwhip.

It made a great wall hanging, but it was not a very appropriate symbol. No party whip would be caught dead using a bullwhip on his colleagues. Maybe that should read, "One who tried to use a bullwhip could end up dead." The House of Representatives is far too complex an institution for that, and the members are too independent, too. The whip's job, I already knew, was much too subtle to allow strong-arm tactics. The hand of the leadership could wield no bullwhip, for a big part of the whip's job was to know the membership and represent it in the highest councils of Congress. When Mr. Rayburn broke up meetings with instructions to "let me know if you hear anything," the whip was expected to do the most hearing and the most letting know.

So a great deal of my new job was just what I had been doing all along during my first eight years. I had to know each of the Democratic members, what made each of them tick, what made each of them vote. The major difference was one of purpose. No longer did I do it from my affection for the House and my curiosity about its members; now my purpose was tied to the highest demands of party leadership in Congress. I had to know what the largest numbers of Democrats would support. I had to know what instruments could increase those numbers, if necessary, one by one. I had to predict how scores of votes—major and minor, procedural and substantive—would turn out. I had to do all of that so that the Democratic leadership could define and could pass a legislative program.

Befitting the institutional significance of the whip's role, Congress gave him elaborate instruments, both formal and informal, to meet his obligations. Back in 1933, the new Democratic majority that was anxious to push through Franklin Roosevelt's New Deal had provided him a system of regional whips as his assistants. Originally fifteen in number, these since had been increased to eighteen. Congressmen from several states usually represented each region, and those members either elected their own regional whips or the delegations' deans appointed them. Each regional whip represented about a dozen or so Democratic members.

The regional-whip system was essential to our operations. Before major votes, we used it to conduct formal polls. I would have the regional whips consult every Democratic member and note their individual opinions ("yes," "no," "undecided") on formal, printed sheets. Armed with that information, we knew what was likely to happen even before a floor fight would begin. We knew

It was a long, braided leather bullwhip.

whether we had the votes to win. If not, we went to work to get them. One way could be to alter a bill just enough to convert a few opponents and pick up some undecideds. Scheduling was another tool. The regional whips were available for weekly attendance polls that let us know when each congressman would be away from the Capitol. That allowed us to set the week's calendar with the most critical votes coming when we could expect maximum support. When those days came, I often had the regional whips check their attendance polls against the first quorum call. If a member whom we had expected had not answered the call, I got on the phone and tracked him down. Just before the vote was to be taken, the regional whips, the Capitol switchboard, and I went to work again, calling every member's office and thereby getting our people on the floor in fifteen minutes' time.

On the really tough votes, the ones where we were close but just short, the whip had the hardest part of his job. I had to get those extra votes. Here I had few institutional devices to call upon. I might have his regional whip or an influential congressman approach a member. In special cases, I could get Mr. Rayburn to use his personal influence. Sometimes, I could call on our outside friends with interest and influence. But in almost every important case these were only aids; the real job of persuasion was the whip's personal job. The job was persuasion. And it was personal.

When people used to ask me about my duties, I sometimes joked that one aspect of my job (maintaining party discipline, the political scientists called it) reminded me of what one of my old Bug Tussle teachers had said about correcting the behavior of an unruly farm boy:

> You should appeal first to his honor,
> Then to his pride,
> Then to his conscience,
> Then to his hide.

The only trouble with that advice was that, aside from wall decorations, party whips did not have much of a way to appeal to an unruly congressman's hide. The folks that gave the fellow his job usually lived a long way from Washington. Once in Congress, he could stay and rise in the House without toeing any party line. No whip, no leader, no one could make a single member vote against his own wishes.

That is what made the whip's job of persuasion such a personal one. In the House of Representatives, if you could not get votes by persuasion, you could not get them at all. In my job, I did not twist a colleague's arm; I shook his hand.

I made sure to keep my friendships with veteran congressmen, and I worked very hard to make a friend of every new member that arrived. My position as whip really helped. I do not know how many times a young member came to me with a problem. I guess that I seemed the most approachable of the leadership team. Members in awe of the towering John McCormack or the legendary Sam Rayburn found it a lot easier to open up with me. I gave them a lot of advice, most, I hope, sound; some, I trust, taken. I also became something of their champion with the most powerful congressmen, men more likely to pay attention to the Democratic whip than to a young representative. In time, they learned that I was their friend and a friend who could help them. I might campaign in their district to tell their constituents how much we needed them in Washington. Or I might help pry one of their project's funds loose from the grip of Clarence Cannon, the money-squeezing chairman of Appropriations.

These favors did not guarantee a single member's vote on a single question, but they did assure that nearly every single time I needed to approach a colleague, I was approaching a friend. And friends are a lot easier to approach than colleagues.

So when the House leaders needed votes, they knew that their whip could approach his friends. I usually began by explaining the merits of the question—the whip had to know that and know it on almost every tough question. My usual closing was simple. "We really need you on this one," I might say, "and I don't see any reason why you can't go along with us." To be sure, those last words required that I know the member's district and its demands as well as he—just one more thing a party whip needed to know.

I kept the leather whip up on the wall. Help with personal favors, concerned counsel, a willing ear, attention to every detail, long and grueling workdays—these were the tools of my new job. They made the leadership's right hand a strong one.

The party that I was serving had a majority, but a bare one, in Congress. When we Democrats took control of the House and I began as whip in 1955, our majority was only twenty-nine seats. No whip and no leadership could expect to push through a controversial program on that thin majority. Any significant issue would open fissures that would doom the question and divide the party. On top of that, we were working with the first Republican president since the Great Depression.

As Allied supreme commander and general of the army, Dwight David Eisenhower easily had been America's favorite soldier in World War II. After the war, he was its most popular citizen. So popular was he that a few liberal members of my own party had toyed with the notion of drafting him to replace the "unelectable" Harry Truman in 1948. The idea went nowhere, but neither did Ike's popularity. In 1952, the Republicans nabbed him as their nominee, but only after Eisenhower had given up the notion of first entering the New Hampshire primary on *both* tickets.

No one seems to doubt that he could have won (in New Hampshire and nationally) on either ticket. That he could have done so testifies to his incredible popularity. That he once considered running on both tickets measures his equally incredible political naïveté. Ike came out of the small pre–World War II professional army. He was part of an officer corps that viewed elective politics with independence, if not scorn. The first ballot he cast was (presumably) for himself, but a landslide of voters voted as he did to propel him into the White House, where his popularity did not diminish.

Neither, it seemed to me, did his political acumen increase much. Like a later immensely popular president, Ronald Reagan, he knew very little about politics or its professional practitioners, particularly in the Congress. Like Reagan, he knew very little, either, about the complex issues of the time. Like Reagan's, Ike's staff and his aides by and large ran the government in his name. As in Reagan's case, that was often to the president's sorrow and the nation's misfortune.

In one respect, Eisenhower had it different from Reagan, and better, too, I think. In Congress, President Eisenhower found Democratic leaders who were willing to give the administration its chance. More than that, we were anxious to let it work. Eisenhower may have been a Republican and he may have been naïve, but we knew that he was the only president we had and that for just those reasons he needed all the help that we Democrats could give him. We gave it to him, often in greater measure than his own party members.

Ike had not been in office long before Sam Rayburn laid down the line that we Democrats would generally follow for the next eight years. First elected in 1912, Mr. Rayburn was one of the few congressmen to have experienced divided government at its worst: just after the Armistice, when a newly elected and vengeful Republican Congress had made war upon Democratic President Woodrow Wilson. That war had cost the nation any chance for international peace and domestic tranquility after the First World War. Sam Rayburn and the Democratic leadership were determined not to repeat the Republicans' mistake when it was our turn.

Eisenhower therefore faced a Democratic Congress that rejected the old notion that it was the duty of the opposition to oppose. Except for one circumstance: we were in no mood to countenance any Republican attempt to turn back the clock to the "good old days," the days before FDR's New Deal, the days without Social Security, minimum-wage laws, collective bargaining, and public power. If Eisenhower sought to consolidate and extend the New Deal's legacy of an activist government, he could count on friendly Democratic cooperation. If he were to try to unravel the New Deal's fabric, he could count on a determined Democratic opposition. As Mr. Rayburn said, "any jackass can kick a barn down, but it takes a good carpenter to build one." My party was

. . . a Democratic Congress that rejected the old notion that it was the duty of the opposition to oppose. Carl Albert at the signing of the first bill passed while he was serving as Democratic whip, 1955. Republican Floor Leader Joe Martin is at Carl Albert's right. Photograph by Abbie Rowe, courtesy National Park Service.

full of good carpenters, and we were not about to allow any jackass or general to undo our work.

Through the fifties, we proved as good as our word. On issue after issue, enough Democrats and I voted to support the president's position to save it from the opposition of the Republicans themselves. In fact, of the first 164 occasions in which Eisenhower's views became law, it was the Democrats who gave him his congressional majority 121 times. Thereafter it often remained Democratic votes that built Eisenhower's record and dragged his party kicking and screaming into the twentieth century.

In 1955, for example, one of my first major jobs was winning Democratic votes for Eisenhower's request to renew the Reciprocal Trade Agreements Act. After two generations of unflinching Republican protectionism, FDR and the New Deal Congress had laid that act as the foundation of American trade policy and the promoter of our expanding exports. When Ike proposed to extend it, I worked furiously to line up Democratic support. We won the critical vote by a margin of 206 to 199. It was 140 Democrats who saved the program from the Republicans, who voted 119 to 66 to oppose their own president and kick down the barn that sheltered America's commerce.

At times, we had to work as carpenters. Our overall approach to divided government was to give the administration much of the legislative initiative. We really had no choice. The decentralized committee structure in Congress, the internal divisions within the slim Democratic majority, the likelihood of presidential veto of any broadly ambitious program—all of these mitigated against trying to assemble an overall congressional program for the nation. Rather, our main effort was to take the administration's proposals, pass or improve the best ones, and defeat or replace the worst ones.

One example important to my other congressional duties involved agriculture. As whip, I continued to serve on the Agriculture Committee. That put me directly in the face of Eisenhower's one attempt to reverse the New Deal. The president raised in Kansas farm country was determined to get the government off the farmers' backs, or at least get its price supports out of their pockets. Since the 1930s, it had been Democratic policy to maintain rigid price supports at 90 percent of parity, a complicated formula that ensured farmers' relative purchasing power, if need be, through government purchases at the parity price. Eisenhower and his agriculture secretary, Ezra Taft Benson, were determined to end that with something they called flexible parity.

However they and their economists might define that, I saw its meaning every trip home. In the 1950s, nature cursed our farmers with drought, the marketplace tormented them with overproduction, and now the administration was ready to afflict them with an insensitive farm policy. It was measurable when my own state lost more farmers to the Republican farm policies of the 1950s than it had to the Dust Bowl of the 1930s.

It seemed every year that we had to fight again in our farmers' behalf the battle that Franklin Roosevelt had won back in 1933. Always the fight was close, for the administration generally held the allegiance of even the farm-state Republicans. In 1955, for instance, I put in countless hours polling members and lining up support—vote by vote in the end—to push through a rigid price-support law by a margin of just five votes, 206 to 201. A year later, I had to do it all over again, this time only to see the effort wasted with Eisenhower's veto.

On the whole, however, the Republican president and the Democratic leadership practiced, in the language of the day, a peaceful coexistence. More often than not, it was even a productive coexistence. Many of us appreciated Eisenhower's success in quieting the noisy right-wing demons of his own party, and he came to appreciate the cooperation that the loyal opposition was extending toward his program.

One token of his appreciation was more informal meetings with us at the White House. At one of them, I remember Eisenhower going over some routine business. As we were breaking up, he called Mr. Rayburn and me over.

"I wish you could do me a favor," he said to the Speaker.

"If I can, Mr. President," Mr. Rayburn answered.

"I remember from World War II how important information can be," Ike went on. "I wish you could get the appropriation for Radio Free Europe kicked up by several hundred million."

Mr. Rayburn asked me whether I could get the Democratic votes for it. I said we could. We did. And Radio Free Europe got its money.

That particular job was not too hard. Like Speaker Rayburn,

Majority Leader McCormack, and myself, most Democrats in Congress were anxious to acknowledge the president's leadership in foreign affairs. The Second World War had taught us all the need for strong executive leadership. The GOP's support of Harry Truman's tough decisions in the 1940s had established a pattern for bipartisanship. Already it was understood that party bickering ended at America's shores. We were determined only to affirm that.

In a series of international crises through the fifties, we did. For all of John Foster Dulles's campaign talk about "rolling back" communism and Richard Nixon's criticism of containment as "cowardly," President Eisenhower, as well as his secretary of state and vice president, followed closely the lines laid down in the Truman Doctrine. The major emphasis was upon refining and applying its terms. Here the president took the initiative, and the Congress unhesitatingly handed him its assent.

One historic example occurred right at the start of my service as Democratic whip. On New Year's Day 1955, Chiang Kai-shek predicted war "at any time" with the Red mainland. Communist leader Chou En-lai instantly agreed; war was "imminent" against Chiang's forces on Formosa and the surrounding island groups. Already Communist forces were moving on some islands and threatening others. America's commitment to "free peoples who are resisting attempted subjugation" was set to be tested, and the test likely would come somewhere in the waters between the mainland and Formosa. No one knew where, but when seemed soon.

In Washington, the crisis was played out against the recent and painful memory of Harry Truman's troubles with congressional Republicans over our Korean intervention. President Eisenhower wanted none of the criticism that Truman had taken for not consulting Congress before committing American forces, so he prepared a formal resolution, the Formosa Resolution, that gave congressional consent for any action he might take, including the use of troops, in the defense of Formosa, the Pescadores, or any other "closely related localities." The precise definition of the last was left to his own judgment. In one and two-thirds centuries of

American history, no executive had once asked Congress for such advance approval of an open-ended policy that could lead to war. Ike got it.

Mr. Rayburn pledged the support of the Democratic members. He, too, remembered Truman's experience in Korea, and when a few Democrats privately protested, he reminded them of how "the Republicans patted Truman on the back when he first went into Korea and kicked him in the pants afterward. We're not going to do that," he promised. We did not. In fact, our own leadership insisted that there be no debate at all on the resolution. There was none, and only one Democrat dared vote in opposition.

I had watched history made. I had seen the opposition party in one branch sign a blank check for a president to do what he wished, when and where and how he wished. I was not the only one who did not notice that we were also watching a precedent being set.

In 1956, American voters seemingly ratified the prevailing cooperation in Washington. Eisenhower won again, even increasing his large margin of 1952 while carrying all but seven states, all of those in the Deep South. At the same time, the electorate returned Democratic majorities to both houses of Congress. In fact, we Democrats got a bit more breathing room in extending our majority to 234 to 201, a gain of four seats. However predictable the outcome, historians noted that Eisenhower thereby became the first winning presidential candidate since 1848 whose party carried neither house in Congress, but then everyone knew that the general's famous battle jacket had no coattails at all.

Still, major figures in both parties were upset. Noting the congressional defeats, a few Republican leaders complained openly of Ike's inattention to the party's fortunes and his subsequent inability to transfer his personal popularity to the GOP. On the Democratic side, a number of prominent men—most northerners, most liberals, and most safely outside the arena of elective politics—complained even louder that the Democratic leadership of

Congress was no help at all to the party's presidential ambitions. A few even judged it a hindrance. Former New York Senator Herbert Lehman, for instance, moaned that

> the mistakes that really hurt were mistakes made in Congress. . . . The Democrats in Congress failed to make issues during the 18 months we were in control. On the contrary, almost everything the leadership did during that time was designed to prevent any controversial issue from being seriously joined or vigorously debated.

The upshot of those complaints was that a few weeks after the election the Democratic National Committee and party chairman Paul Butler announced creation of the Democratic Advisory Committee. Its purpose would be to define the Democratic party line. Twenty people, including such luminaries as Harry Truman, Eleanor Roosevelt, and Adlai Stevenson, would head the group to define the canon of Democratic orthodoxy. Butler also saw fit to include the Democratic leadership of the House and Senate. For us, that was Speaker Rayburn, Majority Leader McCormack, Mike Kirwan of the campaign committee, and myself, the party whip.

Since Congress was adjourned and I was back in Oklahoma, I got wind of this only when I received Butler's telegram inviting me to join the group that he presumptuously had announced. On the next day, I got a phone call from Bonham, Texas. Mr. Rayburn wanted to know if I had received a telegram from Butler. After I told him that I had, he asked me if I had responded yet. My answer was that I was waiting until I could confer with the Speaker and John to get their reaction. My wait was over. "Tell Butler you cannot, as a House leader, serve on such a council."

Each of us did just that. To the press we released a polite response signed by Mr. Rayburn and Lyndon Johnson, by now the Senate's majority leader. Although it graciously acknowledged our interest in "the help of any committee set up by the Democratic National Committee" and expressed a willingness to "consult with them at any time," we explicitly rejected any attempt to assert "outside" influence upon the two deliberative bodies. Our actions spoke even louder: each of us in both bodies' leadership refused to participate. As it turned out, only eight of the twenty did join. Shorn of any of the Democratic congressional leadership, the advisory committee limped along for a few more years, issuing pronouncements and manifestos that nearly everyone ignored.

The result was a major embarrassment for Paul Butler and, I suppose, the national committee. It should be said, however, that they should have known better. Anybody who understood the congressional leadership should have known better. Anyone who wants to understand the Democratic party or the American Congress of the late 1950s has to know better.

The congressional leadership was just that: the leaders of Congress. As Democrats, we supported our party's presidential nominee and worked for his success. I know that I spoke for Adlai Stevenson at every opportunity in both 1952 and 1956. Nonetheless, like Sam Rayburn, John McCormack, and (in the Senate) Lyndon Johnson, my job was not to put Governor Stevenson in the White House. Neither was it to see that his campaign promises or the pronouncements of some appointed advisory committee became law. Our job was to cultivate winning majorities in the two houses of Congress. Our Democratic party was the elected Democratic membership of Congress. The Democratic program was what it would approve. And as we say in Oklahoma, you have to plow with the horses you have.

What we had was 230 or so Democrats in the House. The exact number was just that number of individuals, and some of them were truly individuals, men of independent judgment and pride in that independence. A good whip had to know who they were and how to approach them, and know, too, that he would not often be successful. A large number, however, fell into one of three broad groups.

One was the congressmen, usually northern or eastern, who represented the last of the legendary big-city machines. Their ethnic and working-class constituencies still rolled up huge Democratic majorities that could be delivered with dependable regularity. Those close to the machines' inner councils thereby could count on making careers of Congress, as well as on the ability to make or break their colleagues' careers. Moreover, they tended to maintain alliances with other urban machine representatives on matters vital to their similar constituencies—labor and welfare issues, for example. Thus, Chicago's Tom O'Brien could sit silently on the House floor and with the slightest nod of his head decide the fate of many a bill; he did not have to say a word to do it. He did not even have to stand to show the votes that he carried around in his back pocket.

Another group of congressmen liked to stand and speak on the House floor and anywhere else they got the chance. The liberals were a small but vocal minority. Usually northern or western in origin and younger in age, the liberals shared a common belief in change. That generally meant taking the inherited Democratic agenda both deeper (increasing Social Security's responsibilities, for example) and broader (into black civil rights, for another). Men like Minnesota's Eugene McCarthy and Montana's Lee Metcalfe were tireless champions of both causes and much more, too. As a group, however, the liberal crowd never had anything like the discipline of the machine Democrats. Beyond common convictions, they lacked specific concentration. Moreover, many were mavericks, unwilling to scar their convictions with the branding iron of compromise, either with other groups or even one another.

Neither of these groups had anything like the significance that fell to the southerners. As I write this thirty years after the fact, I put them last. At the time I was my party's whip, they always came first.

One thing that always put them there was simple arithmetic. The South (by which I mean the old Confederacy plus the former slaveholding border states of Missouri, Kentucky, West Virginia, Maryland, and Oklahoma) was still pretty much the Solid South, at least in congressional elections. A very popular Republican like Eisenhower might turn voters' heads in isolated presidential races, but in congressional campaigns, the southerners went right on stamping that Democratic rooster, just as their daddies had done ever since Reconstruction. I do not know that the saying was true that they would have sent a yellow dog to Congress if he were on the Democratic ticket, but I do suspect that they would have kept him there if he were an incumbent.

Nowhere else, except in a few big cities, was the Democratic label as vital to success. For that reason, the sixteen southern states usually sent more Democrats to Congress than did the rest of the states combined. After 1954, for example, they gave us 134 of the 231 Democrats in the House. Nowhere else, not even in the big cities, was a Democratic congressman so secure from competition. For that reason, they stayed on and on. Those southern Democrats who were sitting when I became whip collectively had served 1,248 years, with very many more sure to come.

Although the South had not even a quarter of America's voting population, no minority had ever exercised such power in national affairs. Its hold upon so many Democratic seats was a hold upon the lever that governed the country. More than numbers was involved, though. While there were exceptions—I was one of many—most of those southern Democrats represented a powerful establishment, an interlocking network of landowners, financiers, industrialists, and professionals, all men of power, all men of white flesh. Over generations, that establishment had learned to pick outstanding young men of talent, men imbued with the establishment's views, and send them to Congress. It kept sending them back and watched them grow old as they voted the establishment's way and expressed the establishment's opinions.

Their soft southern drawl sheathed the cold steel of shared convictions. Its highest priority was to maintain that establishment. This meant to discourage voting by blacks and poor whites through poll taxes, literacy tests, and stiff registration laws. It meant maintaining states' rights to keep the federal bureaucrats out of Dixie. It meant minimal welfare laws to turn back the carpetbaggers. It meant harsh antilabor statutes to cast out union organizers. It meant miserly educational programs to ward off alien ideas. Most of all, it meant white supremacy.

Their numbers gave the southern Democrats influence; their common convictions gave them force. What gave them their power was the House's internal structure of authority. The mechanism that America had evolved to guide legislation turned out to be perfectly fitted to the southerners' interest in shaping it.

"Congress in committee," Professor Woodrow Wilson wrote long ago, "is Congress at work." So it remained. No president, no party panel, not even the Speaker and the formal leadership determine what Congress will and will not do. For that matter, neither does the mass of 435 members. The membership, contained entirely within the House walls and answerable only to independent districts, controls the House, but only as that membership is organized into committees. In most cases it is the committees that draft the bills the House will consider. The committees declare what form those bills will take. Often, the committees decide what changes the House can consider in them. The committees determine how long the House will debate. The committees' recommendations usually decide how the House will vote. Congress in committee *is* Congress at work. And Congress in committee was usually the southern Democrats in control. What made that so was the mechanism of committee assignment and the internal structure of committee influence.

Just as I had done back in 1947 when I boldly sought assignment to three prestigious committees, every person who first comes to Congress publicly indicates his committee preferences and privately prays for success. For a Democrat, those prayers and preferences are answered by the party's committee on committees. Between 1910 and my own Speakership, that consisted of the Democratic members who also sat on the Ways and Means Committee. When I went to Congress, six of the ten committee Democrats were senior southerners. By the time I became whip in 1955, it was eight of fifteen, and the same number sat at the decade's end.

Although the Ways and Means Democrats paid some attention to an individual's preference and more to achieving some claim to regional balance, the South's influence was visible in the assignments. A routine committee like Interior and Insular Affairs had in the mid-1950s only six southerners among its eighteen members. For a powerful committee like Armed Services, the proportion was fourteen southerners out of twenty-two.

Far more important even than assignment was the structure of power *within* each committee and thereby for the Congress as a whole. Like other men, all congressmen may be created equal, but in Washington, they do not stay that way. Committee chairmen separately could determine their committee's products; collectively they could decide the Congress's output. Their power was great and its source was singular. Congressmen became chairmen (and thus more equal than others) at the exact moment they had served on a committee longer than any other committee member. Seniority was its name. Southern domination was its effect.

Like so much else, the process dated to 1910, when the Democrats and some rebellious Republicans smashed the power of old Joe Cannon. Like most of his predecessors, Speaker Cannon had assigned committee memberships for both his own party (the Republicans) and the minority, too. He also had selected each committee chairman. In the revolt of 1910, the Democrats won the right to make their own committee assignments, giving it in time to the southern-dominated Ways and Means Democrats. That revolt also overturned the Speaker's power to name chairmen. Heretofore dictated by the whims of one man, chairmanships became the automatic reward of an unarguable process. They were the prizes of longevity.

For all of its apparent irrationality and injustice, the seniority system did have its virtues. It undeniably fostered stability by encouraging members to stick with their committees for their entire careers, and it guaranteed the committees experienced leadership. Because the process was automatic, it preserved Congress's independence from outside pressures, including lobbyists and the White House. Also, it unquestionably was the only way men like Bill Dawson and Adam Clayton Powell could have become chairmen. Despite Powell's later notoriety, the two were capable legislators. For a long time they were the only two blacks in Congress, but precisely because they were there for a long time, both rose to become committee chairmen, Dawson of Government Operations and Powell of Education and Labor.

More noticeable, though, and far more important, were the system's more typical beneficiaries. Because southern Democrats profited most from incumbency, they profited most from the seniority system. When I became whip, New England, the North Atlantic, the Midwest, and the West all combined to provide chairmen of only five committees: Illinois's Bill Dawson (Government Operations), California's Clair Engle (Interior and Insular Affairs), New York's Emmanuel Celler and Charles Buckley (Judiciary and Public Works, respectively), and Pennsylvania's Francis Walter (Un-American Activities.) Everywhere else I looked— across fifteen committees—there ruled a solid phalanx of southern chairmen:

Agriculture—Harold Cooley of North Carolina
Appropriations—Clarence Cannon of Missouri
Armed Services—Carl Vinson of Georgia
Banking and Currency—Brent Spence of Kentucky
District of Columbia—John McMillan of South Carolina
Education and Labor—Graham Barden of North Carolina
Foreign Affairs—James P. Richards of South Carolina
House Administration—Omar Burleson of Texas
Interstate and Foreign Commerce—Percy Priest of Tennessee
Rules—Howard Smith of Virginia
Veterans' Affairs—Olin Teague of Texas
Ways and Means—Jere Cooper of Tennessee

Surrounding them were the ranking members of the majority party. As heads of the chief subcommittees, these men controlled many of the separate pieces of major legislation. In full committee deliberations, their voices spoke louder than others in shaping those pieces into a whole. And because of the seniority system, those voices, too, usually had southern accents. Take, for example, my own committee, Agriculture. Ranking behind Chairman Cooley in order were the following in 1955: Bob Pogue of Texas; George Grant of Alabama; E. C. Gathings of Arkansas; John McMillan of South Carolina; Tom Abernathy of Mississippi; myself of Oklahoma; Watkins Abbitt of Virginia. Altogether, then, the South not only held fourteen of the twenty-one Democratic seats on that committee, but southerners occupied all of the top eight positions. It was the South, then, not Ezra Taft Benson, not Dwight Eisenhower, not the Democratic National Committee, and not some outside advisory group, that wrote America's agricultural legislation. It also was southern committee chairmen, none of these others, who decided what the Democratic House of Representatives would do.

There was not a weak man among the chairmen. All had learned from experience. All were capable. And yet I could not help but reflect upon how accidents of birth in the right part of the country, mixed with some early good fortune, had put them where they were.

Take Carl Vinson, for instance. After he helped me with my Marine and his mother, Vinson and I became close friends. I already knew he had served in the House longer than any current member except Mr. Rayburn (Vinson eventually established the record for continuous tenure: fifty years). I knew, too, that his colleagues admiringly called him the Swamp Fox in testimony to his canniness. In time, he told me how he had come to be in the House.

It seems that back in 1914, when I was just a boy down in Bug Tussle and Dwight Eisenhower was a cadet at West Point, Vinson had announced his candidacy for Congress from Georgia's Sixth District. He had the reputation for a fondness for alcohol, not unique to the district or to Georgia, but enough to cause a certain Baptist preacher to come out strongly against him. The fellow had enough of a following to swing the election, so young Mr. Vinson called on him.

The preacher came out on his front porch early one morning to find Carl Vinson there. He had slept the night on the porch so as not to miss him. The preacher was surprised to find the candidate there, but he swiftly buckled on his moral armor and went on the attack.

"It won't do you any good being here, 'cause I'm not about to be for you," he said. "Georgia cannot elect a man of your sorry morals to the House of Representatives. I will never support a man like you." Vinson's eyes misted a bit as he softly answered, "I didn't come here to ask you to vote for me. I came here to ask you to pray for me." The two went into the preacher's house, and one of them was converted. The preacher came out blazing for Carl Vinson for Congress. Vinson went to Congress, went on going to Congress, and went on drinking, too.

With no real opposition (after the preacher), Carl Vinson rose steadily up the ranks. He rose to head the Naval Affairs Committee and its successor, the Armed Services Committee. Utterly secure, he ran a committee with no tolerance at all for interference. Lyndon Johnson used to tell the story of when he had served with Vinson on Naval Affairs and once had tried to ask a question of an admiral who was testifying. The chairman slammed his gavel down and ruled the question out of order. Lyndon, no shrinking violet himself, got mad. Declaring that he had never once been allowed to speak, he shouted that "after three terms a fellow should be allowed to ask a simple question." "All right," Vinson gave in, "but just one."

Such was part of the power that seniority could give a man. But that was only a part. The bigger part was that Armed Services Chairman Carl Vinson largely made up the defense budget of the United States. Carl Vinson authorized to the penny what the army, the navy, the air force, and the marines would spend. With fellow Georgian Richard Russell of the Senate Armed Services Committee, Carl Vinson determined the exact location and allowable appropriation for every military base in every congressional district in the entire country. Seniority gave him that power. His great expertise, his awesome intelligence, his fierce willpower— these allowed him to make the most of it. Still, I never quite got over thinking how important that preacher's prayer had turned out to be.

That so many legislative committees sat firmly under southern domination explained a great deal of that one region's impact upon congressional affairs. Separately, powerful southerners determined many of the problems that Congress would address.

Each, in his special field, defined the allowable answers. At the heart of the South's powers, however, lay one very special committee, one designed to have no legislative authority at all. Nonetheless, skillful southerners had managed to transform it into the citadel of southern ascendency. It was the House Committee on Rules.

Before 1910, the Rules Committee had functioned as an indispensable arm of the House leadership. It was known as the Speaker's committee because the Speaker named its members, and, befitting its significance, he himself served as its chairman. Once again, however, the revolt against Speaker Cannon had born soured fruit. By barring the Speaker's service on the committee and declaring that its members would be appointed and its chairman selected like those of every other committee, the reformers had made the Rules Committee independent of Speaker Cannon's whims. They also had made it independent of any future Speaker's control.

Attempting to democratize power by dispersing it, the reformers had left it for some group outside the elected leadership to grab. The Rules Committee was the place to grab it, for that one committee sat right at the center of congressional power, not power over a single bill, but power over the entire process of legislating *all* bills. The metaphor commonly used to describe that power was to refer to the Rules Committee as the House's traffic light.

As the legislative committees sent finished bills down the road to consideration by the full House, each bill first pulled up at the Rules Committee. The committee would assign for each a rule that established the conditions for House debate. Commonly, the rule would fix the time limit for debate. In addition, it could specify the number and type of amendments that would be permitted from the floor. Some bills—tax legislation, most notably—usually received closed rules, which allowed no amendments and forced the members to vote up or down on the committee bill. Other bills received open rules, which permitted unlimited amendments. In yet other instances, the rule could specify precisely what amendments would be allowed. Sometimes it would specify the exact wording of the permissible amendments.

The power inherent to defining those different conditions was obvious, but the committee's power ran even deeper. It could refuse to issue any rule at all. When it did, the traffic light burned a steady red and the entire legislative process screeched to a halt. Without a rule, there could be no debate, there could be no amendments, there could be no consideration of the bill at all. Not, at least, without circumstances known to congressional scholars but hardly ever seen by House members.

Four procedures existed to move a bill beyond the Rules Committee's stoplight, but none had much potential. First, the bill could be placed on the Consent Calendar and thereby be called to the floor on the first and third Mondays of each month. A single objection (certain to come on any matter of importance) by even one of the 435 members would close that exit, however.

The second escape was the suspension-of-the-rules process, but it required a two-thirds vote for the bill's passage. No broad bill could press through that narrow tunnel.

A third alternative occurred once a week on Calendar Wednesday when committee chairmen could bypass the Rules Committee to put a bill before the House. That avenue, however, opened only as the Speaker went down the roll of committees in alphabetical order. Moreover, any bill so presented had to be disposed of in that one legislative day; otherwise, the process would begin again a week later. Thus, a chairman of Agriculture or Appropriations could cooperate with the Rules Committee to maintain the traffic jam of Ways and Means or Veterans' Affairs bill that sat idling behind him.

Finally, a bill's supporters could file a discharge petition to pull the bill from the Rules Committee and set it on the floor. All that took was for a majority of the members, 218, to sign the petition. At first glance this might seem a plausible deliverance, since any bill truly desired by the majority could reach the floor if that same majority merely signed a piece of paper. In fact, it probably was the easiest way to bypass an obstructionist traffic light. It was so easy that from 1923 to 1959, some 797 discharge petitions had been filed, but exactly one bill (the 1938 Wages and Hours Act) had made good the escape to become law under this—the easiest—alternative.

Even should a way be found to bypass the Rules Committee, get a bill to the floor, and pass it, the committee had yet another power, this time the power to erect an impassable barricade. If the Senate were to pass the same bill with as much as a single difference—one word more or less, one comma added or deleted—the difference would have to be resolved before sending it to the president. The mechanism was to send the bill to a conference committee, where House and Senate members would iron out the differences. Should a single member object to sending the bill to conference, the Rules Committee first had to approve the submission.

In practice, then, that one committee could serve not as a traffic light but as an execution chamber. That is exactly why every Speaker through Joe Cannon had insisted upon controlling the Rules Committee. When Cannon lost to the reformers, what was lost was the leadership's (and the membership's) right to control the House of Representatives. The people who won it were those brilliant practitioners of congressional politics. They were the southern Democrats.

As long ago as 1937, the southerners perfected the method of their control. Their conservative economic and social views made them the natural allies of equally conservative Republicans. Roosevelt's liberal programs made the two more compatible ideologically. Only FDR's early towering popularity helped hold the southerners to him. In 1937, that popularity was broken when Roosevelt attempted to "pack" the Supreme Court with a bill to increase the number of justices. The public uproar over the move, and Congress's defeat of the bill, signaled that the southern Democrats could safely side with the Republicans against their own president and their own House leaders. Led by Georgia's Gene Cox, a crude but crafty race baiter, they did just that. The three southern Democrats serving on the twelve-member Rules Com-

mittee began voting with the four Republican members to produce a seven-to-five majority that kept the New Deal at bay by
keeping its initiatives off the floor. It is estimated that this little
coalition of seven willful men killed more than twenty bills of
Democratic Presidents Franklin Roosevelt and Harry Truman.
One scholar, James Robinson, has counted exactly eighty-three occasions between 1947 and 1959 when the same coalition similarly
nullified the directions of the Democratic leadership of Congress.

The number would have been larger yet but for the extraordinary personal influence of Sam Rayburn. Mr. Rayburn got along
well with Joe Martin, the former Speaker who stayed on as the
GOP's floor leader. He got along even better with Gene Cox, who,
despite his ideological differences, almost worshiped the Speaker
and loved striking blows for liberty with him at the Board of Education. I do not know how many times a word uttered there by
Mr. Rayburn persuaded Martin or Cox to pressure one of their fol-
lowers into switching a swing vote or arranging a timely absence. I
do know that the number was large, and I know that Sam Rayburn
was the only man with enough personal prestige to pull it off.

That, though, was a consequence of Mr. Rayburn's personal
stature. His institutional power as Speaker over the Rules Committee was much less. In fact, it was almost nonexistent. Only
briefly did the House allow anyone power to bypass the committee. In 1949, on the opening day of the Eighty-first Congress, the
House amended its rules to allow a committee chairman to bring a
bill to the floor if the Rules Committee had not done so within
twenty-one days after receiving it. Only because of the twenty-
one-day rule was the House able to vote on such important legislation as the anti–poll tax bill, as well as on public-housing and
minimum-wage bills. Two years later, after the Republicans had
picked up twenty-nine seats in the 1950 elections, the rule lost to
a coalition of Republicans and southern Democrats. Both recognized the Rules Committee as the traffic light that protected their
minority's pedestrians. Neither was concerned with the traffic jam
that stalled the majority's vehicles.

The Democratic leadership thereupon had only the personal influence of Sam Rayburn to overcome the situation that became unendurable with two events in the 1950s. In 1959, Charles A. Halleck of Indiana engineered a coup that ousted Joe Martin as the Republicans' leader. Halleck won the post after criticizing Martin's "cronyism" toward the Democrats in general and Sam Rayburn in particular. A self-proclaimed "gut fighter," Halleck was not at all inclined to swing an occasional Republican vote on the Rules Committee to benefit the Democratic leadership.

By that time, we needed all the help we could get. In 1955, Howard W. Smith had ascended to the chairmanship of Rules. He was every bit as conservative as Gene Cox, but Judge Smith (he kept the title long after his early service in the Virginia judiciary) was infinitely smarter. In fact, with the possible exception of Sam Rayburn, Howard Smith was the smartest man and the most able legislator that I ever saw in Congress. And, as he often said, he was not serving in Congress to be some traffic cop.

Personally, the old judge was a living monument to Virginia gentility. I never once saw him lose his temper. His floor speeches were models of decorum. Always polite, his innate reserve parted just enough to display his friendliness toward every member. He was the kind who could drape an arm around your shoulder while his free hand was cutting out your heart. He knew the parliamentary rules better than any member and how to turn them to his advantage. When he was working on a bill, he knew as much about it as its authors and more about how to beat it. Most of all, he had a determination that you hardly ever see in people. To Howard Smith, being called a reactionary was no insult. To him, it was a badge of honor, testifying to his consuming faith. Reaction was his religion, and he was its prophet, its messiah, and its apostle, all rolled into one.

So reactionary and so talented was he that even Virginia's other legendary archconservative, Senator Harry Flood Byrd, recognized Howard Smith as his own superior. In the House, every conservative southern Democrat deferred to his leadership. Any

With the possible exception of Sam Rayburn, Howard Smith was the smartest man and the most able legislator that I ever saw in Congress.

bill that threatened their hidebound orthodoxy could count on Judge Smith direct their fight against it. He led it with all the brilliance of a Confederate general—and with more success.

First would come the assembly of the southern high command, the so-called southern caucus, in which the wily veterans of many a fight would gather in a private office. A typical collection might include Sidney Herlong of Florida, F. Edward Hebert of Louisiana, Graham Barden of North Carolina, Jim Richards of South Carolina, and Mississippi's William Colmer and John Bell Williams. Under the judge's leadership, the group would dissect the offending measure line by line, determining what was to be stricken and what was to be amended, how, and by whom. The strategy set, each participant became an emissary to the remaining southerners, marshaling Dixie's troops for battle. Meanwhile, Smith contacted Charlie Halleck to arrange for Republican reinforcements.

As the floor fight unfolded, Howard Smith became the field commander, a master in battle. A salvo of southern oratory might open the struggle, to be followed by brilliant parliamentary maneuvers to outflank and demoralize the opposition. Counterattacks were parried; brief reverses were met with instant tactical changes. Whatever the outcome, it could be said of Judge Smith, as it was said of General Lee, that even his adversaries respected him. Because I was often one of them, I knew that especially his adversaries respected him.

Of course, the judge had one legislative advantage for which Robert E. Lee had no military equivalent. After he became chairman of the Rules Committee, he was in a position to dictate the terms of battle and on occasion win it with a single mighty blow. Working with him on the committee was his faithful lieutenant, Bill Colmer. Bill lacked Smith's brilliance but gave him all the loyalty expected of an awestruck junior officer. In league with the four archconservative Republicans that Halleck put on the committee, Smith always had the easy option of a six-to-six vote on sending a bill to the full House—enough to keep it his prisoner, for release required a majority, at least seven. Even without employing that weapon, the mere threat of it could be enough to compel his foes to accept his views, in effect to surrender the substance of the fight just to get the bill out of committee. During my first term as whip, Howard Smith did exactly that with bills regarding housing, absentee voting, the doctors' draft, and the distribution of polio vaccine. With Colmer and Joe Martin's obstinate Republicans, he refused any compromise to bury outright a bill to provide aid to chronically depressed areas.

As it turned out, the aid bill was one of the items that Paul Butler and his advisory group wanted to place on the Democratic agenda. They were looking for issues that a Democratic nominee could use in the next presidential election. In the House leadership, we were looking not for issues but for laws. They wanted to make a record; we had to make policy.

And we had to plow with the horses we had.

In some circles, there was talk at the time that something had to be done to break the power of the House's southern Democrats. I knew quite well just how much power they had and just how difficult it was to work around. Still, I judged much of that talk to be unrealistic. In the first place, much of it was of the form of what Congress *should* be, entirely unmindful of what Congress in fact *was*. The power of the southern Democrats was a consequence of the internal structure of Congress, not its cause. To break their power would require the complete dismantling of much of that structure. That, in turn, would require the cooperation of precisely all those elements that had benefited from the structure. And nearly every powerful member had benefited from it; it was why they were powerful. Moreover, the experience of the last major reform of congressional procedures—the 1910 Cannon revolt—provided, at best, mixed lessons regarding the salutary effect of breaking up congressional power.

What really troubled me most was the implied (sometimes the explicit) claim that the southern Democrats were not "real" Democrats. This was not just because many outsiders looked upon me as a southerner, too, though many in the news media and the academy did. Neither was it because many southerners were my close friends, though they often were men whose friendships I valued and whose abilities I respected. No, what struck me was the arrogance of the claim that the men who gave us most of the Democratic membership of Congress were not Democrats. If they were not Democrats, who were? What gave any other group an exclusive claim to that title? There was none stronger than the fact that these men had been elected to office as Democrats and were judged by their own constituents every two years to be worthy Democrats. I could not help but notice that few of their journalistic and academic critics could offer the same credentials.

Ours was a diverse party of diverse viewpoints, but our diversity only mirrored that of the American people. No one group had a unique claim to the word *Democrat* any more than to the word *American*. As part of the party's congressional leadership, I never once forgot that.

Neither did I forget the limits to our leadership. Historically, the elected leadership of Congress had maintained its institutional authority by controlling the Rules Committee and the legislative committees, as well as by using the Democratic caucus to shape party policy. In the 1950s, the Rules Committee had become an independent fiefdom. Only on very important matters could Speaker Rayburn step in to direct a committee chairman's work, and even then his entrée was his enormous personal prestige. Sam Rayburn would not cheapen that currency by using it often. The party caucus that other Speakers had used to bind Democrats to a common position had withered to brief biennial assemblies to renominate our leadership team. Mr. Rayburn dared ask no more of it for fear that the party would split wide open.

If these were our limits, then dedication, sensitivity, and a spirit of cooperation became our tools. Because they had them, Sam Rayburn, a Baptist from Fannin County, Texas, and John McCormack, a Catholic from South Boston, worked together. They had a whip (this Methodist from Oklahoma) who worked with them. I was determined to do as much as possible to win as much support as possible on as many issues as possible. Knowing just what *was* possible, I was awfully proud of what we did.

Events at the decade's turn simultaneously highlighted and magnified both the leadership's limits and its possibilities. In 1958, Americans went to the polls amid a major recession, the second

Republican recession in five years. The effects were most severe in midwestern and northeastern industrial areas. The consequence was that those districts turned out Republican congressmen and replaced them with a corps of young, activist Democrats. Altogether, we picked up forty-eight seats, forty-three of them from those two regions. Two hundred eighty-two Democrats gave our party its largest majority since so many had come in with the Roosevelt landslide of 1936. Even more striking, for the first time since FDR the South provided less than half of the Democratic membership.

Many of the new members were beneficiaries of a rare organized effort by liberal Democrats to unite to increase their number and influence. A group led by Lee Metcalfe had provided some eighty northern and western candidates with free (and effective) campaign aids. As the grateful but confused newcomers reached Washington, the group followed up its work by providing orientation sessions, temporary office space, and experienced individual advice. I knew from my own experience as a freshman just how helpful that could be to a new member. I also knew that the veteran liberals had much to gain, too. Familiar with the House's ways, I was not too surprised at the outcome.

Toward the end of the 1959 session, six experienced liberals called a meeting of northern and western Democrats to discuss "imperative issues of concern." About forty came. One who was there described that initial meeting as having the air of an old-time revival. Member after member rose "to confess his own failure or frustration and to signify his own willingness to work for the common good." Other meetings followed. Soon the revival turned into an embryonic organized religion. Calling itself the Democratic Study Group (the title was deliberately neutral), the group selected Metcalfe chairman and surrounded him with capable, experienced assistants. Frank Thompson of New Jersey became secretary. Co-equal vice-chairmen were John Blatnik of Minnesota, Frank Coffin of Maine, William Green of Pennsylvania, and FDR's son James Roosevelt of California.

It was an impressive group. More impressive still was the river of activity that flowed from the DSG's small temporary office. To increase communication and build morale, it sponsored seminars conducted by outside experts. A steady stream of mimeographed papers provided issue analysis and explained congressional procedures, including such arcane practices as Calendar Wednesday. Seven task forces, each directed by knowledgeable members, worked on issues of common concern: civil rights, aid to education, depressed areas, housing and urban renewal, the farm problems, a higher minimum wage, and a medical care program under Social Security. For each, the task forces prepared thorough background papers and mapped legislative strategy. Meanwhile, the initial group of 40 had swollen to around 125, mostly western and northern Democrats—just about the same number, 133, that came to us from the South.

Through all of this, the DSG was careful to pledge its allegiance to the formal House leadership. On our side, my position as whip ruled out any personal participation. Responsible to the entire Democratic membership, I could no more be identified with its efforts than I could those of Judge Smith's informal but mighty southern caucus. Nonetheless, I fully appreciated the DSG's efforts and marveled at its ability to harness so many strong but heretofore free-spirited broncos. This was a group that could do some plowing.

It was also a group that could kick over the traces. Sam Rayburn was at the very peak of his influence and authority. Thus, the DSG emphasized its desire to help the Speaker by cooperating with his leadership. More revealing than its words was its reliance upon Richard Bolling.

Dick Bolling had represented the Kansas City district since 1948. An early member of Americans for Democratic Action (ADA), Dick was a steady champion of liberal causes. He also became something of a protégé of Speaker Rayburn. Perhaps Mr. Rayburn saw him as a bridge to the party's ADA types. Perhaps he believed that Dick's Alabama upbringing and newspaper and academic experience could combine with his liberal sentiments to make Dick sensitive to many party elements. Most likely, Sam

Rayburn saw in Dick Bolling what he had seen in Lyndon Johnson, Hale Boggs, and others (including me): here was a smart young congressman with a brilliant career that the Speaker could promote and shape. In any event, Dick became a regular at the Board of Education. It was natural that the DSG would turn to Dick as a link to the leadership and as a source of important counsel.

For his part, Mr. Rayburn appreciated the group's deference and steadily increased his reliance on Bolling. Publicly, he granted the DSG its office space (one of the Speaker's prerogatives) and told the press that these were "good boys" whose enthusiasm was a blessing. Privately, I learned from John Holton, the Speaker's administrative assistant, that Mr. Rayburn would pace the floor of his office, talking loudly to himself. He swore that if these smart young kids wanted to take him on, he would "tear them to pieces."

It was not Sam Rayburn they wanted to take on; it was the House's structure of power and its conservative consequences. Although the 1958 elections had changed vastly the complexion of the House since I had become whip, there had been virtually no change in its distribution of effective power. Only one southern chairman had been replaced by a nonsouthern beneficiary of seniority, that when Thomas E. Morgan of Pennsylvania ascended to the chairmanship of the Foreign Affairs Committee in place of South Carolina's Jim Richards. Any loss of southern influence there was more than offset by the change in two of our most vital committees. Ways and Means was now commanded by Wilbur Mills of Arkansas, a man just as southern as his predecessor, Jere Cooper, and even more capable. On Interstate and Foreign Commerce, Percy Priest had departed to turn over the chairmanship to Oren Harris of Arkansas, with John Bell Williams of Mississippi as ranking Democrat. Both were close to Howard Smith.

Smith's own influence had weakened none at all. As cagey as ever, he grew even more experienced as he continued to head the Rules Committee. That committee had kept exactly the same Democratic membership in exactly the same order of influence. The only difference after 1958 was that Charlie Halleck stacked the Republican side with four archconservatives. Hence the election of the most liberal Congress since the New Deal and the impressive creation of the Democratic Study Group made no difference at all in the House's decision-making process and little noticeable difference in its decisions. The difference was that Sam Rayburn, John McCormack, and I all found our jobs harder still. Two groups of nearly equal number but quite disparate power were pulling away in two different directions. Caught in the middle was the Democratic leadership, surrounded by questions that begged for answers and issues that cried out for Democratic peace when there was no peace.

And then presidential politics made the cries even louder.

In 1960, General Eisenhower was the grateful recipient of the GOP's anti-third-term slap at FDR. Without the popular Ike to run against, our party's prospects of returning to the White House were good. They were good enough to call forth a small swarm of Democratic contenders. Two of them were friends of mine from the House.

Jack Kennedy had entered the House with me and had gone on to the Senate with impressive election wins in 1952 and 1958. In between was his near capture of the vice-presidential nomination in '56. From that moment on, I knew that he had a national career ahead of him, a career pointed toward the presidency.

As a congressman, Lyndon Johnson had served only one term with me, and he had spent much of it campaigning for the Senate election of 1948. Upon reaching the other body, he soared to singular prominence. As its young majority leader, he made that office what it remains today. His influence in the Senate had but one equivalent: that of his mentor, Sam Rayburn, in the House. Around Mr. Rayburn, at least, Lyndon took no pains to conceal even loftier ambitions. I remember accompanying them on an airplane trip in 1956 when Lyndon Johnson begged the Speaker to help him get that year's presidential nomination. Mr. Rayburn sat embarrassed and silent, but both he and I knew that Lyndon's eye would never wander far from the main prize.

Both Jack Kennedy and Lyndon Johnson were my friends. Either could have been (and both became) outstanding presidents. In 1960, I admired Jack Kennedy for his vigor, his eloquence, and his ability to organize an impressive nationwide campaign. Lyndon Johnson I respected for his masterful legislative expertise. Their combination into one ticket was a formidable alliance that made me awfully happy personally. It did result, though, in one immediate discomfort politically.

Kennedy's Catholicism concerned me not at all, except that I knew it would hurt him badly in my own state. As a young man I had seen Al Smith fall victim to Oklahoma's militant Protestantism, and I had not seen much happen since to convince me that Sooner voters were ready to support a Catholic candidate. In the campaign, I was mighty proud that one thing had changed. Back in 1928, nearly every Oklahoma Democratic politician had made rats' departures from Smith's sinking ship. In 1960, a good number of us came out squarely for John Kennedy and against religious bigotry. In more than sixty speeches and radio addresses, I spoke earnestly of the need for Democratic leadership in the White House, and I mixed reason with derision to take on intolerance directly. Our young governor, J. Howard Edmondson, willingly sacrificed his own shrinking popularity to tell Oklahomans what they did not want to hear. I may never have been prouder of Senator Robert S. Kerr than I was when he forthrightly addressed a hostile crowd at an Oklahoma City rally. Engaged in a tough reelection fight himself, the man famed as Baptist Bob blasted the ugly Know-Nothingness of bigotry to endorse boldly "a patriotic Catholic Democrat for president."

In the end, our appeals did not turn the situation around. Richard Nixon kept the state in the Republican column where Ike twice had placed it. Kennedy carried only one congressional district, my Third. But then I already thought a lot of its voters' good sense. Our efforts may not have been in vain, though. Since the governor, the senator, and many more of us (including Jack Kennedy) took on the issue squarely in 1960, Oklahomans have elected one Catholic governor (Dewey Bartlett), two Catholic senators (Bartlett and Don Nickles), and one Catholic congressman

(James Jones). That is testimony to what may have been the lasting effect of Kennedy's election for Oklahoma and America. It removed the unspoken, unholy religious test for public office.

In the context of the Congress and of 1960, John Kennedy's campaign and election had a different meaning. They triggered the hardest fight I ever saw in the House. At stake was the nature of the Democratic party and control of the legislative process. The battlefield was the House Committee on Rules.

Both houses had recessed for the national conventions and returned in August. Those last few hot days of the Eighty-sixth Congress were important to our party and our nominees, Senators Kennedy and Johnson. Both pledged their "full energies" to pushing a program through to final adoption. At its heart were three bills that had consumed most of the previous two years: an expanded housing program, federal aid to education, and a higher minimum wage. Each died a graceless death in the Rules Committee at the hands of Judge Smith and his gang of five. The postconvention session had been billed as "Kennedy's Congress," a demonstration of the Democrats' ability to "get the country moving again" behind an activist nominee and his running mate, a man chosen for his legislative legerdemain. Instead, it pointed to the paralysis that kept the Congress from moving at all. It turned out to be Howard Smith's Congress, not John Kennedy's and not the Democratic leadership's.

To the press and general public, the issue that Smith's power and obstinacy had raised was singular. Would the new Democratic president control the House or would a tough-minded reactionary from Broad Run, Virginia? To us in the leadership, that question was secondary to other, harder ones. Could we meet our obligations to the House and the nation with an independent and hostile Rules Committee? Could we intervene in the legislative process without upsetting its interlocking machinery of committees, seniority, and procedure? How could a Speaker from Texas and his allies (including this whip from Oklahoma) take on the southern Democrats in the very bastion of their strength? Could we discipline our largest single element without driving them to permanent estrangement? These were the questions with which we wrestled. And we, not the young fellows moving into the White House, were the ones who had to answer them.

We began on a Saturday, the last day of 1960. Sam Rayburn had summoned us to the Capitol early. In the Speaker's office, John McCormack, Dick Bolling, Lew Deschler (the House parliamentarian), a few Texas congressmen, and I met with Mr. Rayburn to consider the options. Doing nothing was not one. The dismal records of the postconvention session had forced the issue.

For some time, the DSG had been pushing one alternative: restoring the twenty-one-day rule. I knew Mr. Rayburn well enough to know that that would go nowhere. The Speaker had been unenthusiastic about the procedure when we had it and had made no effort to block its repeal. He was not about to take away Smith's power to bring legislation to the floor only to give it directly to the committee chairmen. By doing that, a twenty-one-day rule would only further weaken the Speakership.

A second possibility was to expand the committee by adding three members to it, one Republican and two Democrats. While preserving the traditional two-to-one formal party split, two moderate or liberal Democrats would break the informal six-to-six conservative coalition. Mr. Rayburn told us that he had given Howard Smith that option just that morning. But the old judge would have none of it. He was ready to fight any move to alter the committee's makeup and its ability to block any legislation that he felt would bring ruin to America—by building schoolrooms, for example.

One option remained. Bill Colmer, the ranking Democrat and Judge Smith's alter ego, had been removed from the committee once: in 1947, when we had lost four assignments to the new Republican majority. Although there was no requirement that a member be restored to a committee assignment when his party regained the majority, Colmer had pleaded with John McCormack to get the place back when we took control in 1949. John had agreed, out of his friendship with Colmer, and Mr. Rayburn reluctantly had gone along to restore him to Rules. Colmer's mossback sentiments made him the sixth vote of the obstructionists; the same sentiments now made him vulnerable again. With Jamie Whitten, Arthur Winstead, and John Bell Williams, Bill Colmer had been one of four Mississippi congressmen to campaign openly against their party's presidential ticket in favor of a slate of independent electors. Twice before—after Theodore Roosevelt's Bull Moose campaign of 1912 and Robert M. La Follette's Progressive candidacy in 1924—the GOP caucus had punished disloyal Republicans by stripping their seniority and removing them from choice committees. Now, Bill Colmer's party bolt gave us the same option: remove the Mississippian in favor of a moderate or liberal Democrat on rules.

Carefully, we explored every option on that December afternoon. I remember that Sam Rayburn listened closely and questioned probingly. Whatever his own thoughts were, he kept them to himself. All of us knew that the final decision would be his.

The president-elect found out the same thing. When John Kennedy met with the congressional leadership team, he began by ticking off some routine items of business. Quickly disposing of them, he drew himself up and solemnly announced, "Now, I'd like to talk about the Rules Committee." Sam Rayburn's hand slapped the table, sounding like a gunshot. "No, sir," he shouted. "That is House business, and the House of Representatives will decide that. The White House has no business there at all." Kennedy sat silently, as we all did. Awkwardly, he moved on to another topic. Sam Rayburn had made his point. Now he would make his decision. All of us—the president, the floor leader, and the whip—would have to live with it. The president's program and our control of Congress would live or die with it, too.

For all of his apparent simplicity, Sam Rayburn was the most complex man I ever knew. On much lesser problems, I had seen him mull for days, never speaking, but weighing every factor in his remarkable mind. This time, he did the same thing. Not one of us closest to him knew what he would do. What he did was to devise the most brilliant strategy of his long career.

On January 2, 1961, the Speaker met with a group of liberal Democrats. There would be no restored twenty-one-day rule, he said, and Judge Smith had refused the compromise of enlarging the committee. Under the circumstances, he had decided that there was only one recourse: he, Sam Rayburn, would recommend that the Democratic caucus remove William Colmer from the Rules Committee and replace him with a loyal Democrat.

Almost instantly the liberals (never known for their secret-keeping capacity) leaked the word to the press: Sam Rayburn was going to "purge" Colmer. Most of the press and the House members were stunned. I know I was. In 1949, Mr. Rayburn stoutly had refused to punish the bolting Dixiecrats, and he had done the same thing in 1956 when Adam Clayton Powell endorsed Eisenhower. Singling out Colmer, therefore, flew in the face of his own precedents, always a powerful factor to the Speaker. Moreover, it seemed certain to provoke the southerners to revolt.

It did provoke them—to compromise. Even Howard Smith offered one. He agreed to release five bills that the president-elect had declared critical. This time it was the Speaker who would have none of it. The offer itself affirmed the committee's supposed sovereignty. Besides, the new president might end up wanting a hearing on more than five bills. (He did. In three years he sent us 1,034 recommendations.) Judge Smith's compromise was no compromise at all; it was an instrument of surrender, and now it was Sam Rayburn who was determined to fight.

It was old Carl Vinson who offered the only compromise Mr. Rayburn would accept. Fearful of a bloody fight to purge Colmer and of its even bloodier consequences, the Swamp Fox made the Speaker an offer. If Mr. Rayburn would drop the purge notion, Vinson would get him enough southern Democratic votes to add three new members to the Rules Committee. That was exactly where Mr. Rayburn had started and, I suspect, exactly where he wanted it decided. The purge threat had served to make the expansion seem moderate and to flush out the critical support in advance. The fight would be on Sam Rayburn's terms. Vinson's offer meant that whatever its outcome, a twelve-member committee or one of fifteen, there would be no permanent division into embittered southern and antisouthern elements.

Our job was to win that fight, and we called on all the resources we had. I approached every member, listening and persuading. John McCormack did the same. Carl Vinson worked among the southerners to redeem his commitment. Our outside friends, labor unions and civil-rights groups most notably, contacted every member who would listen to them. Our greatest asset, however, was Sam Rayburn. Those few weeks seemed to take thirty years off his tired old body and fifty off his spirit. He monitored, directed, and coordinated all of our efforts. His stout frame, stepping lightly now, roamed the House hallways, where he cornered members and pressed his case. At least one heard it in language that no ambitious member could resist. "The question under discussion is a simple one," Sam Rayburn told the young fellow. "Are you for the Speaker or are you for that old man from Virginia?"

That old man from Virginia, who was two years younger than the rejuvenated Speaker, used all of his caginess, too. He had now an open alliance with the Republican leadership to block the expansion (the "packing," they called it) of the committee. While Charlie Halleck slammed into Republican guts, Judge Smith went his soft-spoken way. That way was to marshal all the forces of the southern establishment—the editors, the bankers, the manufacturers, the professional men—into a mighty force to save Dixie by denying Mr. Rayburn the southern votes he needed to win.

For his part, John Kennedy was publicly detached. At his first press conference, the new president observed that he hoped Mr. Rayburn would prevail, but he emphasized that "the responsibility rests with the members of the House. . . . I merely give my view as an interested citizen."

If that indicated that the president had learned the Speaker's short but forceful lesson in civics, his work behind the scenes showed only that he should have. His chief legislative aide, Larry O'Brien, started contacting members. "Let's win this one for Jack, Jackie, and little Caroline" was his appeal, not yet knowing how lightly those considerations lay upon a congressman's conscience.

Cabinet members, most notably Interior Secretary Stewart Udall, tried to pressure some. Before taking a cabinet seat, Udall had been a reform congressman, and he still could not resist attempting to remake the House, this time by threatening to eliminate the water projects of four wavering Democrats. Other than causing resentment, the results were negligible; all four ended up voting with Smith.

President Kennedy's one known attempt to involve himself had the same result. In the presence of an uncomfortable Mr. Rayburn, Kennedy called Harold Cooley, the dean of North Carolina's delegation. The new administration had been awfully good to that state, the president reasoned, in naming three of its Democrats (Luther Hodges, Charles Murphy, and James Webb) to top assignments (respectively, secretary of commerce, undersecretary of agriculture, and director of the National Aeronautics and Space Administration). Surely, the Tar Heel State could give him more help on the Rules Committee fight. In the end, it gave exactly one vote, Herb Bonner's, and he had been committed to Sam Rayburn before the call. After that vote came, Mr. Rayburn was exactly right when he observed that the White House "did not change a vote." He was right for the same reason that he had been right a few weeks earlier. This was House business.

The vote came on December 31, 1961. Precisely at noon, Sam Rayburn stepped up to the Speaker's dais, just as he had hundreds of times and other Speakers had for 172 years. For the first time ever, this Speaker entered to a standing ovation. The galleries were packed with what may have been the largest crowd in House history. The floor was filled with what was nearly the entire membership. After H. R. Gross, a Republican gadfly, demanded a quorum call, the long-awaited debate began and the long-awaited showdown unfolded. Would the rules for the Eighty-seventh Congress be amended to provide a fifteen-member House Committee on Rules?

Formal House speeches rarely change a single vote, and certainly none would on this question. What the two leading debaters offered was a special glimpse into their talents and their characters. Howard Smith's was the voice of sweet reason, gently but forcefully outlining the arguments against "packing." He repeated the solemn pledge that he had made, and unquestionably had honored, when he took over the committee. "I will cooperate with the Democratic leadership of the House of Representatives," he promised before adding, "just as long and just as far as my conscience will permit me."

At the qualification, the House erupted into laughter. The old judge paused in quiet dignity, let it subside, and then added in a voice as calm as the Virginia countryside and as cold as the outside air: "Some of these gentlemen who are laughing maybe do not understand what a conscience is. They are entitled to that code, and I think I am entitled to mine."

Sam Rayburn had the last word. He handed me the gavel and descended into the House well. His opening words captured his character and the source of his influence perfectly, just as Judge Smith's verbal stab had done for his own. "Whether you vote with me today or not," he began, "I want to say that I appreciate your uniform kindness and courtesy that has been displayed toward me."

The speeches finished, the clerk began the roll: "Abbitt, Abernathy, Adair, Addabbo, Addonizio . . . ." The first three answered no, the second two yes. "Albert . . . ." My vote tied it at three each. So it stayed through the roll call: the two sides even, then first one and then the other inching ahead by two or three. After the clerk reached Jim Wright of Texas, Sam Rayburn led by one, with only twelve votes left. The roll call complete, the clerk handed the Speaker the tally card. Mr. Rayburn did not even smile as he solemnly announced, "On this vote, there being 217 ayes and 212 noes, the resolution is adopted."

Two hundred seventeen to 212. By a margin of just five votes, Sam Rayburn had shown what respect, courtesy, and kindness could do when they were combined with nearly a half-century of legislative experience and brilliance. Howard Smith accepted his defeat gracelessly by refusing to provide the three new committee members with chairs. Only when one's constituents sent him a chair larger than the chairman's did he give in.

Howard Smith was a gentleman of conscience and a legislator of brilliance, but in the end he was just a mean old man.

Not until the House Judiciary Committee voted impeachment resolutions against Richard Nixon did I see a congressional vote as dramatic as the 1961 decision to expand the Rules Committee. Though it was hailed as a great victory for the Democratic leadership and President Kennedy, I recognized just what its limits were. The expected eight-to-seven liberal-conservative lineup only gave the leadership a chance to unstick Howard Smith's blazing red light; it did not put the light's controls in our hands. At best, that belonged to any one of the liberal eight. The loss of a single vote would restore Judge Smith's power of uncontrolled obstruction.

That is exactly what happened on the one domestic issue that the new president judged most important for 1961. At the time, America's schools were groaning from the pressure of the millions of school-age youngsters born to returning servicemen. Those numbers, coupled with inadequate salaries, had caused a severe shortage of teachers, a shortage of both quantity and quality. Bound to tax systems that dated to a simpler and cheaper past, the nation's fifty states and forty thousand school districts were stretched to their financial limits, and those limits were well short of the need.

Congress had not been unmindful of that need. With the added incentive to catch up with the Soviet Union's sputnik of the previous year, we created in 1958 the first specialized federal aid to education in modern times with the National Defense Education Act. In fact, one of my proudest moments as whip came when I persuaded Mr. Rayburn to put the bill on the floor. It was the session's last day and the bill's author, Carl Elliot, was desperate. Every time I asked Mr. Rayburn to call it up, he found some reason to put another matter ahead of it. Finally, I cornered him when there was absolutely nothing else pending, and the Speaker reluctantly called the bill up. He confided to me later that he still believed that school costs should be borne by local districts, but we had managed to open a modern era of educational financing.

In the 1960 session, both houses had passed a general school-aid bill. That bill had died, however, when Howard Smith's six-vote coalition stubbornly refused to submit our slightly different bill to a conference committee. The frustrating episode had given us one of our strongest arguments in favor of expansion. There could have been no better, for that willful band of six thereby had asserted its mastery over *both* the House *and* the Senate. With the final vote on expansion so close, that one episode well could have made the difference.

If so, the experience of 1961 was all the more frustrating. Understandably sensitive to lingering concerns for the separation of church and state, President Kennedy presented us with a school bill that deliberately forbade taxpayer assistance to religious and parochial schools. His own education message cited a "clear prohibition of the Constitution" against aiding such schools, and not even the Catholics' highest prelates could budge him. It may have been that *especially* the prelates could not budge him for when the bishops, archbishops, and cardinals of the National Catholic Welfare Conference vowed to oppose any federal aid that excluded their schools, the president had to refuse them rather than reopen the issue of his alleged subservience to the church.

In that form, the only form the president would sign, the Senate passed its bill in May. The House Education and Labor Committee dispatched ours to the Rules Committee in July. Judge Smith was ready for it. Declaring that the bill somehow would "complete the subjugation of the southern states," he put Bill Colmer in his pocket and lined up the new committee's five Republicans, who seemed more anxious to embarrass a Democratic president than to educate schoolchildren. Then he got the eighth and deciding vote.

Jim Delaney was a veteran Democrat representing the good Democratic Queens district of New York City. Its voters were working-class Catholics, stubborn in their convictions. Jim was just as good a Catholic and even more stubborn in his. If his faith's 12,700 schools, 5 million students, and 102,000 teachers could get not one penny of aid, then no one else would, either. And there was nothing we could do. I talked with him. The two other Catholics on the Rules Committee reasoned with him. Secretary of Health, Education, and Welfare Abraham Ribicoff pleaded with him. Twice, President Kennedy sat him down for long off-the-record sessions. Not one of us could move him. Jim Delaney voted his convictions, and the House Committee on Rules voted not to report the bill to the floor. It was by just the margin, eight to seven, that the expansion had led us to expect. Close, but we had the seven.

It stayed just that close all that year. John Kennedy himself had been elected president with the closest popular-vote lead in American history. Our party had dropped a net of twenty-two seats to the Republicans since 1958, making Kennedy the only president of the century to win the White House while his party was losing strength in Congress. Each of the twenty-two were Democratic liberals from the industrial North and East. Our five-vote victory in the Rules Committee fight had come only because twenty-two Republicans had had the guts to withstand Charlie Halleck's threats. Sixty-three southern Democrats (sixty-one of them from the old Confederacy) had stood with Howard Smith on that one.

What all of this meant was that President Kennedy and the Democratic leadership could expect nearly every vote to be a close one. Mrs. Kennedy could have been describing all of us when she said that her husband was "an idealist without illusions." As idealists, we wanted to get the country (and the Congress) moving again, but we had no illusions about how very hard that would be and how very close every vote would be. When, as whip, I had to line up the votes for something like emergency farm-price supports, I found it every bit as hard as it had been with Ike in the White House. With a Democratic president and a Democratic agriculture secretary backing the bill, we still won that one by just seven votes. Close.

Except for the president's initiatives in military spending and foreign affairs, most of them were just that way. A few we lost. Others we did not force, knowing that we would lose. Some of the ones that we won required all of the parliamentary skills we could muster.

The minimum-wage bill was typical of that, and of just how demanding and frustrating the whip's job could be. Kennedy had campaigned on a pledge to raise the minimum wage to $1.25 an hour while expanding its coverage. The proposal had been another one that Howard Smith's Rules Committee had buried in the dismal 1960 postconvention session. With the restructuring of the committee, we did get the bill to the House floor in 1961. And then the real fight began.

The opposition was ready for us with a substitute authored by Paul Kitchin, son of former floor leader Claude Kitchin and a committed North Carolina conservative Democrat, and William H. Ayers, a wily, chain-smoking Ohio Republican. On the face of it, the Kitchin-Ayres substitute was about as attractive as Kennedy's bill. It, too, offered a higher minimum wage, but $1.15 compared with $1.25. It, too, covered more workers, 1.3 million more, compared with 4.8 million. It was those differences that made it even more attractive than Kennedy's bill to tight-fisted Republicans and southern conservatives.

Back home in McAlester, I got a taste of that. It seemed that every time I walked into a store, the owner would pull me aside to protest a new minimum-wage law covering his employees. Quite often when I left, some of the clerks would follow me out on the sidewalk. Believe me, they knew the difference.

The problem in Washington was that the Republicans and the southern Democrats together held 302 seats. They had the votes to bury Kennedy's bill, and we had to work to resurrect it. In Sam Rayburn's office, he, John McCormack, Dick Bolling, Carl Vinson, James Roosevelt, and I met with Secretary of Labor Arthur Goldberg, several of his Labor Department's technical experts, and Larry O'Brien. Quickly we hammered out a new version of Kennedy's bill, one that we hoped could peel enough votes from the Kitchin-Ayres substitute that we could pass it. Observing how important the southern Democrats would be, O'Brien suggested that I personally present the new bill and lead the debate for it.

All night I studied the bill, pored over committee reports, and prepared my speech. Larry later wrote that I "made an absolutely brilliant presentation when the debate was held." Brilliant or not, we lost to Kitchin-Ayres, 186 to 185. I am told that when Larry broke the news to President Kennedy, the president stabbed a letter opener into his desk. I know what happened when Sam Rayburn and I identified three Democratic liberals who had sat in the House restaurant during the vote and seven others who had not bothered to leave their offices. We made a brilliant presentation.

In the end, we won, but we did it by parliamentary maneuver. The Senate passed a bill close to the president's original. Our conferees who carried the Kitchin-Ayres version to the conference committee had been carefully selected by Speaker Rayburn, whose powers included naming all conference members. They brought back for both houses' approval a bill very much like that which we had produced with Secretary Goldberg in Mr. Rayburn's office. Both houses passed it. It was a decent bill. But I had had to fight for the president—and the store clerks—every step of the way.

I know that the store clerks appreciated it, and I know that the president did, too. That fall, he came down to my Third District to the community of Big Cedar. The *Big* was entirely in the name, since it was but a highway intersection marked by four houses, a barn, and a filling station. But Senator Kerr lived nearby, and Bob Kerr was a man that John Kennedy had to have in the Senate if he was going to go anywhere in 1962.

So John Kennedy went to Big Cedar, dedicated a highway, gave a great speech, and spent the night at Kerr's ranch. The entire community showed up for the speech, though it was many times outnumbered by the friends of Kerr and me, as well as the Secret Service and the White House press corps. The president graciously spoke about the work that I had done for him and his New Frontier, and I was mighty proud of that. Some of the press even read it as a plug for me as the next majority leader once John McCormack moved up to Speaker upon Mr. Rayburn's retirement.

The "Big" was entirely in the name. President John Kennedy at Big Cedar, Oklahoma, 1961. On the platform, left to right: Congressmen Tom Steed, John Jarman, Ed Edmondson, Mike Monroney, and Carl Albert; President John F. Kennedy; Governor J. Howard Edmondson; Senator Robert S. Kerr; unidentified person; Methodist Bishop Angie Smith.

We knew that the Speaker had left Washington early to rest. We did not know that Sam Rayburn was dying.

Mr. Rayburn had never been sick a day in his life, but his life was seventy-nine years long. His sight failed him badly that year. His daily two-mile walks around the Capitol took him longer. What troubled him, though, was a gnawing pain in his lower back. Several Washington physicians tried to treat it. Nothing they could do made any difference. Sam Rayburn's own diagnosis was just as

Now he can say in the language of the apostle Paul, 'I have fought the good fight.' Sam Rayburn's funeral, Bonham, Texas, 1961.

plain as he was. "I've got lumbago," he said, "and no one's ever died of lumbago."

What he had was cancer, and several Rayburns had already died of that. In time, we learned that it had started as pancreatic cancer, a particularly vicious form because it does not appear on X-rays or in other tests until it has metastasized through the lymphatic system. Until then, it steadily gnawed away at him.

It was doing so that summer when, on June 12, the House of Representatives officially honored Mr. Rayburn. That date marked his sixteenth year and 273d day as its Speaker. On that day he had served more than twice as long as any other Speaker in House history, twice as long as the only man who could contest him for greatness in the office, Henry Clay. He spoke that day of his love for the House of Representatives. His dimming eyes wept as he spoke, too, of his gratitude to the people of his district for trusting him all those years.

At the end of August, it was to those people that he returned. Bonham, Texas, he had always said, was the kind of place "where people know when you're sick and they care when you die."

He did not expect to die. He kept telling everybody—himself, too, I suppose—that he would whip this lumbago and be back to the House he loved. He surely was not going to die in any hospital bed. No, Sam Rayburn said, when he died he wanted to have his boots on his feet and a gavel in his hand.

The doctors at Baylor University Medical Center put him in a bed. That is where he was when they finally found his cancer. By then, it was so far gone that they gave him a week to live, two at most. He lived six weeks more. I visited him once, but I hardly recognized him. Gone was the gleam of his eye, gone with most of the weight of his body. About all that was left was his fierce will. It, too, left him early on the morning of November 16, 1961. For his last two weeks, he had been at his home in Bonham, "where people know when you're sick and they care when you die."

In Sam Rayburn's case, many people cared. A 74-year-old country preacher from the Primitive Baptist Church performed the funeral service. His congregation, heretofore never larger than forty-five, was in the thousands and included three American presidents and the next one: Truman, Eisenhower, Kennedy, and Lyndon Johnson. The preacher pronounced the judgment that we all shared. "Our good friend," he said in Sam Rayburn's soft Texas accent, "made himself a servant, not of the classes but of all of the men and women and the boys and the girls and the children. . . . Now he can say in the language of the Apostle Paul, 'I have fought the good fight.'"

Surely some of us remembered and repeated to ourselves the words that Sam Rayburn had choked out in his own eulogy for his friend Alben Barkley: "God comfort his loved ones. God comfort me."

CHAPTER SEVEN

Congratulations, Mr. Majority Leader

Sam Rayburn did not get his wish. He had not died with his boots on his feet and a gavel in his hand. But he had died as Speaker of the House of Representatives, and his death left vacant the Speaker's chair for the first time since William Bankhead's death put the gavel in Mr. Rayburn's hand. That had been back in 1940, before World War II, before the Cold War, before either Dwight Eisenhower or John Kennedy was involved in politics. Of the 435 House members serving at the time Mr. Rayburn died, only the most veteran members, 14 of them, had known a Democratic leadership other than John McCormack's and Sam Rayburn's.

Most of us had sensed that this would end in 1961; Mr. Rayburn would not be back. As the reality of the situation sank in, fifty or sixty members must have approached me; it was always at their initiative, and their message was always the same. "You've worked hard as whip," they said, "don't just sit here and be done out of what you're entitled to." A few even offered that I was entitled to the Speakership and could win it against seventy-year old John McCormack. Those always got the same answer, an answer that I meant as much as I had ever meant anything in my life: John McCormack had earned the Speakership; he had the qualities that would make him a great Speaker. Above all that, John McCormack

253

was my friend. He and Mr. Rayburn had put me in the leadership. To oppose him for the post that was his due would be the act of an ingrate. It would never be the act of Carl Albert. But Carl Albert did know what his own due was. I believed that my six years as Democratic whip had prepared me to succeed John as majority leader. I believed that I could handle the job. I believed that I could win it in the Democratic caucus vote. And I knew that I wanted it.

After Mr. Rayburn's funeral on a Saturday, I returned to McAlester. I already had planned to announce my candidacy for majority leader on the following Wednesday. On Sunday, however, I got quite a shock. Charles Ward, my administrative assistant, called me from Washington. He told me that Dick Bolling had just announced that he was running for majority leader. I knew Bolling well, and, as most members did, I respected him. I had seen how close he and Mr. Rayburn had become, especially in the Rules Committee fight, when Bolling had kept the liberals in line and twisted many an arm for the Speaker. I knew that he was esteemed by the party's most liberal interests outside Congress: the labor unions, the civil-rights groups, and the many reform clubs. I knew that he had a warm relationship with the New York and Washington political writers. I knew that his candidacy was no attack upon me, any more than mine would be upon him. I knew that outside the walls of Congress many people honestly believed that Dick Bolling would be the more forceful advocate of Democratic liberal programs. But I also knew that the decision was going to be made within the House walls.

Once I had confirmed Bolling's announcement by hearing it on national radio and reading it in the McAlester paper, I made my own press announcement by calling Bill Arbogast, the Associated Press's congressional correspondent. Then I called Western Union and dictated a simple telegram:

> I take this means of advising that I am making the race for majority leader of the House subject to the action of the Democratic caucus. I

will greatly appreciate your support and help. I would like to talk to you about the matter at your convenience.

Kindest regards
Carl Albert, M.C.
Third District, Oklahoma

The company billed me $399.99 to send that message to 269 individuals: a few friends and the entire Democratic membership of Congress. Then I started calling each of them personally, just as I had in making whip polls for the past six years. I started with the western states (I suppose because Bolling might have had an initial advantage there), and I started with my friends there.

As I was reaching for the phone to make another call, it rang for me. It was Bob Kerr, Oklahoma's senior senator and one of the Senate's richest men. He was ready to use his money to help Oklahoma, as he saw it, and that meant he would use it to help me. When he asked what help I needed, I told him that all I could use was a little help with the phones. Within the hour, three telephone workers installed a bank of telephones that covered most of the vacant space in my offices in the McAlester Federal Building. I do not know what it cost Kerr (I bet it was more than $399.99), but I trust that it ended up helping Oklahoma. I do know that I stayed at that phone bank for the next four days. By the first one's end, I had lined up endorsements from all but four or five western Democrats. Then I went to the other states.

While I was doing that, I began to take calls from members who had received my telegram. One of the first was from John Fogerty from Rhode Island. John told me that Mike Kirwan had contacted him and the two of them were going to go all out for me. Those two fighting Irishmen—fighting for me—meant a lot of votes from the big-city northern Democrats.

The next call was more of a mixed blessing. I picked up the receiver to hear the familiar voice of Adam Clayton Powell, Harlem's flamboyant black representative. "I'm for you a 100 percent," Adam vowed, "and I'm issuing a statement to the press." I thanked him even while wondering whether his endorsement would cost me more than it gained me. I really wondered after the phone rang again. It was Judge Howard Smith, and he wanted me to know that not only was he backing me, he wanted to work with the southerners on my behalf. I had to tell him, "I really appreciate that, Judge, but you need to know that Adam Clayton Powell just called me and he's going to put out a press release supporting me. I wouldn't want you to be embarrassed."

"Don't worry, Carl," the old judge chuckled, "I figure a guy's got to get a vote anywhere he can get it, and you still have mine." As always, Howard Smith was true to his word and a real pro. He helped get me a lot of votes where only he, certainly not Adam Clayton Powell, could have gotten them.

The rest I got myself. As I went through the states, my usual strategy was to contact each delegation's dean and work downward through the ranks of seniority. That way, I could meet any resistance within the delegation by mentioning the senior men who already had endorsed me. In a few cases where I was less certain of the veteran's attitudes, I reversed the process. I started with the younger members, the ones I had helped as whip. By the time I got to the top, I thereby was able to tell the old-timers that I already had most of their delegations behind me.

Either way, I never once mentioned Dick Bolling (or, for that matter, John Kennedy, the New Frontier, or any issue). I just asked my listeners for their support, and usually I got it. The people I was calling knew me, knew my talents, knew my habits, knew my record. If that would not earn me their support, nothing I could say about any transient issue would.

Nonetheless, the press tried to play the contest up as some sort of liberal-versus-conservative battle. The fact that Bolling and I had almost identical voting records made no difference. Neither did the fact that we both had supported President Kennedy's program in more than 90 percent of the 1961 roll-call votes. Some ignored that, too, to write it up as a struggle over the fate of Kennedy's program in the House.

For his part, the president knew better. Publicly, he never wavered from neutrality. Privately, he knew that the New Frontier could not lose between Bolling and me. Everyone knew his respect for Bolling, but to all who asked, he acknowledged his gratitude for my work on his program's behalf in the long session just ended. Meanwhile, I stayed at the phone bank, doing House business.

By the time I was through going down every state and every member, I had enough votes pledged to win the job when the caucus met in January. I went to Washington early and made an appointment to meet with John Kennedy. On a bright, crisp winter day, I walked into the Oval Office and shook the hand of the man whom I first had met fifteen years earlier, when Representative Kennedy had asked if I was the new congressman from Oklahoma who had been a Rhodes scholar. This time, when I released the same hand, I said, "Mr. President, I have enough votes pledged to make me the next majority leader of Congress." The president replied, "Congratulations, Mr. Majority Leader."

My election was a formality. On January 3, a week before the 1962 Congress convened, Dick Bolling made a short announcement to the press. "I am withdrawing from the race for leadership of the House," he said. "Developments of the last few days have convinced me that I don't have a chance to win."

At the party caucus to name our leadership slate, neither John McCormack nor I drew an opponent. That was expected for John, since the majority leader's elevation was an unbroken tradition in this century. My unanimous selection—it was Dick Bolling who made the motion for unanimity—was rarer, and for that reason I treasured it more. I thereby became the first majority leader in the twentieth century to win his party's initial caucus election without opposition. As the second session of the Eighty-seventh Congress opened, my selection as majority leader was announced and the House voted, as always, on straight party lines (248 to 166) to elect John McCormack its Speaker.

Our first order of business was to name our party's whip. The new Speaker and I were in complete agreement: my old job would pass to Hale Boggs. As majority leader, I made the announcement. Hale was a Louisianan of distinguished southern lineage. His grandfather had been a major general of the Confederacy, and Hale was a Tulane journalism and law-school graduate. Tall, striking, blessed with a melodious voice, he first went to Congress from the New Orleans district in 1941. Hale lost his reelection bid in 1943, joined the Navy, and came back in 1946 to retake his House seat. This time, he stayed in it. With a voting record that was liberal by southern standards, he earned a place on the Ways and Means Committee and steadily moved up its seniority ladder. Like me, he also became an early protégé of Sam Rayburn. The lonely bachelor loved eating dinner with Hale and his charming (and very astute) wife, Lindy, and played with their children, Barbara, Tommy, and Cokie. Lindy, though, was the one who best explained Mr. Rayburn's interest in Hale. "Mr. Sam," she said, "just liked smart southerners."

Hale was smart, and he profited from the Speaker's interest. In 1955, when Mr. Rayburn and John McCormack had picked me for whip, they also had created a new party post especially for Hale: deputy whip. When John and I both moved up one rung on the ladder, it was only natural that we reached down to pull Hale Boggs up one rung with us.

To the new Speaker, the new whip, and I fell the task of guiding a Democratic program through Congress. To help us, we had a Democratic president who already had created a remarkable liaison operation in the White House.

Prior to John Kennedy's administration, both Republican and Democratic presidents had dealt with the congressional majority in a haphazard fashion. White House legislative initiatives usually fell to the affected department for oversight; the Agriculture Department looked over farm bills, for example, or the Labor Department worked with Congress on minimum-wage proposals. Only on very special matters did the president or a top staff

Hale was a Louisianan of distinguished southern lineage.

assistant try to coordinate the legislative strategy on several diverse bills.

John Kennedy brought to congressional relations the same talent for organization that had won him nomination and election in 1960. Every proposal on every subject in every field passed through the White House and stayed under its steady eye. In charge of the operations was one of the ablest politicians and finest men I ever knew, Larry O'Brien. The son of Irish immigrants, Larry's entire life had been spent in Democratic politics. He had signed on with Kennedy for his first Senate campaign and stayed with him into the White House. There he had a first-rate staff of bright young men to help him. The president's other aides, particularly Theodore Sorensen, Kenny O'Donnell, and Pierre Salinger, also lent their considerable talents and energy to working directly with the congressional leadership.

Ready to join them were the other administrative officials. Sargent Shriver, the president's brother-in-law and choice as first director of the Peace Corps, practically moved into my Capitol office while we were working on the agency's creation. I never had seen a man as dedicated and energetic as Shriver was with the Peace Corps. I sometimes said that Kennedy's labor secretary, Arthur Goldberg, was better than any professional lobbyist in Washington. When Goldberg was working on a bill, he would come into my office with an informed count on where it stood, a carefully detailed legislative strategy to move it, and a thorough analysis of what it would take to pass it. More than once I suggested that we needed some of the members to make floor speeches on his bill's behalf. Agreeing, Goldberg would tick off the names of the most appropriate ones, reach into his briefcase, and pull out typed speeches—just in case they needed them.

Every Tuesday morning, the congressional relations people, affected White House officials, the president, and the vice-president met with us for breakfast at the White House. Speaker McCormack, Hale, and I represented the House; Mike Mansfield, who had won Vice President Johnson's old job as Senate majority leader, and Hubert Humphrey, the Senate's Democratic whip,

John Kennedy brought to congressional relations the same talent for organization that had won him nomination and election in 1960. President Kennedy with Senate Majority Leader Mike Mansfield, Senate Democratic Whip Hubert Humphrey, House Democratic Whip Hale Boggs, House Majority Leader Carl Albert, and Vice-President Lyndon Johnson.

came from the other body. Over a good American breakfast—ham, eggs, toast, juice, and coffee—we would go over the week's legislative business. The president always took the initiative, but we offered the benefit of the Speaker's long experience in congressional strategy, Hale's latest whip counts, and my knowledge of the status of the committees' work.

Another of our jobs was to help the White House people best

use the tools of influence available to them, all the while knowing just how limited those tools were. The president could pick up a few votes by the adroit use of his few patronage powers and the executive branch's control over certain federally financed projects. Campaign help (an endorsing speech before a member's constituents or just a picture of Representative X counseling with the president) could add a few more. A few members were susceptible to the flattery of presidential attention at formal dinners or public receptions. Added together, those were about all that the president had available.

On the other side, President Kennedy had some disadvantages, inescapable disadvantages, that neither he nor his liaison team nor the House leadership could ignore. Congressmen may be fond of White House attention and executive assistance, but they can be awfully resentful of White House pressure. Of course, it was often hard to draw the line between attention on one side and pressure on the other. A good general rule, though, was that the more powerful a congressman was, the more attention looked to him like pressure. Eight years of independence from a Republican White House only added to that tendency.

The circumstances of Kennedy's election did nothing to help. Whether they liked the president or did not, whether they believed in his programs or did not, the fact was that few congressmen owed him anything. The great bulk of Democratic members had run well ahead of Kennedy in their districts; his own contribution had been negative, sometimes powerfully so. The most powerful congressmen tended to come from safe, one-party Democratic districts in which any subsequent challenges would surface not in the general elections but in a party primary. In these future contests, there was little the president could offer them. Local business, commercial, and professional interests could offer a lot, but those were precisely the settled groups furthest removed from the New Frontier.

Finally, there was the inescapable power of simple arithmetic. In 1962 as in 1961, the nearly two-to-one formal party lineup ripped open on the stubborn rocks of southern regionalism. With nearly every Republican committed to opposing nearly every Democratic initiative, we would have to keep fifty to sixty southern Democrats with us in order to win—by five or six votes. After we lost five seats in the 1962 elections, even that arrangement would have us losing—by five or six votes. It was going to stay just that close.

Altogether then, the new leadership team, the president, and his staff had our work cut out for us. President Kennedy and we could not win on every fight. We could not always get the country moving again. But we did get Carl Albert moving quite a lot.

On some matters, it was easy to move the Congress with us. President Kennedy entered the White House after eight years of Republican devotion to tight defense budgets. American conventional forces had deteriorated steadily in favor of an overreliance on nuclear weaponry. Eisenhower had called it his New Look, while Secretary of Defense Charles Wilson had caught its appeal when he labeled it "a bigger bang for the buck." The problem was that it left the country with few military options short of the big bang. Threats to American interests could be met by either doing nothing or blowing up the globe. Those were pretty poor choices.

In 1962, we addressed that with overwhelming bipartisan support for the president's efforts to restore balance to our defense capacity and options to our military. Congress voted the funds to put one-half of our bombers on fifteen-minute alert, to increase our antiguerrilla forces by 150 percent, to add seventy-four ships to the active fleet, to bring our NATO forces to full strength, and to step up M-14 rifle procurements from 9,000 per month to 44,000. When added to the continuing buildup in strategic forces and delivery systems that Kennedy and Congress had inaugurated the year before, it meant an American military supremacy not seen since 1945.

In foreign affairs, too, Kennedy found a steady ally in Congress. The tradition of bipartisan support for presidential direction of foreign policy that dated to the Second World War and had been strengthened by the Cold War still held firm. An occasional congressman might speak out against some immediate action, and a few senators discovered that criticizing the president's foreign policy could get them before the television cameras. By and large, however, the powerful leaders of both houses agreed with nearly all of their members: the president made our foreign policy; we supported it.

Three stunning examples occurred in my first fall as majority leader. With Nikita Khrushchev rattling his missiles and threatening to end Allied occupation rights to West Berlin, President Kennedy turned to Congress to support his determination to keep the city and to keep it free. In October, we rushed through a resolution authorizing the president "to prevent by whatever means may be necessary, including the force of arms," any Soviet attempt to interfere with Western rights in Berlin.

Only a month earlier, we had used exactly the same words regarding Cuba. Fidel Castro's betrayal of any hopes for Cuban democracy, his steady barrage of anti-American harangues, his declaration to be a Marxist-Leninist, his thirst for Soviet aid and arms—all of these added to a mounting crisis. In September, we had passed an official resolution that authorized *any* presidential action to prevent the export of Castro's revolution or any "externally supported military capability endangering the security of the United States." As we had done for Eisenhower with Formosa, we did now for Kennedy with Berlin and Cuba. We signed a blank check authorizing the president to do whatever he wanted whenever and however he wanted. We did it with hardly a murmur of dissent.

In Cuba's case, the check came close to being honored in blood and nuclear ashes.

On a Monday afternoon in October, I was summoned to the White House to meet with the president at five o'clock. When I got there, I found the entire congressional leadership of both houses, including the Foreign Affairs and Armed Services committees' chairmen. The president got straight to the point. Only six days earlier, he had received incontrovertible evidence that the Soviet Union was installing nuclear-equipped ballistic missiles in Cuba. Continuing surveillance indicated the near-completion of the missile sites, and more Soviet nuclear hardware was crossing the ocean bound for Cuba. He would inform the nation by television of the situation and announce his decision to "quarantine" Cuba with a naval blockade to turn back the Soviet freighters while negotiating for removal of the existing installations. His speech would air in exactly two hours.

As we sat there talking on that autumn afternoon, American missile crews were already on maximum alert. Already troops were headed for Florida and Georgia to join five divisions poised to move on Cuba. One hundred eighty warships already surrounded the island. Already the Strategic Air Command had been dispersed to civilian landing fields to lessen its vulnerability. As we sat there conferring, America's B-52 bombers, their bellies engorged with atomic bombs, already were in the air. The instant one landed for fuel and a fresh crew, another climbed into the sky. In those circumstances, we leaders of Congress learned just what "whatever means may be necessary" meant.

The only dissent was in favor of stronger action. Richard Russell, chairman of the Senate Armed Services Committee, spoke first and most forcefully. He said that he could not live with himself if he did not state in the strongest possible terms that a quarantine was too weak a response. What we needed to do and do now was invade the island, destroy the missile sites, and get rid of Castro once and for all. President Kennedy listened calmly and offered his view that an invasion likely would trigger a nuclear war. If the blockade were unsuccessful, it might come to that. He hoped it would not, but he was ready if it did.

John Kennedy left us to prepare for the television address. As he did, he was obviously shaken by the criticism. Still, he knew that what I told him at the end was true. Any misgivings expressed in that room would be forgotten. He was our president. He would get our support. He did, and he proved to be right; we soon recognized that. Only later did we realize where the precedent pointed.

Cuba had been a moment of singular crisis. Powerful legislators had buried their differences with John Kennedy when we all might have been buried otherwise. A president could expect that, but he had to expect also that without such a crisis other differences would arise. They did in the House, and powerful legislators demonstrated just how much power they had.

Not many members had more power than Wilbur Mills. Part of it was due to his native Arkansas intellect, an intellect sharpened by Harvard schooling. More of it was due to his position. In 1943, at the beginning of only his third term, Mills had landed a seat on the Ways and Means Committee. Such a prized assignment was rare for one so new, but Wilbur Mills was another of those smart southerners that Sam Rayburn liked to help. The assignment surely helped Mills. In fact, it made his career. By 1957, he was chairman of Ways and Means, probably the most powerful committee in the House.

One reason for its power was its immediate jurisdiction. The one great power constitutionally assigned to the House alone is the power to initiate all revenue bills. Since the earliest days of the Republic, the responsibility for writing tax legislation had fallen to Ways and Means. From that power more followed, so that the Ways and Means Committee became a web of immense scope and power. Because America's first tariffs were *taxes* on imports, Ways and Means grabbed control of anything involving foreign trade. Because the Social Security System was financed by a payroll *tax,* Ways and Means assumed authority over anything touching it. Because the first federal welfare plan was incorporated in the 1935 Social Security Act, Ways and Means took over the nation's entire welfare system. And so it had been continued.

Despite its many responsibilities, Ways and Means had no subcommittees at all. Every title, every section, every paragraph, and every line of every bill on every subject was worked out by all fifteen members of the entire committee, with Wilbur Mills presiding. Its craftsmanship complete, its bills went to the Rules Committee, which traditionally assigned them closed rules, forbidding amendments from the House floor. The consequence was that the other 420 members could only approve or disapprove its bills; they could not change them.

The final element of Wilbur Mills's power was that he was Wilbur Mills. No one—no one in the House, no one in the Senate, no one in the Treasury Department—knew more about the incredibly complex tax code than this Democrat from tiny Kensett, Arkansas. So thorough was his knowledge and so complete his preparation that the members would often accord him a standing ovation when he presented a bill.

Such expertise had not come easily. One of the first bills that he had presented as chairman had come out of a divided committee and was beaten on the floor. Wilbur Mills never forgot his humiliation. From that day onward, he never produced a bill until he was certain it would pass. He was absolutely obsessed with having the overwhelming support of his committee, including the support of its ten Republican members, before producing a bill. He was determined to have the votes on the floor before presenting it. Until he was sure, his committee would conduct hearings, it would debate, it would work its way line by line. And it would do that on just one major bill at a time.

The Ways and Means Committee was, then, in a position to make or break much of John Kennedy's New Frontier. Sometimes it was Wilbur Mills who made it. In my first year as majority leader, the president's central legislative effort was a trade-expansion bill. Eight years of Republican inactivity had bequeathed America a stagnant economy at precisely the moment that the birth of Europe's Common Market threatened our markets abroad. By granting the president the authority to negotiate with the Europeans mutual tariff reductions ranging to 50 percent, the bill would get our exports and America moving again.

Larry O'Brien and I put everything we had behind that one. I must have talked with every Democratic member. I kept O'Brien's people informed of just where the administration might use just what influence. Between updates at our weekly breakfasts, the president threw himself into it with exceptional vigor. But the legislative craftsmanship was Wilbur Mills's. Patiently, he brought his committee to consensus behind the Kennedy bill. When the

White House and I had the floor votes, and the Speaker and I had the schedule set, he undraped the bill. Wilbur Mills got the members' applause that day, but it was all of us who won the key vote, 253 to 171.

One vote we did not even take testified to Mills's ability to break the New Frontier. Medicare, the payment of the elderly's hospital expenses under Social Security, had been a proposal of Senator Kennedy and a campaign promise of candidate Kennedy; now it was a White House bill of President Kennedy. Offered in 1961, the bill went to Ways and Means, where the chairman put it behind other bills. His committee started its hearings just before adjournment. In 1962, the hearings continued, with no end in sight.

I knew that what Wilbur Mills was after was not more information from more witnesses but a consensus on his committee. I knew, too, that he was not going to get it. Medicare was just too much for the ten Republicans and the eight southern Democrats. Because the president wanted the bill so badly, my advice was that he would have to get it from the Senate. If Medicare were attached to a Senate welfare bill, we could bring it to the House as a conference-committee report on our own welfare bill. What my strategy did not calculate was the influence in the other body of a man just as powerful and just as resourceful as Wilbur Mills. He was my own state's senior senator, Robert S. Kerr.

John Kennedy had known what he was doing when he came down to Big Cedar; it simply had not worked. Amid the championship Angus on Bob Kerr's ranch, the two had talked about Medicare, to no resolution. Kennedy wanted it; Kerr did not. As the president and his entourage were leaving, Kerr told me in tones as calm as they were confident, "He thinks he can beat me on this, but I'm gonna beat him."

I already knew that Bob Kerr was a man not likely to lose any fight that involved such immense determination. My only wonder was at his determination on this one issue, a determination on an issue that seemed to have nothing to do with his one great fixation, Oklahoma. After we got back to Washington, I found out why: Medicare touched the one matter that counted for even more to Bob Kerr. Riding in his car up Independence Avenue to the Capitol, the senator told me that he did not care one way or the other about Medicare, but his wife, Grayce Breene Kerr, was a Christian Scientist. Like her faith's other believers, Mrs. Kerr did not want Social Security paying for medicine, doctors, and hospitals.

Senator Kerr was going all out to beat the president for his wife and her church.

Beat him he did. In a masterful bit of maneuvering, Kerr won for the Christian Scientists by keeping Medicare out of the Senate welfare bill, fifty-two to forty-eight. There was no medicare amendment to the conference report. There was no vote on the House floor. And the hearings went on.

There were not many things more frustrating than something like that. One of them was dealing with Clarence Cannon. Cannon first came to the Congress back in the early 1900s as a secretary to Champ Clark. For a time, he served the House as its parliamentarian. In fact, his codification of House rules and procedures, *Cannon's Precedents,* stood for decades as the bible of the legislative process, or at least as its ten thousand commandments. In 1923, Clarence Cannon took Clark's old seat and in time rose to become chairman of the House Appropriations Committee.

Eighty-two years old when the 1962 session opened, Clarence Cannon was set in his ways. He knew the House procedures, and he knew the Constitution. He took very seriously that language of ARTICLE I, SECTION 7: "All Bills for raising Revenue shall originate in the House of Representatives; . . . ." Our power of the purse was one that he cherished. It came awfully close to being *his* power of the purse.

Cannon's equivalent in the other body was a lot like him. Carl Hayden also came to Congress in the early 1900s: as the voteless delegate of Arizona Territory. The state of Arizona sent him to the House when it entered the Union in 1912. In 1927, he went to the Senate. By 1962, when Carl Hayden was eighty-four, the Arizonan was the Senate's president pro tempore and head of the Appropriations Committee. He cherished his great power, including the constitutional power granted by the closing clause of ARTICLE I, SECTION 7: ". . . but the Senate may propose or concur with Amendments as on other Bills."

In 1962, these powerful and willful men each stood stubbornly on his respective constitutional clause. Caught in the middle was the entire United States government. Each house had passed appropriations bills but in different forms for different amounts. All of them had to go to a conference committee, its members including and chosen by Chairmen Cannon and Hayden. That was not the problem. The problem was where to have the meeting. Asserting the House's prerogative and his committee's responsibility, Clarence Cannon refused to meet on the Capitol's Senate side. Proclaiming the Senate's rights and his committee's authority, Carl Hayden refused to meet on the House side. For more than two months, each stood his ground. Two months was not long from the octogenarians' perspectives, but it was an awfully long time for us. Unless one of them would budge, the government would go out of business, unable to pay its bills or honor its payroll checks.

At the weekly leadership breakfast, President Kennedy would turn to us for some help out of the impasse. Declaring that Cannon would not even return his calls, the president dispatched me to have Cannon call him. I took him the message, and old Clarence Cannon responded like a shy adolescent. "Why, I'm just a little bitty congressman from Missouri," he said. "I'm not a big enough person to trouble the president of the United States with a phone call."

I tried a different strategy. I told Cannon that I needed to meet with him in a Capitol room to discuss some other business. When he showed up, Larry O'Brien and some of the White House people were waiting there to reason with him. I left them, and in a few minutes Clarence Cannon came storming out. "Damn you, Carl Albert," he roared. "This is too important for a bunch of damn kids in the White House." So much for the little-bitty-congressman bit.

I finally did find a way out. After poring over the building's blueprints, the Capitol architects found me the one place, Room 101 of the East Front extension, that could hold the conferees in a place exactly halfway between the Senate and the House wings. I took the drawings to Clarence Cannon, and he agreed to meet Carl Hayden on that neutral site. Each (literally) met the other halfway. So it was that the government was empowered to pay its bills.

It was not always that frustrating. As majority leader, I was working on legislation that did get America moving again. The president's bold initiatives to move the economy took us a lot of time, but it was paying off. The trade expansion bill was law by the end of 1962. In that year, we also completed the first major overhaul of the federal tax system since 1954, winning the decisive vote with only twenty-three to spare. A year later, we took up Kennedy's proposal to slash taxes across the board. With its customary thoroughness, Wilbur Mills's committee spent two months in hearings, another two in closed executive sessions, and four months drafting a bill. When everything was in place, the House passed it on September 25 by a comfortable margin of 271 to 155. Republican conservatives had howled that the bill's deliberate creation of a deficit was heretical and dangerous, but combined with our previous steps, the tax cut's stimulus sparked the longest and greatest sustained period of economic growth in the nation's history. National production soared, inflation remained minimal, unemployment virtually disappeared. The government's revenue rode with the economy, leaving John Kennedy just short of an overall budget surplus for his period in office.

I am proud to write these few sentences, and it is easy to do it; it was not nearly so easy to win some of the battles. Some we lost. Ways and Means continued to hold up Medicare through all of 1962, 1963, and 1964. Clarence Cannon and his foreign-aid subcommittee chairman, Otto Passman, cut billions off that necessary program. It was all we could do just to save it. We did not even try for a general aid-to-education bill. The need was great, but the continuing church-state controversy was greater.

These we could not turn around, but others we could. This happened when the majority leader was doing his job well, and it made his job fun. Particularly when it involved agriculture, it also was mighty important to this leader's district.

For all of his learning, John Kennedy knew almost nothing about agriculture and had to find an agriculture secretary who did. He first had leaned toward a recognized farm leader, a real, live practicing farmer. The president-elect had met with the fellow at his Georgetown residence, had interviewed him, and had become so bored that he actually fell asleep. He finally settled on Orville Freeman, the former governor of a farm state (Minnesota), deliverer of Kennedy's convention nomination speech, and a man who needed a job, for Freeman had lost his reelection contest in 1960.

In 1962, Secretary Freeman gave us a complicated new proposal to establish supply-management controls for milk and feed grains, including wheat and corn. I knew the vote would be close, and the harder I worked on it, the more certain I became. In the last days, I was fighting for it one vote at a time until I had every vote that it could get, including four members who intended to vote no but agreed to switch to aye if that would save it. As the House voted on June 21, I watched the count. It turned out to be 215 to 205 against us. A fifth switch would have saved it because Speaker McCormack would have voted to break the tie, but I could still be one short, so I spared the four to fight another day.

It came on September 20. The Senate's farm bill had secured supply management for wheat but not the other commodities. Our conferees brought that version back to us and gave me one last chance to turn it around. The odds were not good, though. Back in June, every Republican but one had voted against the bill. As the clerk went down the roll, it was obvious that the GOP was still determined to beat us. I just about gave up on it.

Steadily, the margin against us rose. At one point, it reached twenty-one. And then it began to drop, slowly but consistently. As the clerk read on, we climbed within seventeen, then sixteen, then fifteen, then fourteen. We had broken the momentum. We could turn it around. As more Democratic members filed into the House to vote, Hale Boggs and I grabbed them. "If you come with us," I pleaded, "we can win this thing." Speaker McCormack called a few northeasterners up to his chair and pressed the case to help us.

The margin kept dropping. It was eight, then seven, then six. With just a few more minutes, we could win it. I bought them by dispatching a few rank-and-file members into the House well. "Mr. Speaker," each asked in turn, "how am I recorded?" As the clerk patiently looked up each member's name and told the member what his own vote had been, I scurried around the floor, picking up a new vote here, gaining a switch there. Furious, the Republican leadership tried to cut us off. Charlie Halleck rose to shout out a point of order. "Members are asking how they are recorded," he declared, "for obvious purposes of delay." John McCormack overruled the objection. "The Chair cannot look into the minds of members and determine their motives," observed the old veteran of many a fight.

Finally, I had cornered every entering member and had persuaded three to switch their original votes. The clerk completed the long-delayed roll call and handed the Speaker the official tally. We had won by 202 to 197. This time, I had the three switches that were exactly what we needed.

During my first year in Congress, I got one of those letters that Sam Rayburn had told me about. It was from a poor fellow who wanted some help. It read, "We Okies expect you to uphold our interest in this nigger question."

It was an attitude not universal in my district and not unique to it, either. You could find it all over America. I had been raised among people who held it. Most of them had voted to send me to

Congress to be their representative. Theirs was a view centuries old; it was the custom of our daily lives; it was enshrined in the laws of our states and localities. What is remarkable is not its existence, not its expression, not its strength. What is remarkable is that my district, my state, and my nation have overcome it. It happened while I served in Congress, most of it while I served as majority leader.

In a sense, it began with Harry Truman, the Missouri courthouse politician who became the first president in this century to ask Congress for civil rights legislation. After the 1948 Democratic National Convention committed the party to a civil rights program, Harry Truman boldly made the commitment his own. It split the party and came to nothing legislatively, but it secured Harry Truman's election and his place in history.

However meager the immediate results, the issue, once raised, did not go away. In the most important constitutional case of this century, the United States Supreme Court, in the 1954 *Brown* case, unanimously forbade the racial segregation of students in American schools. Subsequent decisions steadily chipped away at segregation's foundation. In Montgomery, Alabama, a young minister, the Reverend Dr. Martin Luther King, Jr., took up the cause of a middle-aged seamstress, Mrs. Rosa Parks. In the streets of the Cradle of the Confederacy he forged the tactic, the passive resistance of nonviolent protest, that made her cause his people's cause as it blazed across the South and seared the nation's conscience.

Cautiously, almost painfully, Congress began to move. In 1957, we marginally strengthened black voting rights with the first civil rights act since Reconstruction. I remember that when it came up, I sought the advice of Sam Rayburn. Mr. Rayburn represented the same kind of people I did. In 1948, he had had to save his seat from a vicious demagogue by swearing his powerful opposition to any civil rights laws. But I still remember what Sam Rayburn told me that day in 1957. "Carl," he said, "under the Constitution, every man has the right to vote. You can defend the position before any audience in this country." That cleared it up for me immediately. Any other consideration slipped away, and I saw the issue in moral terms. On the decisive teller votes, I marched down the House aisle with the civil rights people. I voted for the act on final passage. I did the same thing three years later when Congress passed a second (though still weak) civil rights bill.

Still, the issue did not go away. By endorsing stronger action and dramatically securing Dr. King's release from a Georgia jail cell, John Kennedy won the overwhelming support of black voters and, only because of that, the presidency. But if black votes at the polls had made him president, southern votes in the Congress would decide his fate. For that reason, he (and we in the leadership) moved cautiously. In 1961, we worked on only one civil rights measure, an act to extend the Civil Rights Commission created in the 1957 law. Candidate Kennedy had roundly criticized the Eisenhower administration for failing to end discrimination in Federal Housing Administration loans by executive order—with "the stroke of a pen," he had said in 1960—but it was November 1962 before President Kennedy moved his own pen under such an order. Even as late as February 1963, Kennedy's eloquent message on civil rights led only to meek White House proposals to tighten existing laws and provide assistance for school districts that were integrating voluntarily. Nothing was said about the thousands of districts and entire states that still refused to integrate nine years after the *Brown* decision, and little was done to push the little that was proposed.

If political reasoning seemed to compel such a lack of vigor, events far removed from the Capitol moved to their own logic. In April of 1963, Dr. King took his cause to Birmingham, Alabama, the city that he described as "the most thoroughly segregated big city" in America. Mass demonstrations, many involving schoolchildren, followed. The city's police commissioner, Eugene ("Bull") Connor, met the children with fire hoses and attack dogs. Scores were injured, and 3,300 demonstrators were arrested and herded into pens. In early May, a bomb destroyed the church that Dr. King was using as his headquarters. Four little black girls, each clad in her Sunday-best dress of white, lay crushed beneath the rubble. More bombings followed. Eventually, and inevitably, some blacks put down their picket signs and picked up rocks. Spasms of rioting, looting, and terror threatened to tear the city apart. In other cities, from Cambridge, Massachusetts, to Cambridge, Maryland, mass protests in the streets marched a hot breath from violence.

Atop it all, Governor George Wallace finally got his chance to keep his campaign promise to "stand in the schoolhouse door." After long and tedious litigation, a federal court had ordered the University of Alabama to admit two black students. Deputy Attorney General Nicholas Katzenbach personally delivered and read the order at the Tuscaloosa campus. Standing before him was the cocky little governor, who melodramatically read his statement of defiance. Standing metaphorically behind the governor was the possibility of mob rioting, such as had injured hundreds a year before at the University of Mississippi. Standing literally (if somewhat distantly) behind Katzenbach were army troops already aboard helicopters at Fort Benning, Georgia. It was George Wallace who stood aside. Neither the spirit of defiance nor the prospect of violence budged at all.

Beginning in May, the president had talked in the leadership breakfasts about withdrawing his original meek proposal in favor of a real civil rights act, one with teeth like Bull Connor's dogs. He told us that his Justice Department already was working on just such a bill. On June 11, 1963, he told the nation. It was on the evening of George Wallace's stand in the schoolhouse door. It also was John Kennedy's finest hour. All of the eloquence that he always had displayed and all of the passion that he heretofore had withheld went into his speech. Observing that the events in Birmingham and elsewhere had "so increased the cries for equality that no city or state or legislative body can prudently choose to ignore them," the president outlined the legislation that he would submit, but he added that the nation faced not "a legal or legislative issue alone" but rather "a moral issue. It is as old as the Scriptures and is as clear as the American Constitution. . . . Those who do nothing are inviting shame as well as violence. Those who act boldly are recognizing right as well as reality." The moral issue was the nation's, but the legislative issue fell to the Congress. The time had come for us to act boldly.

Most people recall the events that surrounded our deliberations. The president, his brother (Attorney General Robert Kennedy), and his entire administration seized every public forum to urge the bill's passage. Dozens of labor unions, church groups, and reform bodies mobilized their moral energies and mounted lobbying campaigns. In the summer, a quarter of a million people marched on Washington as a human petition for civil rights. Gathered around the reflecting pool of the Lincoln Memorial, they were stirred by Dr. King's great "I Have a Dream" speech, and they left most of the country ready to make that dream come true.

To the congressional leadership fell the undramatic task of turning the dream into a law. In the nature of things, we would have to do it first in the House of Representatives. Submitted directly to the Senate, the bill would fall into the clutches of Mississippi's James Eastland and his fellow southerners on the judiciary committee, the unhappy hunting ground of civil rights. Because Senate rules allowed a bill already passed by the House to bypass committee assignment and go directly to the floor, we would have to produce the bill for them.

On our side, we were lucky. The House Judiciary Committee was one of the few not headed by a southerner. Emmanuel Celler was chairman of the committee. For forty-one years he had represented an ethnically diverse and intensely liberal Brooklyn district. There may have been no firmer friend of civil rights in the House of Representatives.

Working closely with Speaker McCormack and me, Manny Celler made his first decision. It turned out to be the most important (if unpublicized) decision in the long legislative battle to come. That decision—not a passionate speech, not a massive march—made the 1964 Civil Rights Act. It was Celler's designation of the subcommittee that would take up the bill.

The Judiciary Committee's original work on the bill, including its initial drafting, would fall to the subcommittee of Manny Celler's choice. That was one of his prerogatives as a committee chairman. Unlike those of most legislative committees, Judiciary's subcommittees were designated by number, not by narrow and hard lines of jurisdiction. Celler therefore was free to choose any of five subcommittees. His choice was Subcommittee 5, the only one not headed by a southerner or a southern sympathizer. Its chairman was Manny Celler himself, and its Democratic membership included some of the most enlightened members of the House: Pete Rodino of New Jersey, Byron Rogers of Colorado, Harold Donohue of Massachusetts, Herman Toll of Pennsylvania, Robert Kastenmeier of Wisconsin, and Jack Brooks, a Texan who was one of the strongest and most determined men in the House. Heading the subcommittee's four Republicans was William McCulloch of tiny Piqua, Ohio. McCulloch was the full committee's ranking Republican and a man respected on both sides of the aisle. Much of that respect flowed from his absolute devotion to principle.

Manny Celler's subcommittee took up President Kennedy's bill and proceeded to rewrite it. Its symbolic heart, Title II, remained the same. In one strike the bill outlawed discrimination in public accommodations, forbidding the awful system of whites-only practices in privately owned facilities that served the general public. Everywhere else, the subcommittee improved the bill by strengthening it. It added a new section outlawing employment discrimination. It fortified Title III by empowering the attorney general to initiate suits to desegregate public facilities and to intervene in suits brought by citizens seeking equal protection of the laws. Kennedy's bill had sought a four-year extension of the Civil Rights Commission; the subcommittee went all the way and made the commission permanent. The president had sought the discretionary power to deny federal funds to discriminatory programs; Manny Celler's subcommittee gave him no choice: it *required* their denial. All in all, it was Subcommittee 5 of Manny Celler's House Judiciary Committee that made John Kennedy's civil rights bill.

It was the job of the House leadership to sell it, and the first person we had to sell it to was the president.

John Kennedy feared that a bill too strong would never pass the full House or the Senate. In fact, he had dispatched his brother the attorney general to testify in the subcommittee against most of its changes. When the subcommittee went ahead anyway, he called us to the White House. Speaker McCormack, Chairman Celler, and I went, along with several rank-and-file members of the full committee. Bill McCulloch, Charlie Halleck, and a few others represented the GOP. Late into the night we argued with the president for the subcommittee's version. It was the right thing to do, it was the right time to do it, and we believed we could pass it. Judging the House's mood, I figured we could get as many as 140 or 150 Democratic votes for final passage. If the Republicans could get us even half of theirs, we would win it. Halleck and McCulloch said they could do that and declared they would. It was our bill that we took out of the White House that night, and it was our bill that the full Judiciary Committee overwhelmingly reported to the House of Representatives.

First, though, it would have to go before Judge Smith's Rules Committee. Knowing what to expect, Manny Celler was preparing a discharge petition the day he submitted the bill, November 20, 1963. The next day, President Kennedy left for Dallas.

I had first heard of Kennedy's trip from Lyndon Johnson; I thought it a bad idea. Dallas had become something of the capital of right-wing extremists, some of whom recently had heckled and assaulted United Nations Ambassador Adlai Stevenson. But the thing that struck me when Johnson told me about it was LBJ's mood.

Lyndon Johnson had left the power and the action of being Senate majority leader for the vice-presidency. Apparently he had believed that he could use the vice-president's constitutional role as the Senate's presiding officer to make himself John Kennedy's chief of Congress. He and Mike Mansfield had cooked up a scheme to make him head of the Senate's Democratic conference, but his former colleagues would have nothing of it since it jeopardized their independence from the executive branch. Johnson thereby was left with the empty honor of the vice-presidency. I suspect that he soon agreed with one of his predecessors' view of their job.

The vice-presidency, Texas's John Nance Garner had said, is "not worth a bucket of warm spit."

While he served as vice-president, Lyndon Johnson seemed a changed man. Usually active, assertive, even aggressive, he meekly went about his duties. He publicly spoke for the president's policies; he headed a few committees and boards. I saw him most frequently at the weekly leadership breakfasts. Lyndon Johnson, a man once hailed as a legislative magician, rarely spoke except to answer a question. His answers usually were short, and frequently they sounded detached. Otherwise, he sat passively, his face drawn, his eyes wandering.

That is what made so memorable an evening in the fall of 1963. Mary and I were leaving an after-work press-club reception when a long, black limousine pulled up to the curb. It was the vice-president's official car. Its darkened window dropped, and Lyndon Johnson leaned out to invite Mary and me over to his northwest Washington residence for dinner with him and Lady Bird. We piled in and had a fine meal: corn bread, black-eyed peas, and peach ice cream. Afterwards, Johnson and I sat out on his patio. I had not seen him so animated or so enthusiastic in years. He told me about a private poll he had commissioned down in Texas. It looked like John Kennedy could not carry Texas in 1964; the president would have to visit the state to rally his troops. What accounted for his exhilaration, though, was his belief that he was getting another chance to do something important. If John Kennedy was going to Texas, he would need Lyndon Johnson.

On the morning of Thursday, November 21, President Kennedy had a meeting with the Democratic leadership of the House and Senate in the Cabinet Room just before he was going to leave for Texas. When the meeting was over, he asked me to come into the Oval Office with him to discuss a legislative matter. While we were talking, his helicopter flew up and landed near the Rose Garden, just south of the East Wing of the White House. He turned around and watched the helicopter as it was stopping, then turned to me and said good-bye. He left the Oval Office for the helicopter, boarded it, and departed for Andrews Air Force Base. I was the last person to visit with him in the White House.

On Friday, November 22, I was eating lunch in the Congressional Hotel when Lydia Vacin, a secretary for the House Agriculture Committee, ran up to me. She said television had just carried the news that the president had been shot in Dallas; no one knew his condition. I rushed over to my office and learned that Ted Sorensen, President Kennedy's top aide, was calling me. I picked up the phone and he told me the president was dead. I walked into my inner office, closed the door, and turned out the lights. I railed against the madness of the assassination. I said over and over that he never should have gone. Standing in the darkness, I wished I could cry.

That night I accompanied a group of Lyndon Johnson's oldest House friends to Andrews Air Force Base. *Air Force One* rolled up, and a military guard removed a coffin. When Johnson got out, he joined us, and we drove over to the Executive Office Building. Through a little side door, we went into the White House. Nobody had said much of anything by the time we broke up an hour or so later. No one had to.

The whole country needed Lyndon Johnson.

Almost instantly Lyndon Johnson became once again a changed man. All the energy, all the ambition, all the talent that had frustrated him so in the vice-presidency now drove him, even consumed him. My phone never seemed to stop ringing. It was the president, not a secretary, not an aide. Lyndon Johnson wanted action, and he wanted it now.

In the few weeks left to 1963, I learned just how much I had ahead of me with Lyndon Johnson beside me, behind me, and seemingly all over me. The hard work that we had been doing on civil rights had put more routine bills in jeopardy. At the time of Kennedy's murder, we had passed only one of twelve general appropriations bills. Johnson drove us to get the others through, and he never let up. Finally, we were down to the last one. It was

The whole country needed Lyndon Johnson. Carl Albert with Lyndon Johnson at the White House, December, 1963.

the foreign aid bill, and I never had seen a bill so hopeless. After months of wrangling, each house had passed a bill and we finally had gotten a conference report acceptable to House and Senate negotiators. But Clarence Cannon, chairman of Appropriations, opposed it; Otto Passman, chairman of the Foreign Aid subcommittee, opposed it; Charlie Halleck and the entire Republican leadership opposed it.

The immediate problem was that the conference bill was lodged in the Rules Committee, awaiting dispatch to the floor. Sure, Howard Smith opposed it, and the Republican committeemen literally had taken their opposition with them when they left Washington to return to their homes. I could not really blame them, though. Several Democrats on Rules had done the same, and for good reason: it was December 23, only a few hours before Christmas, and this one bill was preventing the end of what was already the fifth-longest session in American history. When some Democrats and all the Republicans left, we were one vote short of the quorum necessary to get the bill out of Rules.

Even had we wanted to do so (and we did not), Lyndon Johnson was not about to let us end without getting the money to run a foreign aid program. Thus, I spent the night of December 23 at the White House. The president, the Speaker, and I moved into the Oval Office and worked the phones, trying to find that one vote for a quorum on rules. We could not even locate most of its members; those we did find were neither happy nor cooperative. It was 2:00 A.M. before I reached our last possibility, Bill Colmer. He was in a Mississippi hospital tending to his sick wife. I did not waste time arguing the bill's merits because I knew that it had none for Bill Colmer. What I said was, "Bill, we need you, your party needs you, and President Johnson needs you. We all need you to give us a quorum."

Bill Colmer left his ailing wife's bed, boarded a plane, flew through a blizzard, and reached Washington that night. At 7:00 A.M. the next day, he voted not to discharge the bill, but his presence gave us a quorum to take the bill to the House. The House passed it, and we voted adjournment on December 29. Gene Mc-

With Lyndon Johnson beside me, behind me, seemingly all over me.

Carthy joked that Sam Rayburn had died before teaching John McCormack and me how to adjourn Congress, but we finally managed that. What we were learning was how to deal with Lyndon Johnson.

Right from the start I learned that I was working with a man utterly consumed with politics. Lyndon Johnson ate, drank, breathed, and lived politics every minute of every day. He must have fallen asleep by counting votes. I never saw a man so obsessed with anything as Lyndon Johnson was with politics, especially its legislative expression. I can remember visiting him down at his ranch and trying to make some small talk. "Those are some fine-looking cattle," I might say, and Johnson would not miss a beat. "Yeah," he would answer. "That old bull over there looks just like Chairman So-and-So. What do you think we can do to move such-and-such a bill out of his committee?"

That total absorption found expression in his matchless gift for one-on-one persuasion of legislators. When he was a senator, he was famed for The Treatment, and as president he used it just as Rowland Evans and Robert Novak had described it:

> He moved in close, his face a scant millimeter from his target, his eyes widening and narrowing, his eyebrows rising and falling. From his pocket poured clippings, memos, statistics. Mimicry, humor, and the genius of analogy made The Treatment an almost hypnotic experience and rendered the target stunned and helpless.

But Lyndon Johnson was neither a hypnotist nor a magician. He was a consummate politician who made it his business to know what mattered to whom and why. Through individual contact and hard bargaining, he knew just what each congressman needed. And that is why he usually got for himself exactly what he wanted.

In 1964, he got a big chunk of it when we finished action on John Kennedy's two chief proposals of 1963. Although it had taken Wilbur Mills's Ways and Means Committee eight months to produce a tax-cut bill, it took only eight weeks for the Senate to pass it and the president to sign it once the session opened.

In even less time we got a civil rights bill to the Senate. Howard Smith used all of his legislative skills to delay it in his Rules Committee, but he no longer had the power to block it entirely. Manny Celler had gone ahead and filed his discharge petition, and its signers steadily climbed toward 218. Dick Bolling, committee member and fearless student of parliamentary procedure, kept the heat on Smith by finding an obscure procedure to make the committee meet over the chairman's objections. Recognizing the inevitable, Judge Smith allowed his committee to vote a rule on January 30. All five Republicans honored Charlie Halleck's commitment, and with the six nonsouthern Democrats, the committee voted eleven to four to release the bill.

The old judge assembled about sixty southern Democrats that same afternoon to plan a strategy, but Howard Smith's long night had passed. Manny Celler and Bill McCulloch handled the floor debate brilliantly. They hurled scores of emasculating amendments back into Smith's face. The one successful amendment of substance involved the subcommittee's outlawing of employment discrimination on the basis of race, color, religion, or national origin. To those forbidden categories the House added another: sex. Thus, the bill became a landmark in the cause of women's rights as well as black rights. It was an odd fate, for the amendment's purpose had been either to damn the bill as unenforceable or defeat it as too strong. Never before had its author made such a blunder—or such a contribution. That author was Representative Howard Worth Smith of Virginia.

So amended, the bill won overwhelmingly, 290 to 130. We got 152 Democratic votes, losing only 4 outside the South (and getting 11 there). The Republicans honored Charlie Halleck and their country by going for the bill 138 to 34.

Two White House aides who watched the final vote went out in the hall to congratulate themselves. As they stood there celebrating, a pay telephone began ringing in a nearby booth. Curious, one of them answered it. The caller was Lyndon Johnson. All he said was, "All right, you fellows, get on over there to the Senate because we've got it through the House, and now we've got the big job of getting it through the Senate."

It was a big job. Only after a three-month southern filibuster did the Senate vote, seventy-one to twenty-nine, to shut off debate. The margin was just four above the two-thirds needed. Its battle of words lost, the South lost the war, seventy-three to twenty-seven, on final passage. That vote came on June 19, 1964, exactly one year to the day after John Kennedy had submitted his bill. It had been a much longer time coming.

Presidents Kennedy and Johnson deserved all the credit they got. Manny Celler and Bill McCulloch deserved far more credit than they received. Dick Bolling deserved far more than the public ever knew. I guess I deserve some credit, too. I finally had answered that old letter wanting me to do something about the race question.

By 1964's end, Lyndon Johnson and the Congress had passed most of John Kennedy's program, but not all. Federal aid to education still tossed around the rocks of religious controversy. After Bob Kerr's untimely death in 1963, the Senate attached a Medicare amendment to the next year's Social Security bill. Wilbur Mills killed it in conference because he knew that it could not have gotten through ways and means and feared it would not pass the House.

In one stunning particular, we had gone far beyond Kennedy's public agenda. With Walter Heller, chairman of his Council of Economic Advisers, President Kennedy had talked privately about making poverty a vague campaign issue in 1964 and introducing antipoverty legislation after the election and after the tax-cut and civil rights bills had been cleared. On the evening of November 23, Lyndon Johnson's first full day as president, Heller had told Johnson of those plans. Lyndon Johnson had jumped all over the poverty issue. "Go ahead," he had told Heller. "Give it the highest priority. Push ahead full tilt."

"Push ahead full tilt" was exactly what Lyndon Johnson himself had done. During the Christmas holidays of 1963, he had put his staff to work on framing antipoverty legislation, not campaign speeches, and for 1964, not down the road. In his January State of the Union message, the new president was ready to swear that "this administration, here and now, declares unconditional war on poverty in America." The legislative expression of that was the Economic Opportunity Act of 1964. The president built a national consensus for the measure with dramatic televised tours of poverty regions and persuasive personal appeals to groups ranging from the Daughters of the American Revolution to the Socialist party. Sargent Shriver, his designated commander of the war as director of the proposed Office of Economic Opportunity, moved into my office again to help direct the congressional fight. Knowing the significance of southern Democratic votes, we assigned the bill not to education and labor's chairman, Adam Clayton Powell, but to a respected Georgian, Phil Landrum. The work that Landrum, Hale Boggs, and I put in with the southerners paid off on August 8. We got exactly the two-thirds southern Democratic support that I had figured would be our maximum, as 60 southern Democrats voted with 144 nonsoutherners and 22 Republicans to give us a comfortable 226-to-185 majority. Hale and I called the president just after the vote and I confessed my surprise at winning that easily. He thanked us, and I got ready to push ahead full tilt again and immediately.

Congress had recessed for the Republican National Convention in July, and I had taken a brief but singular vacation. Mary and David and I decided to drive up to Canada to get away. For the only time ever, I told no one on my staff even where I was going. I wanted this occasion to be a real getaway, so I made sure that no one on earth could find me. Or so I thought.

We went up to Quebec, where we visited with Paul Bouchard, a Rhodes scholar who had gone up to Oxford with me in 1931. After a nice dinner with Paul, David and I were watching Canadian television in our room. Right in the middle of the news, an announcer broke in with a bulletin: "The Royal Canadian Mounted Police is endeavoring to locate Congressman Carl Albert. He is believed to be in Canada and driving a 1964 Thunderbird, Oklahoma license PB 827. Anyone knowing the whereabouts of Carl Albert will please immediately notify the Royal Canadian Mounted Police." David looked at me like he expected Sergeant Preston to bust down the door any minute. I hurried to a phone and called the Mounties, wondering why I was a wanted man. The fellow I asked laughed. "Sir," he answered, "you're not wanted by us. Your President Johnson is the one who wants you." It figured. The president had put the FBI, the RCMP, and the White House switchboard to work finding me. It had taken them several hours, but they had done it. The president wanted me to direct his own convention's platform committee, and he wanted me to start now.

It turned out to be a pretty good job. It was a sign of how rapidly and how tightly Lyndon Johnson had seized the fallen reins of leadership that we produced a platform exactly to his liking. In fact, the only dispute involved a minority that wanted an extreme civil rights plank that was sure to touch off a bloody floor fight. Manny Celler, whom I had put on the drafting subcommittee because of his responsible leadership for civil rights, took care of that. Like the entire platform, the final plank was a testimony to Democratic unity behind a progressive yet realistic program.

That was a mighty big asset in the 1964 election. At San Francisco's Cow Palace, a fractious Republican National Convention had chosen as its candidate a man regarded as neither progressive nor realistic. Barry Goldwater had built a reputation as a conservative ideologue. He welcomed hardly any major advance of the past third of a century, not Social Security of the 1930s, not public housing of the 1940s, not his own party's moderation of the 1950s, not even civil rights of the 1960s. In hundreds of speeches, a syndicated column, and a widely read book, Goldwater also had revealed a disquieting tendency to shoot from the lip. He wanted to call nuclear weapons "nukes," apparently to make them seem friendlier. At a moment of international crisis, he had offered the discomforting advice of "lobbing a few into the men's room of the Kremlin." All of this had made Goldwater something of a hero to every right-wing extremist group in the country, and the candidate had not shunned their sweaty embrace. On the contrary, he had bellowed at San Francisco that "extremism in the defense of liberty is no vice; moderation in the pursuit of justice is no virtue."

By the time of our own convention, Republicans everywhere had displayed his picture: steel-gray hair; square, set jaw; black lensless glasses. The last eliminated the photographer's glare but did nothing to improve the Arizonan's peculiar vision. Beneath it ran the 1964 slogan: "In your heart you know he's right."

In Atlantic City, we Democrats had our fun with candidate Goldwater. Hubert Humphrey's speech accepting the vice-presidential nomination ran through the litany of recent reforms backed by our party. Each, he added, was embraced by the vast majority of

Americans. Soon the crowd was chanting with him the line that followed: "But not Senator Goldwater." I made my own contribution to Democratic humor when I said of the opposition's slogan, "In your heart you know he's right—too far right."

Our good spirits continued right through Election Day. Lyndon Johnson carried all but six states (five in the Deep South, plus Goldwater's home state) in rolling up 61 percent of the popular vote, a new national record. All across the country Democrats owed their elections to him, or, perhaps, to Barry Goldwater. That was surely the case in Congress, where we added two seats to our already substantial Senate majority and another thirty-eight in the House. In both chambers the Democratic party held its largest advantage since the Roosevelt landslide of 1936. The tide that Lyndon Johnson had mounted in 1963 was rolling along. In 1965 it reached flood proportions, crested, and fell.

When the 1965 Congress had completed its work, President Johnson gave me a present that I promptly put on my office wall. Today it is one of the few souvenirs of those days that I display in my office at the Federal Building in McAlester, Oklahoma. It is a framed set of fountain pens, each bearing the title of a separate bill. At the bottom is a plaque engraved with what must have been dictated by the president. Who but Lyndon Johnson would say "With these fifty pens, President Lyndon B. Johnson signed into law the foundations of the Great Society which were passed by the historic and fabulous first session of the 89th Congress"?

"The historic and fabulous first session of the 89th Congress" was indeed the most remarkable Congress of my generation. In its 293-day session, it passed the bills that completed the Democratic agenda that had been stalled since the 1930s, bills that established Lyndon Johnson's reputation, bills that defined national priorities into the 1980s and beyond. Since I had become party whip, I had become accustomed to settling for half a loaf; sometimes I had gotten the crumbs. In 1965, we got the whole loaf with the meat, the condiments, and the beverages thrown in to give us a real legislative feast.

It was the House's leadership that made sure we got it, and we made sure we got it by the end of the session's first day. After the election, Speaker McCormack, Hale Boggs, and I resolved to make the most of our majority. We knew that thirty-eight new Democrats would not automatically change the decisions of Congress, not unless the decision-making process changed. That is what we set out to do. We told the president and he was more than sympathetic, but he recognized that these were House matters. This was our fight, and it was the leadership of the House that won it.

One change gave us more leverage over the Rules Committee. Having made the 1961 expansion permanent in 1963, we now added a twenty-one-day rule. Unlike that of 1949, this one took some of the committee's power and gave it directly to the Speaker, not other chairmen. The Speaker gained the discretionary power (not the obligation) to recognize *any* member of a committee who wanted to call up a bill on the floor if the Rules Commitee had not reported it favorably within twenty-one days. In addition, we eliminated outright the Rules Committee's power over the submission of bills to the House-Senate conference committees.

The other change involved the critical Ways and Means Committee. For years the committee's membership had been frozen at fifteen majority members and ten minority members, regardless of the party ratio in Congress. In 1965, we insisted that the overall ratio (more than 2:1) prevail on that vital committee. The result was that the GOP slipped to eight seats and we went to seventeen. With one vacancy otherwise, we then added three moderate-to-liberal members: Richard Fulton of Tennessee, Phil Landrum of Georgia, and Charles Vanik of Ohio. Down the road was the promise of a more representative Congress, since the seventeen Democratic members would continue to make our committee assignments.

Without those changes—entirely conceived and executed by the House leadership—that framed gift on my wall would hold very few pens. It was on that day by those deeds that we made it possible for the Congress to have a "historic and fabulous" session.

The president was ready to make the most of those opportunities. The drive that I had seen in 1963 and 1964 only increased in 1965. Lyndon Johnson had the big majority that every Democratic president since Roosevelt had wanted and needed. He had the House leadership and internal structure that even Roosevelt had lost, he had the momentum of a national mandate of record proportions, and he had the sense to know that he must use them all while he still had them. Use them he did with 469 legislative proposals. At the session's end, we had approved 323 of them, giving Lyndon Johnson a batting average of .689. No president since FDR had won nearly so much; none since LBJ has, either.

Many of them he won only because of our internal reforms. If Lyndon Johnson had had to deal with Howard Smith's old Rules Committee and Wilbur Mills's old ways and means, he would have gone down swinging. As it was, the changes engineered by the House leadership allowed the president to set a record. In many cases, that record also was indebted to the long labor of unsung congressmen. Take Medicare, for example. Presidents John Kennedy and Lyndon Johnson both had fought hard for the bill, but the original idea belonged to neither president. Back in the 1950s, Representative Aime J. Forand of Rhode Island had introduced the first bill to pay the elderly's hospital expenses under Social Security; that was essentially the bill that President Johnson sent us in 1965. What the leadership had done ensured that Congress would pass it.

Even before those changes, the election results already guaranteed there would be some health-care legislation for the elderly that year. Even the Republicans and the American Medical Association knew it, so they aimed to defeat Medicare with something called Eldercare. Unlike the Forand proposal for compulsory hospital coverage, theirs would pay only the elderly's doctor bills through voluntary contributions. The battle would be fought in Wilbur Mills's Ways and Means Committee, and our changes in that committee won it. In a brilliant maneuver dictated by the altered memberships of both his committee and of the House, Wilbur Mills outflanked the opposition by coupling its alternative to Representative Forand's original idea. The compulsory payroll tax of Social Security financed the elderly's hospital costs; voluntary supplementary coverage (at a cost of three dollars monthly) would cover the participants' doctor bills.

The same principle applied to the landmark Elementary and Secondary Education Act of 1965. For years, general aid to education had stalled because of the church-state issue. Lyndon Johnson and the White House finally found a way around it, but it was the way that had been blazed by Representative Cleveland Bailey of West Virginia. Back in the 1950s, Congressman Bailey had put through Congress a number of specialized aid-to-education bills. Because heavy federal employment at untaxed federal facilities took money away from local school boards while it put children in their classrooms, the Bailey Acts distributed money in proportion to the federal impact upon enrollments. From that precedent came the 1965 proposal. Since the government was waging a war on poverty, general education aid could be made available to any school (public or sectarian) impacted by large numbers of poor students. So conceived, the bill passed handily.

Another example is the 1965 immigration-law reform. Back in the 1920s, the Republicans had pushed through an act placing a tight lid on the total number of immigrants allowed in the United States. Worse, the act had adopted the notorious national-origins system of quotas. Seeking to freeze the nation's racial mix as it had stood before the influx of southern and eastern Europeans, the act had assigned each nation a quota of allowable immigrants on the basis of that nation's proportional contribution to the American population *of 1890.* In 1965, we got rid of that once and for all. Lyndon Johnson signed our bill before the Statue of Liberty, but the bill he signed was essentially the one that John McCormack and Manny Celler had called for in their maiden speeches in Congress, both delivered before Lyndon Johnson was old enough to serve there.

That is not to say that the president deserved no credit and made no contribution. Manny Celler lived to put the bill through his Judiciary Committee, and John McCormack lived to sign it as Speaker, but when its time came, Lyndon Johnson was behind the bill all the way. His Justice Department prepared the detailed "blue books" that went to every member and persuasively made the case for reform. His press office recorded messages in forty languages and distributed them to 250 radio stations to stir up popular support. And it was Lyndon Johnson himself who sat down and reasoned with the chairman of the House Judicial Subcommittee on Immigration, Michael Feighan. It was The Treatment that finally washed away Feighan's objections and made the bill possible.

On other bills, too, the White House's influence was undeniable. The Voting Rights Act of 1965, the one law that has most revolutionized American politics in my lifetime because it made southern politicians answerable to millions of black voters, was described by the press as Johnson's hurry-up answer to Martin Luther King's march in Selma, Alabama. Though that march dramatized the need, the fact was that the president, the Justice Department, and the congressional leadership were preparing to write and pass a voting-rights bill before a single marcher ever set foot on Edmund Pettus Bridge. This simply was an act whose time had come.

The same story stands behind almost all the pens that rest in that maple case in my office. Their time had come. We were no rubber-stamp Congress blindly catering to the president's ego. Lyndon Johnson was harvesting the work of those who had gone before him. He could do it because we stood by him. We knew our part, and we did it; he did his better than any president in my lifetime.

Until Vietnam.

Before the Eighty-ninth Congress, before the Johnson landslide, on August 4, 1964, President Johnson asked me to stay after our regular leadership breakfast to go over some other business. We had just begun talking pleasantly when the president received a phone call. His mood changed abruptly. He said to the caller, "They have?" He silently took the answer, then he shouted into the phone: "Now, I'll tell you what I want. I not only want those patrol boats destroyed, I want everything at that harbor destroyed,

I want the whole damn works destroyed. I want to give them a real dose." With that, he slammed the receiver down. Awkwardly, we finished our business without another word on the subject of the call.

Not until that evening, when I was called to be at the White House at seven o'clock. Joining me were six other congressmen and seven senators. Collectively, it was the entire bipartisan leadership of Congress and the Foreign Relations and Armed Services committees. With the president were Secretary of State Dean Rusk, Secretary of Defense Robert McNamara, Central Intelligence Agency Director John A. McCone, and General Earl Wheeler, chairman of the Joint Chiefs of Staff. Clearly, this was no routine assembly, a judgment confirmed by the president's opening words: "Some of our boys are floating around in the water."

Quickly, the administration's leaders outlined the circumstances that had brought us there. McNamara explained the morning's phone call when he told us that for the second time in as many days, North Vietnamese patrol boats had attacked an American naval vessel routinely patrolling waters forty to sixty miles at sea in the Gulf of Tonkin. Rusk ran through the immediate diplomatic background and sketched the responses already unfolding. McCone gave us the intelligence estimates regarding the involved North Vietnamese forces, and Wheeler read the message that he had dispatched to the commanders of our men serving as advisers in South Vietnam. After some general discussion, President Johnson told us his purpose—and ours.

He had prepared a resolution, based directly on the Formosa, Berlin, and Cuban resolutions, that he would present to Congress the next day. The resolution authorized the responses already made (as he read it, American planes were warming their engines for a retaliatory strike) and much else besides. In language used before, it generally empowered the president "to take all necessary steps, including the use of armed force" to assist any allied nation of Southeast Asia "in defense of its freedom." Explicitly, it expressed congressional approval and support for the president's "determination . . . to take all necessary measures to repel any armed attack against the forces of the United States and to prevent further aggression." From the entire assembly there was not one word of opposition. Each of us praised his resolve; each of us predicted overwhelming congressional approval. We departed with Senator George Aiken's comment, "By the time you send it up, there won't be anything for us to do but support you."

Lyndon Johnson sent it up and we did. The resolution cleared Thomas Morgan's House Foreign Affairs Committee without debate and without opposition. On August 7, Morgan presented it to the full House. No one spoke against it, and I was one of those to speak for it. "The president has asked us as representatives of the American people for our support," I said. "It is now time for all of us to join together as a nation firmly united behind our Commander-in-Chief and to express our complete confidence in him and in his leadership." In the House, we all did. The vote was 416 to 0. It had taken us just forty minutes.

Behind those minutes were years of experience. Not once since the sobering episode of Woodrow Wilson's Versailles treaty had an American president sought the support of Congress for his foreign policy and failed to get it. The world's bloodiest war had followed that failure. Since that war, both parties in both houses had stood united behind the critical policy decisions of four presidents. Both parties had acknowledged the chief executive's primacy in foreign policy, and every time America had stood united behind the president, peace had prevailed. Both Eisenhower and Kennedy had committed us to maintain the independence of South Vietnam. Every commitment we had made everywhere we had honored, and peace was the product. In an American election year, with a president and a candidate I knew to cherish peace, with the American flag under armed assault, this was no time to forget those lessons. When we voted that resolution, we were not making a military decision at all but a decision of the highest politics, and we made it with that past before us.

Few doubted our choice. Before the episode, opinion polls recorded that two-thirds of the American people cared little or not at all about Vietnam. After it, 85 percent expressed their approval of what we and the president had done. Otherwise, the immediate political effect was to defuse recent Republican charges that we were letting down our guard in Vietnam and to add to Lyndon Johnson's majorities. Compared to Barry Goldwater's rhetoric, President Johnson's acts were reasoned and responsible, firm but unthreatening. When he told a campaign crowd in my own district that "we don't want our American boys to do the fighting for the Asian boys," all of us—the president, the crowd, and I—believed that what we were doing was the one thing that could keep American boys out of the fighting. We believed because it always had in the past. This time it did not.

In South Vietnam we were setting our feet firmly upon an unstable slope that dropped to chaos. Following the military's 1963 overthrow and murder of Premier Ngo Dinh Diem, a series of governments, each more inept than its predecessor, came and went. Determined to take advantage, the Vietcong and North Vietnamese came and fought. Poorly led and demoralized, South Vietnam's army rarely stood to fight back, never successfully. The emboldened Communist forces even struck at American targets. In November 1963, they shelled our air base at Bien Hoa, destroying five planes and leaving four Americans dead. At Christmas, they bombed a Saigon hotel that housed both military and civilian personnel, killing several. On February 6, 1964, they assaulted a military outpost at Pleiku, killing nine of our soldiers.

Never before had a Communist force dared directly provoke a power such as the United States. Never before had there been such a power. In the mid-1960s, the United States produced half the world's wealth. Eleven of our states outproduced the entire Soviet Union; California alone outproduced Red China. A few good American counties generated more economic might than did all of North Vietnam. No one—not the Vietcong, not North Vietnam, not Red China, not the Soviet Union, not the entire Communist block—could match the military resources of the United States. Intelligently and carefully brought to bear, those resources surely would end the aggression. The military leaders told us it could be done with air power alone. Having seen the devastation that ruined Japan even before Hiroshima, I wanted to believe them. Lyndon Johnson did, too.

Two hours after the Pleiku attack, the president ordered a series of retaliatory raids directed at specific North Vietnamese targets. Two days later, those raids became a sustained and graduating air war that eventually would drop on North Vietnam more tons of high-explosive bombs than had fallen on Japan or on Germany or on all military targets in the history of warfare. It would not be enough.

By the summer of 1965, that was already clear. The Vietcong and the North Vietnamese had not cowered from American might, they had taunted it by stepping up the pressure of their attacks. Our military saw the bloody consequences and the certain outcome: the imminent collapse of South Vietnam.

On July 27, the congressional leadership met again with President Johnson to discuss the situation. With him were all of his top aides, both military and civilian, as well as our ambassador to South Vietnam, Henry Cabot Lodge. The collection told me how important the meeting was. Again the president's opening words told us why. The situation in Vietnam, he said, was critical. The Communists had rejected his recent calls for peace. The only change was that South Vietnam's army was nearing disintegration. General William C. Westmoreland had requested a real commitment of American power, manpower, for a land war. The general also had declared that South Vietnam could be saved only if the United States military shed its role as advisers and "put its finger in the dike" by taking charge of the war in the south.

Calmly, Lyndon Johnson described for us five possible responses to the dire situation. One was to destroy North Vietnam utterly and totally by unleashing the full might of America's war power. A second was just as extreme: we could walk away. The third was to cling to the status quo—as he put it, "hope Lodge can pull a rabbit out of the hat." Not even Ambassador Lodge smiled at that or at the fourth option: to proclaim a national emergency, call up the reserves, and declare war. His last option was to increase draft calls to meet Westmoreland's immediate requests, seek supplemental appropriations to pay the bill, and trust that that measured commitment would be enough. If not, we could always add to it.

Not one person in that room believed either one, two, or three was even an option. The experience of China's intervention in the Korean War made the first a potential disaster that no one would risk again. The experience of appeasing Hitler at Munich ruled out the second, a point that John McCormack particularly stressed. The evaluation of Lodge and Westmoreland made the third a thinly disguised version of two; it was appeasement on the installment plan. No one in that room doubted that Lyndon Johnson's only real alternatives were either the fourth or the last. We all could tell—his tone, his words, even the ordering gave it away—that the last was his strong preference. Perhaps it was already his decision. Without dissent, we each agreed to back him. No one wanted another Korea or Munich, but no one wanted to declare war in Vietnam. No one thought it necessary; no one thought it prudent; no one wanted a third-rate Communist state to stop our progress toward a Great Society.

A few days later, President Johnson announced that he was sending 50,000 American boys immediately to Vietnam, toward a year-end total of 175,000. Moreover, he would grant General Westmoreland whatever additional numbers were necessary to do the job that was now our job. He did not say that we were going to war. We did not know that we were—on the installment plan.

The overwhelming majority of Americans supported that decision. I think they did so for the same reason I did: we had the experience of the past, and we had confidence in our capacity to shape the future. But we could not have foreseen or even have imagined how that future would unfold.

We could not know how little the material might of the world's greatest industrial power would affect events in the jungles of Vietnam. We could not tell that the government we were backing there would waste the lives of our men (and its own, too) with ceaseless scheming and unbounded corruption. We could not imagine that the military superiority of the United States could not break the will of an insignificant state equipped with no navy, no air force, and a peasant army. We could not envision an on-again, off-again war. We could not foresee that the enemy would use negotiations as its military weapon. We could not imagine an enemy ready to die faster than our weapons could kill. We could not foresee that one escalation would beget another and the sum of them all would be the most divisive national experience since the Civil War. We could not know that this war might be lost but not lost before it had provoked a constitutional crisis in our own country. I do not know what any of us—the president, the leadership, the American people—would have done had we foreseen the unforeseeable. I know only that we were all summoned to honorable purposes, not to prophecy.

Most of Vietnam's worst effects lay down a long, twisting, and bloody road. One, however, surfaced immediately. After our commitment was made, the Great Society's momentum broke and then retreated. I could see it as early as the 1966 session, and I saw it up close. We had declared a war on poverty, not on Vietnam. While fighting the undeclared war, we had to finance the declared one.

Knowing it would be too little, the Democratic leadership got an antipoverty authorization of $1.75 billion, every penny that could be gotten through the Appropriations Committee or the House. Events showed just how close we had cut it, for when we put the bill on the House floor, the Republicans moved to strike the enacting clause, thereby killing the bill and eliminating any funds at all. They carried the motion 128 to 118 on a teller vote. Hurriedly, I called for a roll-call vote and rounded up every Democratic vote I could find to save the program. We did, 259 to 157. Still, I doubted that it even would have come to that only twelve months earlier.

Because we had the numbers, we won that one, and many others besides. For all of our difficulties, the two sessions of the Eighty-ninth Congress proved what we could do with a decent number of Democrats. A Harris Poll showed what the public thought of that: 71 percent gave the Congress a favorable rating, 4 percentage points above Lyndon Johnson's best rating and 36 points above our own rating in 1963. Our major accomplishments—Medicare, aid to education, tax reform, and voting rights—earned favorable ratings of 82, 90, 92, and 95 percent respectively. Never in my lifetime had Congress been so highly regarded, and rightly so. On that record we should have swept the 1966 congressional elections. But we were not judged on that record. The poll came before Vietnam was nightly bad news; before war spending began to overheat the economy and send inflation soaring; before the terrible summer riots in Chicago, Atlanta, Cleveland, and New York City; before the disruptive demonstrations on college campuses. The congressional elections came after those, and they gave the Republicans forty-seven new seats. That broke the back of the Great Society right there.

A restored Republican–southern Democrat coalition immediately repealed the measures that had made possible the 1965 burst of congressional energy. Its members ended our twenty-one-day rule, thereby weakening the leadership's control of House business. They restored the old fifteen-to-ten split on ways and means, thereby giving the coalition control over important decisions. Thus fortified, they proceeded to turn back new initiatives and reduce old ones to sepulchers haunted with dead promises of what might have been.

Symbolically, the end came on July 20, 1967, when we debated House Resolution 749, the Rat Extermination and Control Act of 1967. All of the fun that we Democrats had poked at candidate Goldwater came back at us as Republicans hooted about a "civil-rats" act and jested at the notion of "throwing money down a rat hole." Their chief fun maker, Joel Broyhill of Virginia, urged that "the 'rat smart thing' for us to do is to vote down this rat bill 'rat now.'" And they did, 207 to 176. That afternoon, I told Barefoot Sanders, President Johnson's top legislative assistant, that no new programs should even be sent to the House thereafter. All we could get him were the bare essentials, and we could not always get those.

In a few months, I had seen Lyndon Johnson move from a symbol of national unity to a source of national division. Vietnam literally was consuming and destroying him. At our leadership meetings he would go over the war again and again, and in time it became an intensely personal matter. I remember that at one of those in February 1968 he made the wounded comment, almost enraged, almost tearful, that "nobody says anything about Ho Chi Minh. Ho has a great image. But they call me a murderer."

Vietnam consumed him politically as well. Campaigning on a peace platform, my old friend from the House Agriculture Committee, Gene McCarthy, came within a few thousand votes of beating him in the New Hampshire primary. Days after that vote, Robert Kennedy announced his own candidacy, it, too, demanding an end in Vietnam.

By the end of March 1968, I knew just how hopeless his situation had become. On March 28, I gave a rousing partisan speech before a strangely somber crowd at the South Carolina Democratic Convention. I understood the quiet only afterwards when the state chairman told me that Lyndon Johnson could not carry even one of the state's six congressional districts in a Democratic primary. McCarthy or Kennedy would get every district in South Carolina, one of the nation's most conservative states. The next day, I went to New York City to help Representative John Murphy's campaign. The professionals there told me that Johnson would finish third in New York, one of the nation's most liberal states.

For those reasons, I probably was the least surprised man in America when Lyndon Johnson called me two days later, on March 31, 1968. I knew that he had a major television address scheduled only a few hours later, but President Johnson wanted to tell me personally: he was withdrawing from the presidential race. Soon it would all be over for him.

It was left to our convention to decide on a candidate, and the president was leaving me with one last mighty responsibility: I was to be chairman of the 1968 Democratic National Convention, scheduled for Chicago, Illinois, at the end of August.

That is when it is always hottest in Chicago.

It was hot. It is odd, but one of the things I remember most

When it is always hottest in Chicago. Carl Albert at the 1968 Democratic National Convention.

clearly about that convention was the air conditioning. It blew straight at the rostrum, hurling chilly blasts at the presiding officer. That was I, and within minutes of going to the platform, I developed a cold that first became laryngitis and then impaired my hearing. I was coming down with that when I addressed the convention upon my formal election as its permanent chairman. I said: "Our actions here will be viewed around the world. We will be judged by our decorum. We can make this convention a showcase of democracy or a shambles of discord. We might even make it lively and spirited." I never uttered a grander understatement. It was plenty lively and spirited, but no one can convince me that it was a shambles.

Discord there was, in abundance. Johnson's withdrawal had not ended our party's division. Robert Kennedy's assassination had added to the strife, as had the earlier murder of Martin Luther King. Thousands of antiwar protesters, ill barbered, ill clothed, and ill tempered, descended on the city, determined to close the proceedings in the name of peace. They were ill housed, too, and when they met Mayor Richard Daley's policemen in the city's parks (some of which were under the Vietcong flag), riots resulted. All of that the television cameras picked up, and most of the nation saw it.

We in the convention hall were among the few who did not. Inside the hall, we had our own discord. A sizable body of delegates was there in Gene McCarthy's name. These had no chance. Others, originally selected as Kennedy delegates, had no candidate. Both were determined to have their way on the one issue, Vietnam, that united them and gave them moral fire, the moral fire that, like the religious zealots', would be quenched with no compromise. So intense was their hatred of the war that they placed its ending, or even the opportunity to denounce it, above the convention's real purposes.

The unavoidable result transcended liveliness and spiritedness. Every attempt to transact orderly business (no easy task, at best, with more than five thousand delegates and alternates plus packed galleries plus wandering newshounds) ran headlong into all of the bitterness, all of the divisions, and all of the frustrations that our assembly only mirrored. If the result looking confusing to a politically inexperienced television viewer, I can only say that it looked and sounded awfully confusing to the presiding officer up there on the rostrum. Confusing, yes, but I got the job done. The job was not to entertain a television audience, it was to see that every view was heard in an orderly fashion. It was. Our second day was given over completely to the platform and debate on it. In past conventions, the tradition was that minority views on individual planks were granted thirty minutes of debating time. Knowing the significance of the issue, I got those rules amended to grant two full hours of orderly, informed debate on the Vietnam plank. Amid the millions of angry words over Vietnam, those were two rare hours of structured and responsible debate.

We had to select a candidate, and we did. Hubert Humphrey deserved our nomination. For sixteen years he had been a fighting liberal in the United States Senate, the kind of liberal who early advanced the issues to which the nation later came. It was Hubert Humphrey, for instance, who had first committed the Democratic party to the cause of black civil rights when he carried the minority civil rights plank to the floor and won back in 1948. It was the same Hubert Humphrey who later guided the 1964 Civil Rights Act through the Senate's dangerous shoals. In Hubert Humphrey we also had the one Democrat who stood a realistic chance of winning the election. Robert Kennedy might have done it, but he was gone; Gene McCarthy never could have. Hubert Humphrey, starting so far back, came as close as he could get to winning it, and given a few more days or a couple of breaks, he would have won it.

Humphrey did get one break. Since the advent of saturated network coverage of convention proceedings, one of a convention's functions has been to present its nominee in prime time, before the maximum television audience, for what will be his most important single address. For all the comments about disorder, anyone who turned on a television at exactly 9:00 P.M., eastern standard time, saw Hubert Humphrey speak his opening sentence, not some riot. I thought of that four years later when a hand-picked, stacked convention nominated George McGovern and put him on the air at 3:00 A.M., thereby gaining the insomniacs' votes but (judging from the count) few others.

There is one last contrast I can mention. People commented about the businesslike efficiency of the Republicans' earlier convention in Miami, the convention that nominated Richard Nixon and Spiro Agnew. Few remember that outside its doors the police killed three rioters and shot five others. In Chicago we had an open convention, chose a strong candidate, and gave him our best possible sendoff. And no one was killed. We did not laugh as often as we had in 1964. When the Chicago convention ended, I went home and to bed. I was sick and I was tired. And I was not one bit ashamed.

CHAPTER EIGHT

What Happened to Ernie Albert's Boy

It was a hard winter back home in January 1971, especially hard for the old folks, especially the ones without good heaters and decent houses. One of those was an elderly fellow named Walter Johns, a veteran of the First World War and a retired miner. One night in early January, his gas heater ignited his leaky frame house, and it burned to the ground. Destroyed with his house was everything the old man owned: his clothes (except what he was wearing), his furniture, even his glass eye that he had set beside the bed. He stayed the night in the only shelter he could find from the winter's cold, the Pittsburg County Jail.

The next morning he came by his congressman's office. Sara Lane was working there, and she told me later how Walter Johns had tried to cover his empty eye socket with his smoke-blackened hand. He did not want to embarrass her any, but he thought that maybe she could get him some help, maybe a little money, maybe just another glass eye from the Veterans Administration. He told her how he had fought in the first big war and how his son had fought in the second one. The boy had been killed in action, and the government had sent Walter Johns a form letter of condolence and an insurance check for his boy's life. He told her that he had sent the check back, wrapped in a hand-written note on ruled paper. The note thanked the government but explained that his boy was not for sale.

307

Sara Lane got hold of the nearest VA office and called some McAlester folks who pitched in to help out my constituent, Mr. Johns. Very grateful, he thanked her, apologized for troubling her, and told her why he had called on my office first. "I used to mine coal with Ernie Albert," he said, "and I just knew that Ernie Albert's boy would help me."

Sara later told me that she answered Mr. Johns with a smile moistened by tears and asked him, "Don't you know what happened to Ernie Albert's boy?" Mr. Johns said no. All he knew was that I was the son of a man who had dug out a living with him, underground in the coal mines.

Three days later, on January 21, 1971, Ernie Albert's boy took the oath as forty-sixth Speaker of the United States House of Representatives.

The man I was succeeding had been my leader, my mentor, and my friend for a quarter-century. John McCormack is little remembered now. For more than twenty years, he had labored in the living shadow of the legendary Sam Rayburn. Even as Speaker, McCormack's steady work was lost to the glare of President Kennedy's glamour and President Johnson's energy. By the time of Richard Nixon's presidency, most Americans outside Congress thought of Speaker John McCormack (if at all) as a feeble old man, a sepulchral figure sitting behind the president at his annual State of the Union addresses.

Inside Congress, we knew better. Yes, John was old (he finally achieved the Speakership at age seventy, after thirty-four years of congressional service), but Speaker John McCormack kept all the intellectual tenacity and physical vigor of men not half his age. Anybody who thought him a doddering old man never saw him in debate or ran up against his towering will. In his seventy-third and seventy-fourth years, he presided firmly over the Eighty-ninth Congress and its burst of legislative energies. In the Ninetieth Congress, John kept the Great Society alive, his few defeats sharing but one cause, or maybe forty-seven causes: the exact number of Democrats replaced in the 1966 elections. In the first years of

Ernie Albert in 1947, the year of his death and Carl Albert's first year in Congress.

his presidency, Richard Nixon learned that the thin man behind him on the television screens was no lightweight. Like a Democratic rooster, John McCormack's age just made him tough.

Nonetheless, he was a product of another time. The Congress that John McCormack first entered in 1928 was nearly as far removed from that over which he presided as was Henry Clay's or Joe Cannon's. It grew more diverse as he remained constant. It grew unruly as he remained gentle. It got younger as he grew older. Every ambitious member expected his appearance at every evening fund-raiser, but John McCormack kept his evenings private, sharing them only with his beloved Harriet. Reformers hoped to open an avenue for themselves into the leadership's narrow ranks by creating a policy council after Mr. Rayburn's death. John gave them their answer at his first press conference: "A policy council is out." It stayed out, and they did, too. Excluded from John McCormack's narrow circle of old friends and committee chairmen, the reformers called for breaking up the seniority system. John answered that with the same thing that Sam Rayburn had said every two years at every organizational caucus: the seniority system was not going to be disturbed.

First singly, then collectively, first privately then publicly, some of the brightest young men in Congress moved to challenge John McCormack's ways, even his power. Dick Bolling, Sam Rayburn's young liberal protégé, disappeared from our informal gatherings. In two widely discussed books (*House Out of Order,* 1965, and *Power in the House,* 1968) Bolling openly questioned the Speaker's ability. In 1969, Arizona's able young congressman, Morris Udall, mounted a rare and open attack. At our organizational caucus, Udall challenged John's reelection as Speaker. It did not get very far—John won in the caucus by a 178–58 vote—but even to have a contest was almost unheard of.

Of course, the public heard of it, and some heard the continuing rumbles of discontent that periodically reverberated through the Capitol's marble halls. In December 1969, for example, Speaker McCormack met with Democrats serving on the Education and Labor Committee; the members were complaining about his handling of an antipoverty bill. John McCormack, who had been pushing "progressive" legislation for decades, patiently tried to counsel the young members on the need for patience. They would have none of it. "Look," 37-year-old Bill Clay exploded, "I'm not interested in what you did before I was born." John kept his own counsel, patience, and closed the meeting by saying, "I think some of you want to run the House." New Jersey's Frank Thompson retorted, "That's perfectly true. Some of us do."

But John McCormack, not Bill Clay, not Frank Thompson, ran the House. I believed he ran it well, very well considering what he was running up against. I knew that neither Mo Udall, Dick Bolling, Bill Clay, Frank Thompson nor any of his young critics could ever depose him. They (and I) knew that there was only one member who might beat John McCormack out of the Speakership, and we all knew who he was. His name was Carl Albert.

Few approached me openly about it, I suppose because they knew my position. As majority leader, I was John McCormack's ally and supporter. As a man, I was his friend. As a congressman who had worked with him for decades, I regarded him the world's chief legislator. I knew John McCormack as well as I knew any man in the House, and I respected him more than any other. If it took Carl Albert to defeat him, nobody would.

Those circumstances weighed not at all on my conscience, but they weighed heavily upon my time. The social obligations that accompanied the Speakership fell to me to fulfill. More importantly, I became the intermediary between the established leadership and the young reformers. The former never doubted my loyalty; the latter always expected my sympathy. Both were correct, and because they were, I became the conciliator working behind the scenes to maintain public harmony while carefully weighing and quietly promoting the allowable measures of change.

A small change (small at the time, central for the future) came in 1969, when I persuaded John McCormack to reawaken the Democratic caucus. Back in Woodrow Wilson's presidency, the caucus of all Democratic members had been the instrument of party discipline and the tool of party governance. Leaders like Oscar Underwood and Jack Garner had convened it regularly and directed it to party positions binding upon all Democratic members. In time, though, it had withered to nothing, nothing except biennial assemblies to ratify committee assignments and our leadership slate. Sam Rayburn had distrusted the caucus as much as he had feared its potential for opening bloody regional wounds. John McCormack fully shared that distrust, but he reluctantly agreed to call caucus meetings monthly after January 1969 to allow both the leadership and the rank and file to discuss party strategies. For a while, there was a lot more discussion than strategy, but the caucus had been reborn.

One of its first substantive decisions was to appoint in March 1970, a committee on organization, study, and review. Headed by Julia Butler Hansen, a very capable congresswoman from Washington, the committee would meet regularly during the next four years. I helped Mrs. Hansen select its members, like her, careful to build a committee representative of our party's many interests and elements. In the critical caucus meeting that defined its responsibilities, I took the floor to speak directly for explicitly including study of the one institution of the House that, "if valid, can stand the test of study." Over the united protest of the southern chairmen, we charged the Hansen committee to examine the heretofore unstudied (and untouchable) seniority system.

In that same year, I worked quietly on behalf of the first act to modernize congressional procedures since the La Follette-Monroney Act, passed in the year of my first election. A complex bill that generated enemies with every complexity, the new proposal had been tossed around for years. Finally, Dick Bolling and I got the votes to take it out of the Rules Committee and to the floor. Once there, I used every single lever I had available to add the one amendment that towered over every complexity in the existing bill: it was the amendment to provide for recorded votes on amendments to any bill thereafter considered in the committee of the whole. That amendment may look small now, but it ended the practice of a member's concealing his position on critical votes by marching past tellers, who announced the totals without recording a single individual's vote. We carried that amendment and the entire bill, the Legislative Reorganization Act of 1970, and every member knew what he had won: a major step toward opening our deliberations to public scrutiny.

Each change was a step, but only a step, toward internal changes impossible to foretell at the time, impossible to contemplate only a few years earlier. I gladly let others lay claim to making the footprints, and I never let a single one fall on the toes of my friend the Speaker. Even had I wanted to (and I did not), I knew better. John McCormack could accept changes, but he was not going to let anyone walk over him.

Like the country preacher who prayed that God would tell him when it was time to retire before He told the congregation, John had the faith to stay in the Speaker's chair rather than let anyone run him out of it. John himself decided when it was time to walk away. That was toward the end of the 1970 session. Announcing his retirement, he fielded a few press questions. His personal choice as successor? His answer was as decided as his own career. He was endorsing Carl Albert for Speaker and nobody else for any other job. I liked that.

In January 1971, John McCormack left the Capitol that he first had entered as a young man in 1928. On his last day in Congress, his other friends and I spoke of his many contributions and long leadership. His last words from the podium were these: "Next to God and Mrs. McCormack, I love the House of Representatives best." With that he walked away, the failing Mrs. McCormack at his side, and he left us that he might spend all of his time as he always had spent his private time: at Harriet McCormack's side. To her death and beyond, to his own, John McCormack kept his pride and his dignity. The first Speaker in more than a century to step down voluntarily, he knew when God wanted him to retire. I liked that, too.

With Sam Rayburn's death, I had mounted a vigorous campaign for the majority leadership. With John McCormack's retirement, I needed none for the Speakership. Within days, nearly every state's delegation endorsed my election. Nearly every powerful and re-spected member added his individual voice. One had the soft Arkansas accent of the one member powerful and respected enough even to mount a serious challenge. "If you're campaigning to be Speaker," Wilbur Mills said, "forget it. You've got it sewed up." He was right—Wilbur Mills always knew how to count votes—and only a last-minute and half-hearted challenge from Michigan's John Conyers denied unanimity to my caucus nomination. I won it 220 to 20, the latter, like Conyers's candidacy, a symbolic pro-test to the caucus participation of Mississippi's all-white and thor-oughly segregationist delegation. Shortly thereafter the entire

Carl Albert presiding as forty-sixth Speaker of the United States House of Representatives.

House elected me its forty-sixth Speaker. I accepted the office from the same dais where I had watched John McCormack and Sam Rayburn preside, the same dais from which Champ Clark was speaking when I was Ernie and Leona Albert's boy in Mr. Craighead's class at Bug Tussle.

There to share it with me were many of the people who had put me there, people who had shaped my biography. There was Bill Anderson, Mook, my earliest playmate in Bug Tussle. At his side was Lottie Ross, the first-grade teacher who taught me how to read. Mary, David, and Mary Frances were at my side. Working her way through some of my McAlester High and University of Oklahoma classmates, Sara Lane whispered Walter Johns's story . to me. Political supporters dating to my very first campaign congratulated me. Sitting before me were 434 members of Congress, 32 of whom had seen me enter Congress in 1947, when Sam Rayburn's secretary had thought me a page. It was to all those members that I directed the last line of my brief acceptance speech. "The biography of this Congress," I said, "will shape the legislative history of the seventies." Even as I spoke the biography of that Congress was changing, and those changes, which only accelerated through the 1970s, would largely shape my Speakership.

Of course, Congress is a living institution, one constantly changing. Nonetheless, it seemed to me in my six years as Speaker that I was watching more changes in that body's inner makeup than had occurred in any in so short a time since the Civil War. There were reasons for it. The black migration from the rural South to the urban North became complete in the early seventies. In northern city after city and district after district, blacks overwhelmed the old majorities of immigrant stock who long had sustained the urban machines. Many of the machines' veteran spokesmen left Congress, their places often taken by young, ambitious black members.

Down South a long-delayed revolution was smashing the white conservative Democratic stranglehold on power. The 1965 Voting Rights Act directly enfranchised millions of black voters, who took their ballots and their demands to Democratic primary boxes. Indirectly, the same law, with the national party's other commitments to black equality, helped drive southern whites finally out of the party of the Confederacy and into the party of the union, not Abraham Lincoln's Union but Richard Nixon's union of political, economic, and social conservatives. It seemed that every election brought news that first this southern state then that one, first this district then that one, was sending to Washington its first Republican congressman since Reconstruction. They took the places of the old Solid South, the southern establishment, which had figured so decisively during most of my own earlier tenure. Other establishment types wisely retired or lost their seats to young Democratic challengers, challengers elected with black votes and therefore even more different from the old Dixiecrats than were the new southern Republicans. Already (in 1966) black votes had defeated the old South's formidable champion, Howard Smith. Every year, others joined him in the graveyard of the white man's Democracy.

Smith's defeat had another explanation, too. In the mid-1960s, the federal courts directed that every district in every state be apportioned strictly on the basis of "substantial numerical equality." District lines were redrawn, adding to the political influence of cities and suburbs at the cost of farms and small towns. The kind of voters (college-educated white suburbanites) who helped retire Howard Smith did the same for others, North and South, East and West.

By 1972 yet another change had altered the national electorate with other effects upon the collective biography of Congress. In that year, eighteen-year-olds, heretofore young enough to fight but usually not old enough to vote, went to the polls throughout the nation. When the 1971 session passed the resolution that made it possible, I pronounced it to be akin to the abolition of slavery and the removal of property, racial, and gender qualifications for voting: it was another step in "perfecting our democracy." Thereafter, the new faces in Congress confirmed my expectations that new voters would demand new representatives.

New voters—something of a new electorate—is what I saw as Speaker. What I had to deal with was a new Congress that that electorate summoned forth. As early as 1973, the start of my second term as Speaker, fully half the members of Congress had begun their service after 1966. Representing new voters, they brought new experiences with them. Unlike my own generation, few of them had reached political maturity during Franklin Roosevelt's New Deal, when my party had assembled a coalition of the dispossessed around the bread-and-butter issues of the Depression. Few had followed either the bitter debates before Pearl Harbor or Harry Truman's refashioning of American military and foreign policy in the cold years that began the Cold War. Many had not even marched to John Kennedy's New Frontier or helped Lyndon Johnson push its borders outward to the furthest reaches of social change. For many of them, the defining global experience of their own political orientation was Vietnam, not Munich. The domestic concerns that moved them involved inflation and the environment, not unemployment and civil rights.

Despite all of those differences, the overall quality of Congress changed not at all, except possibly to improve it. We added two additional black women as members, but representatives like Barbara Jordan and Yvonne Burke would have added luster to any assembly. Pat Schroeder was every bit as outstanding as any male veteran, even as good as any of the few women with whom I already had served, women like Margaret Chase Smith, Martha Griffiths, Leonor Sullivan, Katherine St. George, or Julia Hansen. Other minorities, too, finally took their rightful places in Congress, adding both to its diversity and its distinction. Spark Matsunaga, Patsy Mink, and Norman Mineta followed the indomitable Daniel Inouye as outstanding members of Oriental ancestry. Henry Gonzales, Kika de la Garza, and Ed Roybal rose to the top as Hispanic members.

Representatives like these flew right in the face of the prevailing stereotype of Congress. During my first twenty-four years of service, I already had seen the Congress either attacked or ridiculed by nearly every pundit. As Speaker, I knew that most Americans still regarded it as a somber, cumbersome, unappealing body of anonymous men and women, mostly old. They blindly plodded along, insensitive to pressing problems and content to idle while others made progress and headlines. If that were ever true, it was not while I served in Congress, and it was never less so than when I was its Speaker of the House of Representatives. Most of the criticism of Congress overlooked that last word. Its members are representatives, not merely in title but in fact. The altered electorate and the transformed membership only made us more representative. What we represented was a nation of diversity, a nation divided by interest, philosophy, and values on every important issue of the day. Some criticized us for never speaking firmly and decidedly in a single voice, and we did not, for we spoke the many voices of the American people. We were their representatives and what we represented was the collective judgment of the American people.

Our forefathers had meant it to be that way. Originally, the Constitution had made members of the House the only federal officials directly elected by the people. Senators were to be chosen (and were well into the twentieth century) by the state legislatures. The president and vice-president were selected by the Electoral College, which was intended to be a body of independent electors of superior judgment. Judges and cabinet officers were presidential appointees, the former for life. For all the evolution of America's constitutional forms and its political practices, senators, judges, cabinet officials, even the president and vice-president— all still may be appointed to office. Only the members of the House of Representatives hold their seats exclusively by the ballots of the American people, ballots cast every two years in 435 separate districts, not one just like another.

None of those 435 members, not even their Speaker, pretended to represent the entire nation or labored under the illusions that he either could or should. Our Constitution cast us as a deliberative body. Our selection guaranteed that our deliberations would represent all of the conflict, all of the contention, even all of the confusion of the American people. Nearly two centuries of experience had shaped our procedures purposely to forestall hasty action without full consideration of all of the needs and all of the interests of all of the people. Some regarded this as plodding, but neither our forefathers nor political philosophers ever listed speed and efficiency among the virtues of a representative assembly. They were right. Not one weighty issue is ever amenable to overnight solution. Hasty action too often exchanges new dilemmas for old. Too often, today's unsolvable problem arises from yesterday's ill-considered solution.

As Speaker, I understood that. I understood, too, just what responsibilities my position involved. First, I was spokesman for the entire House of Representatives, including the Republicans and the Democrats, the conservatives and the liberals, the young and the old, the ambitious and the satisfied. Speaker for all, I first must listen to all, particularly regarding the institutional business of our assembly. There was nothing so sacred about our procedures, however old and however entrenched, that they could not be altered to make us more representative. There was, though, something sacred about our assembly's power, within the framework of American government, and it must always be defended. The speed and efficiency our forefathers had sought in the executive branch had to be balanced by the deliberativeness they had vested in our own. Defending that balance transcended defense of the House of Representatives, for that defense was of nothing less than the United States Constitution.

As Speaker, I also was leader of my party in the House. Because I was destined to be the first Speaker in modern times to serve entirely with the opposition in the presidency, it was a mighty responsibility, since I occupied the highest elected position of any Democrat in the country. I took that job seriously, but it was more than my natural modesty that allowed me to see its limits. I had no claim to speak for Democratic senators, governors, mayors, or presidential candidates. Every day's headlines showed me they could speak for themselves. Within the ranks of the House, the Speaker had exactly one vote in the Democratic caucus and, by custom, rarely one on the floor. The transformations of the late 1960s and early 1970s broke up old Democratic blocs and replaced them with temporary coalitions, reforming with every new bill, sometimes with every new amendment. Unchanged was the fact that no Speaker since Joe Cannon had had any real power over legislation. That fell to the chairmen of 20 standing committees and 138 subcommittees, each with power independent of the Speaker.

I was that Speaker, but I was also Carl Albert. When I took the Speaker's chair, I took the prize toward which I had directed my entire life. I knew what put me there. I was there because I worked hard, because I was loyal to my friends, because I tolerated differences, because I practiced conciliation, because I wanted the possible, not the ideal, because I sought compromise, not headlines. For better or worse, what had made me Speaker would have to make my Speakership, too.

I understood the Congress. I understood my job. I understood myself. Richard Nixon I never understood.

I had known Richard Nixon since that day back in 1947 when we were both freshmen congressmen and he was the first Republican member I met. From that day onward, I never found him anything but friendly personally. After he went to the Senate, even after he became vice-president, I never saw him anywhere without his coming over, calling me Carl, and chatting a bit.

Politically, I appreciated his abilities early on. I sensed that only Lyndon Johnson may have been more consumed with politics or in greater command of its strategies. In Nixon's case, however, that command early was tied to the lowest form of partisan tactics. I regarded his House work on the Un-American Activities Committee, particularly his crude use of the Alger Hiss affair, as partisan demagoguery incidentally clothed in fact, with only the outer trappings distinguishing it from Joseph McCarthy's tactics in the Senate. I knew that leading Democrats never forgave him for the Red-baiting campaign that beat Helen Gahagan Douglas in the Senate campaign of 1950. His charge of "treason" against high Democratic officials during the Eisenhower campaign of 1952 earned him the undying enmity of both Harry Truman and Sam Rayburn. The earthy former president thereafter always referred to Nixon as "a snaky-eyed son of a bitch." Nixon's name never came up at Sam Rayburn's Board of Education without the Speaker's saying that he, Mr. Rayburn, had looked out over the House into more than three thousand faces in his day and Richard Nixon's was the only one that would have looked more in place in a prison.

From time to time, Nixon watchers (a sizable, somewhat masochistic band, particularly in the press) pretended to have discovered a "new Nixon." Theodore H. White was absolutely sure that a more statesmanlike Nixon had emerged during the campaign that he chronicled in *The Making of the President, 1960*. White was equally sure of the same thing when he wrote *The Making of the President, 1968*. After that campaign, editorial cartoonist Herblock even granted Nixon's caricature a free shave to distinguish the dignified campaigner and chief executive from the crude, unshaven partisan of past drawings. An able public speaker, Richard Nixon could deliver statesmanlike addresses. Men who heard them and then engaged him in friendly conversation over political strategy understandably came away impressed. Maybe their fault was not in judging the new Nixon so uncritically but in thinking of the old Nixon so simplistically.

The Richard Nixon I knew—old, new, or otherwise—was anything but simple. He remained a brilliant political strategist. After the debacle of the Goldwater campaign, when some Republicans had suggested disbanding the party, Richard Nixon did more than any man to restore it to respectability two years later and to power two years after that. No Republican since Lincoln had done more for his party. Neither had any Republican since Lincoln won the White House after suffering such bitter personal defeats, in Nixon's case the 1960 presidential race and the California gubernatorial campaign of 1962 that seemed to have ended his career permanently. In the White House, he stayed just as friendly. I was still Carl, just like always, but even so, he could show a streak of vindictiveness, even meanness. In formal meetings with the congressional leadership, he often would bring up some small slight of years past. The give and take that we professional politicians accepted as the routine stuff of politics apparently was intensely

I knew that Richard Nixon saw politics as a personal battle.

personal to Richard Nixon. When he would attack Adlai Stevenson for some unremembered remark or President Truman for some forgotten misdeed, I knew that Richard Nixon saw politics as a personal battle, a series of interwoven and unending crises. For that reason, Richard Nixon was a man incapable of either forgiving or forgetting.

What united this personal Nixon with the public Nixon was the same thing that bound in one the partisan Nixon to the statesmanlike Nixon, the old Nixon to the new Nixon. From his very first race in 1946 through every campaign to follow, Richard Nixon had been a master of negative campaigning. He had run best when he had something to run against. Without it, he had never won. In his earliest races, he had to manufacture his enemies: Jerry Voorhis, the incumbent Democratic congressman he ousted in 1946 by identifying him with socialists and Communists; Helen Douglas, whom he made his victim as the "pink lady" of 1950; and the entire Democratic party, which he portrayed as leading to "ultimate national suicide" in 1952. In 1968, circumstances conspired to produce Richard Nixon's enemies for him: an endless war in Asia, race riots and antiwar protests in America. In no case was there either an old Nixon or a new Nixon. There was only Richard Nixon, a complex man who needed, publicly and privately, enemies to campaign against. Finally winning the White House, he had to govern for the first time in his political career, and he needed something to govern against. It was the United States Congress.

Though he had served in both houses, Nixon was accustomed to running against Congress. Particularly as Ike's vice-president, he had campaigned against what he perceived as its excesses in the midterm elections of the fifties. More than anything else, it was the same tactic, generously donated to countless Republican candidates, that allowed his political resurrection with the midterm elections of 1966. As president, he attacked Congress with a rare vigor. Presidential news conferences and television speeches scored us for our delay in ratifying his proposals and our dispatch in passing our own. The latter often met his veto, usually on pretended grounds of economy. In January of 1970 he even took the unprecedented step of vetoing a bill—a $19.7 billion labor-health, education, and welfare appropriation—on television, melodramatically signing the veto beneath the glare of camera lights before a nationwide audience.

What the cameras did not record and the audience did not see was the pattern of the administration's dealing with Congress. The president met rarely with the Democratic majority leadership, and he often left even the Republican leaders blind to his intents and purposes. Even they complained that as many as eighty calls from Republican congressmen daily went unanswered by the White House. Nixon's aides, most inexperienced, all ambitious, many arrogant, made no effort to understand Congress except to deride it. The same administration that castigated us for our delays routinely followed stirring presidential messages with weeks of inactivity during which it provided no detailed proposals for our deliberations. By 1971, the new legislative liaison director, Clark MacGregor, was wearing a button: "I Care About Congress." No one else in the White House wore one, and neither MacGregor nor the attitude lasted long.

Meanwhile, the rhetorical attacks upon Congress continued, reaching a frenzy in the 1970 elections. Vice-President Spiro Agnew fired the first blast during a national campaign tour in September. As the Senate's presiding officer, the vice-president and I shared many responsibilities, and I thought that I had come to know him well: a quiet, modest, genteel, and honest man. During that campaign, however, he revealed a surprising talent for invective unheard since the old Nixon of the early fifties. It was Agnew who set the election's shrill tenor by reducing every issue to one: "Will America be led by a president elected by a majority of the American people, or will we be intimidated and blackmailed into following the path dictated by a disruptive, radical, and militant minority—the pampered prodigies of the radical liberals in the United States Senate?" Unstated was the assumption that radical liberals also infested the House and pampered our own prodigies. Unacknowledged was the fact that these same senators and representatives themselves had been elected by a majority of the American people, while this particular president had won a three-cornered contest against Hubert Humphrey and George Wallace with less than 44 percent of the vote.

By mid-October, that president had thrown himself directly into the elections. Attacking "permissiveness," "terrorism," and "crime," he attempted to identify his congressional opposition with all that was abhorrent in national affairs, with nothing that was at issue in any race. The Election Eve commercial that was broadcast nationally closed it all with a voice-over of deep concern: "Support men who will vote for the president, not against him. Bring an end to the wave of violence in America." On Election Night, the administration could count the scalps of two senators. We added a net of nine Democrats to the House and eleven governorships. Whatever those results said about the president's tactics, they testified to the common sense and basic decency of the American people. The entire episode both completed two years of unprecedented executive-legislative discord and introduced my greatest challenge when I became Speaker two months later. I presided over the House that was elected in that campaign and served with the president who had conducted it. Demographic, electoral, and membership changes already were transforming the House. I would have to complete that transformation if we were to face that president.

The transformation began in the January 1971 organizational caucuses, in which my party first began to assemble its leadership team. My fellow Democrats named me their candidate for the Speakership. John McCormack's retirement and my own elevation opened a slot, majority leader, and it was opened to an intense competition that registered the changes already moving the House. Hale Boggs had served right below me since 1955, when Sam Rayburn and John McCormack appointed me whip and gave him the new post of deputy whip. In 1962, John and I named him our own whip. As the man most experienced in our leadership councils, he figured to have no more trouble winning the majority leadership than I had had when I eventually won it unanimously. Arguably, he might have had even less trouble, for Hale was a southerner born and bred, and he had worked well and closely with the northern big-city Democrats. Since the 1930s, that coalition had dominated our party councils. In 1971, it did not.

A small army of determined challengers aggressively contested Hale's election. Their number, and their bases of support, testified to the recent changes within the party. Mo Udall represented a rising number of young, ambitious members who were united by a faith in liberal issues and a dislike of the House's crusty ways. Bernie Sisk, a Californian of Texas birth, hoped to assemble a new coalition of the South and the West in place of the fading southern-northern machine combine. Jim O'Hara of Michigan sought to go entirely outside the House's internal structure of power to build a candidacy on the external power of organized labor. Ohio's Wayne

Hays, chairman of the House Administration Committee, went just the other way. That chairmanship gave him his only power, but great power it was, for Hays had turned the heretofore clerical job into an emperorship with oversight into every member's allowances and perquisites.

Though I could have worked with any of those men as my majority leader (except maybe Hays, whom no one could work with in any capacity), Hale was my own favorite. I made no effort to help him, since I could think of no worse way to enter my Speakership than to antagonize so many different groups. I let Hale Boggs make his own fight, and he won it, though it took him two ballots to secure his majority by a margin of only twenty-five votes. The press pronounced it a victory for the House's old ways of a simple regional coalition, but its old ways would not even have seen such a fight.

The press overlooked the most important election in that caucus. With the revitalization of the caucus as an ongoing party mechanism, its elected chairman became a member of the informal House leadership. Dan Rostenkowski, a big-talking, big-living former car salesman turned agent of Mayor Richard Daley's big Chicago machine, was that chairman. I thought he was my friend, though hardly my brainiest one. At the 1968 convention, I had done him what I thought was a favor when I handed him the gavel to preside briefly and ceremoniously over the delegates assembled in his hometown. I had forgotten the whole incident by the time the story began to circulate that big Dan Rostenkowski had wrestled the gavel out of the hands of little Carl Albert because only big Dan Rostenkowski could bring order to that convention. If that were so, no one had told me about it at the time. But it was pretty plain who was telling it later.

Maybe Dan was busy telling that story in the days just after John McCormack announced his retirement. I do not know. But I do know that as state delegation after delegation lined up behind me for Speaker, one state was conspicuously absent: Illinois. Mel Price, one of my oldest friends from there, could not understand

Illinois's delay, and he offered to call a state caucus to learn why. Afterwards, Mel told me straight out that the entire delegation of Illinois was for me to a man, except one: Dan Rostenkowski, who refused to issue an endorsement of the only candidate groomed for the job or even seeking it.

By the time the Democratic caucus met to approve my nomination, enough of my friends shared enough of my wonder about Rostenkowski's attitude and sense to do something about it. They had come together to oust Rostenkowski as caucus chairman in favor of a man loyal to me—at least to a man with enough brains to climb on board a bandwagon while it was roaring out of the station. Olin ("Tiger") Teague, was that man, and he was a dandy. Born in Woodward, Oklahoma, Teague got his nickname on the football fields of Texas and the battlefields of Europe. His adopted state sent him to Congress in 1947, and he had risen to become chairman of veterans' affairs. Though intensely conservative in his voting, Tiger had not a single enemy, liberal or otherwise, in the House. When the time came to vote on caucus chairman, someone put Tiger's name in nomination. The surprised Teague marched forward with his own ballot held high, showing it already marked with Rostenkowski's name. The even more surprised Dan Rostenkowski watched it become one of the 91 votes he received, compared to 155 for Tiger. Still surprised, the loser told the press, "I got my brains beat out." I was not surprised at all.

A few days later, Hale Boggs came by my office to complete our leadership slate. It was still the tradition that the majority leader appointed the party whip, subject only to the Speaker's veto. Hale wanted to give the job to the man who had sat with him on ways and means, Dan Rostenkowski. He got the Speaker's veto instead. Hale did get a list of ten names, any one of which I would accept as whip. One of those was Tip O'Neill's.

Tip had been around Congress since 1953, when he took the seat John Kennedy left to go to the Senate. Big and gregarious, his earliest attribute seemed to be his laziness. He was what we called a "Tuesday-Thursday congressman," one who spent four days a

Tip had become a protégé of John McCormack. Thomas P. O'Neill, Carl Albert, and John McCormack.

week back home and three on House business. When I was appointed whip myself, Tip had come by, had spun a few stories, and had told me that he would not have the job; it took too much work. Nonetheless, Tip had become a protégé of John McCormack, who eventually got him a seat on the Rules Committee. In 1970, Tip still ranked behind Chairman Bill Colmer and three other Democrats on the committee, and he had no other basis of power. But he had started to work a little harder, he had friends all over the House, and his New England district and liberal orthodoxy represented important elements in the party. When Hale suggested that Tip's appointment would please John McCormack, I agreed.

To help him, we also selected two others to become deputy whips. John McFall was Hale's choice. One of Hale's eighteen regional assistants, John represented an agricultural district in California. His selection thereby broadened the Southwest–New England regional axis that had dominated Democratic House affairs since Sam Rayburn and John McCormack had become Speaker and majority leader back in 1940. My addition was a midwesterner, Indiana's John Brademas. Representing the South Bend area, John already had established his mark as education's most articulate champion in the House. Besides, he had two personal qualities that I much admired. One was tenacity—he had won his seat in 1958 only after suffering two earlier defeats. The other was brains—John Brademas had been a Rhodes scholar and had had an outstanding record at Oxford. He belonged on our team.

Carl Albert, Hale Boggs, Tiger Teague, Tip O'Neill, John McFall, and John Brademas—that was the Democratic leadership team that had taken shape by mid-January of 1971. Among us, we represented every region of our country and every element of our party. We were men of diverse viewpoints and diverse talents. If we had to, we could take on the men, all so similar and all so ambitious, sitting in the White House. Not one of us ached to do it. For myself, I would have preferred the nonconfrontational relations that President Eisenhower and Speaker Rayburn had conducted in the 1950s. But if Richard Nixon wanted to make Congress his enemy, we had the talent to make it a contest.

We certainly had the issues.   ·

As a boy, I had been taught down in Oklahoma's Little Dixie that there was a difference between Democrats and Republicans. My folks and I belonged to the party that cared about average, working Americans. Republicans spoke for the wealthy—belonged to them, some said. At best, they might let prosperity trickle down to the little people; at worst, they would keep it for themselves; at a minimum, they just did not care about the common folks.

As a student of government in two universities and as a congressman, I learned that things were not always that simple. There were quite a few rich and insensitive Democrats and there were plenty of hardworking and generous Republicans. Nonetheless, what I kept seeing never did erase that first impression. The common, average, working American man or woman was more likely to get a better shake from the party of Jefferson and Jackson than from the party of Coolidge and Hoover. I know that the party that controlled both houses of Congress was ready to give them better than the party of Nixon and Agnew.

We already had given them a sustained prosperity never before achieved in this century. The stock market reached a record level; bank deposits did, too. Personal income climbed to a figure never before seen in the world. Unemployment dropped out of sight as the rate (3.4 percent) that stood at 1969's beginning met the economists' definition of full employment. Even though much of President Johnson's Great Society went underfinanced, the rising tide of prosperity raised many of the poor to a better life and gave all the promise of a better future.

It was Vietnam that bled the Great Society of its funds, and it was Vietnam's costs that explained the one sour economic note of the late sixties: inflation. Candidate Nixon had made much of the issue—inflation, not Vietnam's expense—in the 1968 campaign, and President Nixon was determined to do something about it. It was the same thing that Republicans usually offered: economic policies that promised to exchange inflation for recession.

He could not even do that.

We got the recession, all right. At the touch of his misguided wand, Nixon magically transformed the prosperity that was his presidency's inheritance into the first full-blown recession since that last Republican president's, back in 1958. Steadily, the economy's production slipped below its capacity. At the end of Nixon's first year in office, the gap between performance and potential was $25 billion annually and growing. Through 1970, national production actually declined. In 1971, it rose, but only by 3 percent, enough for the president to declare a recovery, even though it was a recession by any measure other than his own dismal record.

The cost of that recession fell disproportionately on working Americans. The lucky ones suffered a decline in real wages, the first decline since the 1930s. The unlucky ones had no wages at all, for the unemployment rolls grew with every presidential pronouncement of prosperity. By 1971's end, the unemployment rate was 80 percent above what it had been at Nixon's inauguration. The percentage difference obscured the human cost: two and one-half million Americans who had lost their jobs, plus another half-million uncounted because they had given up on finding any work at all. Even that number left untold the price paid by the neediest: those in central cities, sixty of which were declared to be depressed (compared to six in 1969); black teenagers, who suffered from an unconscionable unemployment rate pegged at 44.9 percent; returning Vietnam veterans, 375,000 of whom came back to an America that had no jobs for them.

Knowing where Nixon was leading us, I knew that it was the job of the Democratic Ninety-second Congress to lead us out. I knew also that it was the job of the entire Congress, not just its House Speaker, to do it. Senate Majority Leader Mike Mansfield and I began to meet regularly with the press, a practice rare since the days of Sam Rayburn and Lyndon Johnson, to reveal the dismal economic record that lay beneath the administration's slick public relations. While our young reformers berated the seniority system, I worked quietly and realistically to include the committee chairmen in a united and effective legislative leadership. For the first time since the New Deal, the Speaker and appropriate chairmen also met with the press to discuss our own legislative initiatives to replace the executive's inactivity. They got the publicity, which was fine with me, since they, not I, would have to craft our bills and get them through their committees. Behind the scenes, I met with those same chairmen, the rest of our formal leadership, and leaders of every one of the House's many new factions. We coordinated our bills (another innovation), planned our calendar, and mobilized every vote we could get. We could not always get enough, for no one said that the House's collective judgment should be the same as the Speaker's judgment; least of all did this Speaker even think it. Nonetheless, we did get bills written, we did get them out of committee, we did take them to the floor, we did pass them, and we did send them to Richard Nixon. He vetoed them, twenty of them in the Ninety-second Congress alone.

Most of the twenty were bills that had taken months to fashion and to pass, bills that would have primed the economy's dry pump and eased the recession's worst immediate burdens. One of the most disheartening for me was H.R. 15417, a $30.5 billion appropriation for desperately needed employment and welfare programs. Declaring that it was too expensive by $1.8 billion, the president wiped out the work of months and the hope of millions with a stroke of a pen. Seeking compromise, we passed it again at the same level but authorized the president to withhold up to $1.3 billion if he wished. This time, it died without a pen's stroke as President Nixon pocket-vetoed the entire act. So it went: Appalachian regional development, economic-opportunity amendments, promotion of family medicine, expansion of public works and employment, medical care for veterans, rehabilitation for the handicapped, assistance to the elderly, aid to schools—every one of them terribly needed, every one of them tragically vetoed.

For each one, Richard Nixon offered the same set of tired excuses: the bill was inflationary because it cost too much; the economy could not afford it because the debt was too high. The congressional leadership knew better. Though such bills did exceed the administration's niggardly requests, we also were cutting its requests in other areas. On balance, we appropriated each year less total money than the president had requested. The issue was not the level of spending but the form of spending, and the president did not have a monopoly on the wisdom of setting those priorities. Was the economy too small and the debt too large? The

Nixon recession was what was shrinking the economy. That recession cost the Treasury $50 billion in reduced tax collections over the life of the Ninety-second Congress, enough money to have erased the entire federal deficit of fiscal year 1971 and most of it for fiscal year 1972. Instead, the Treasury was hemorrhaging with billions of dollars ($10 billion in 1972 alone) flowing out unproductively in unemployment compensation and welfare payments.

That is what gave Congress the issue to take on the White House. What gave it the reason was the fact that the avowed object of the president's policies and his vetoes was the war against inflation. Soaring unemployment was costing the economy twenty million man-days lost per year, a cruel draft to enlist unwilling soldiers in that war, and it was a war that inflation was winning anyway. The cost of living rose steadily, right along with the unemployment rolls, a paradox never before thought possible in an industrialized nation. One other thing rose with them, and its rise resolved the paradox. Between 1971 and 1973, corporate profits shot up 36.3 percent. That money went straight to those who owned corporate stock, and half of all corporate stock was owned by less than 1 percent of the American population. The net result of unemployment or wage declines for the working people and healthy dividend checks for the well-heeled was a silent transfer of income unprecedented in American history: $10 billion a year moved from the pockets of the poor to the bank accounts of the wealthy.

Maybe the folks back in Pittsburg County, Oklahoma, had a point when they talked about the difference between Democrats and Republicans.

As Speaker of the House, I never believed that the difference was all that simple. Neither did I believe that the effect, however real, of the president's policies, however misguided, were all that deliberate. Nixon and his advisers just believed in something that did not exist. Their policies would have worked in Adam Smith's eighteenth-century world of small producers competing for buyers in an unfettered marketplace in which an invisible hand set prices fairly and automatically. But that world was as dead as Adam

Smith. The marketplace was fettered, not by government, but by giant corporations that dominated every segment of the economy to palsy the hand of free competition. Thus, policies born in illusion matured to enrich the comfortable few and torment the hardworking many.

The latter were the ones the president called the "silent majority," the ones he thought of as "the forgotten Americans." If his economic policies forgot them, his social views tried to pander to them. Years after the Supreme Court had outlawed state-written prayers in public classrooms, the president and his allies piously demanded a constitutional amendment to restore the practice. As the federal courts were following out the logic of the 1954 *Brown* decision to include the transporting of students as one tool to integrate schools, they raised a howl of protest against "busing" and again demanded a constitutional amendment to deny the practice.

For me, those issues went to something far more important than an appropriations bill or an economic index. What was at stake was what had brought me to Washington, not as a new congressman in 1947, but as a high school senior twenty years earlier. It was the Constitution of the United States. If I would let the committees handle our legislation, on that matter the Speaker had to speak out, forcibly, directly, and immediately. I did. When Louisiana's Joe Waggoner tried to use the Democratic caucus to support his antibusing bill this particular member rose to answer him. My answer hardly used the word *busing* at all, for that was not the issue. Not even civil rights was the issue. The issue was the U.S. Constitution, the separation of powers, the subversion of the independent judiciary. On that basis, maybe by that speech, we voted the thing down on May 17, 1972, the eighteenth anniversary of the *Brown* decision.

I also had spoken six months earlier, that time on the House floor. Over the stout opposition of Manny Celler, an outright majority of our members had signed a discharge petition to bring a school-prayer amendment before the House. The petition's success pointed to an easy victory, not for school prayer but for those who would tamper with our heritage of constitutional government in the momentary heat of public passion. I closed the debate with the same thoughts, almost the same words, I had expressed back when I was a college freshman orating on our Bill of Rights: "Any interference by any official at any level is a violation of freedom of religion. I am not prepared to let the hand of government of any level, of any degree, to be placed on any man's altar."

We beat that amendment by a handful of votes. I understand that House veterans, both Republicans and Democrats, still talk about that speech, pronouncing it one of the few that ever changed a vote's outcome. I do not know about that, but I do know that I kept and treasured a letter thanking me for "standing twenty feet tall" in turning back a step that would have "cut the artery of our freedoms." What made it special was that it was from Herschel Hobbs, pastor of Oklahoma's largest Baptist church. I was even prouder—not for myself, but for them—of the church leaders and Christian worshipers from all over my Third District who wrote or called in their support. I always understood that there is a lot of common sense in the common people.

If the president wanted a confrontation with the Congress over the Constitution, I never doubted our need to join the fight or our ability to win it. If he chose to fight us over his sorry economic record, I knew that we had the common people on our side. What happened, though, was that many of my colleagues chose to engage him in another war. It was the war in Vietnam.

Even at the time of the Gulf of Tonkin Resolution and Lyndon Johnson's subsequent injection of American power, I had had no great enthusiasm for the Vietnam War. The thing that I had seized with most optimism was the military's 1964 and 1965 assurances that the thing was winnable with neither great expense nor long fighting. It was not long before I learned that that prediction never changed. However dismal the reports from Vietnam, the military never tired of the prediction of imminent victory. It was a rare moment of candor when General Earl Wheeler, Johnson's chairman of the Joint Chiefs of Staff, interrupted his rosy forecasts to the congressional leaders to speak of the conflict as "this miserable war."

It was miserable, miserable for all of us. It dragged on and on with no end in sight. Even after our negotiators sat down in Paris with North Vietnam and Vietcong representatives, the war went on until it tore at the fabric of American society. In the process, it helped drive Lyndon Johnson from the presidency and put Richard Nixon into it. Though he had talked as a candidate of a "secret plan" to end the war, Nixon turned out to have no secret at all, at least none except for the secret bombing of Cambodia that he launched (and covered up) in 1969. Publicly, he did announce a policy and gave it a label: "Vietnamization." Masters of coining new words to mask old errors, the White House officials actually were offering what the French had tried back in the early fifties under the name *jaunissement*. Translated literally as "yellowing," the French policy was to force upon the Vietnamese the combat manpower requirements for the war. Cynics referred to it as "changing the color of the corpses." It did do that but little else. Defeated and exhausted, the French had left Vietnam to its fate in 1954.

Years later it was Richard Nixon's fate to try to get America out, not defeated and before it was exhausted. That meant ending the steady escalation and the perpetual quest for tomorrow's victory in favor of an orderly withdrawal of American ground forces, their places taken by an American-trained, America-financed, and American-armed South Vietnamese army. It also meant extending the war to include enemy sanctuaries in Vietnam's neighbors. Constant was the commitment that was ours since Harry Truman's day: the United States would do everything within its power to maintain an independent and anti-Communist government in Vietnam. Vietnamization was, at last, recognition of the limits of our power.

Under the miserable circumstances of that miserable war, I felt it was the best that the president, and the country, could do. Precipitate withdrawal of all our forces and all our power would not end the war, not even our involvement. The killing would continue, doubtlessly through the ranks of both South Vietnam's soldiers and its civilians. The certain collapse of its government to a Communist foe would involve us in a moral indictment for the murder of a government that we had conceived and birthed. It also would be the repudiation of a policy that generally had preserved the world's peace through the maturity of my generation. Starting down another road, the American feet fleeing from Vietnam would wear a path to no certain end and none not filled with potentially greater perils. That was what gave Vietnam a significance too great for easy solution, that and thirty thousand American deaths already.

One was Allie Brannon's boy's.

Allie was a Bug Tussle girl, born in the community in a house that still stood. I had known her all her life and her husband, Roy, for forty years of his. Allie worked in a garment plant in McAlester, and Roy farmed at Bug Tussle in sight of the house where Allie was born. I used to go by and talk with them about the old-timers when I was home from Washington. As my leadership duties became heavier, I did not have much of a chance to do it, though, because I just did not have the time. In 1969, I made the time. In their front yard I talked with Allie and Roy, not about the old folks but the young ones, especially their son. He had been a Bug Tussle boy, too, had gone to the same little two-room school as I, and had gone to Vietnam. Now he was dead. Vietnam was personal to people like Allie and Roy Brannon. It was to me, too. And it was a miserable war.

Its politics could be just as miserable. The people wanted out, the president wanted out, and Congress wanted to help. Between 1966 and 1972, Congress voted 145 times on Vietnam. Right up until the very end, it gave two presidents everything they wanted. To Lyndon Johnson it gave the authority to commit our forces and the money to equip them. To Richard Nixon, it gave support for Vietnamization and the money to execute it. With each vote, though, the politics became more miserable.

Over in the Senate, a large and growing number felt that the president was moving too slowly to withdraw, too rapidly to spread the conflict. Because the Constitution bestows only upon the Senate the power to approve or reject all treaties, the other body has always given great weight to its responsibilities in foreign affairs. The evolution of modern politics—the centrality of foreign policy, the televising of Senate hearings, the use of the Senate as the launch pad of presidential aspirants—has also served to make foreign affairs more important to the Senate than to the House. Vietnam was a nasty and divisive issue, one that raised incomparable public passion. Their six-year terms and statewide constituencies gave senators the opportunity to speak out on that issue without immediate fear of electoral retribution. Year by year, they spoke louder and louder.

By 1969, what had been the lone voice of Mike Mansfield's early protest was joined by influential senators—William Fulbright, Frank Church, Gene McCarthy, Ted Kennedy, John Sherman Cooper, and others. Starting in that year, the Senate began to debate amendments to foreign-affairs and military bills that would restrict the president's policies around Vietnam and hasten his withdrawal from it. By 1971, the first year of my Speakership, the Senate twice passed the so-called Mansfield amendment, attaching it once to the draft-extension bill and again to the defense-procurement bill. In each form, it would have compelled the withdrawal of all American combat forces in Indochina within six months, pending only North Vietnam's release of our prisoners of war.

On both those occasions and others, a large majority in the House rejected the Senate's amendments. My chamber was more inclined to give the president a free hand in the war, the withdrawal, and the negotiations going on in Paris with the Communists. Unlike the situation in the Senate, where the Foreign Relations Committee was a center of dissent, our Foreign Affairs Committee and our most influential members in the field tended to back Nixon's policies. Subject to elections every two years in districts small enough that any one issue could tip the balance, we knew that the public was fed up with the war but was gagging on the antiwar movement of students and chronic critics.

Vietnam was, then, no easier a question for public policy than for military strategy. Any attempt to make it simple was misguided from the start. To try to make it a partisan issue or an issue that divided the Congress from the president was worse than wrong, it was stupid. An extreme antiwar position, one demanding immediate, unconditional withdrawal, would divide my party, paralyze the House, and hand Richard Nixon the one political issue that he could dominate. Some wanted to do just that.

A minor but frustrating example of this involved the reborn Democratic caucus. When I had persuaded John McCormack to restore it, I had hoped it would become a party tool in which the leadership and membership could reach consensus for effective legislating. As Speaker, I learned that it too easily became a target of a righteous antiwar minority who sought to turn the caucus into a forum of protest. New York's Bella Abzug, for one, took the floor at every early meeting to urge this or that motion against the war. Sometimes she just wanted a chance to denounce it. Undeterred by her motions' one-sided defeats, Bella would be back at the next caucus with another motion and another speech.

Congressmen can be a patient lot, but after awhile enough Democrats began boycotting Bella's tirades that most meetings adjourned without a quorum. On one notable occasion, I had wanted to use the caucus to discuss overall federal spending, but Bella got the floor first, began another speech, and continued as more than half the membership sullenly walked out. Shorn of a quorum, that caucus adjourned with no discussion of spending, no discussion of anything, just Bella Abzug's speech. Eventually, Tiger Teague and I amended the caucus rules to permit the chairman (Tiger) to set a definite agenda and give the Speaker and majority leader the floor at any point. Even if the war issue thereby lost its power to kill the caucus, it always stood ready to disrupt it.

It could do the same thing—and did—to something much bigger than the House Democratic caucus: the national Democratic party. By 1972, Richard Nixon's economic record had made him exceedingly vulnerable, but a gaggle of presidential aspirants chose to squawk most loudly on the war. Moderate views went unheard in favor of denunciation of the war's "immorality" and the need for a "new politics" to end it. Mobilizing a determined minority, George McGovern demonstrated that minority's power in a divided field of a divided party seeking to govern a divided country.

George had worked with me on Agriculture's wheat subcommittee when he served in the House. I thought him a man of unbending character and burning idealism. In the Senate, he turned both against the Vietnam War. After the 1968 convention, he had used them to rewrite the Democrats' party rules to require the open participation so esteemed in the new politics. During the campaign season, he used those rules to pile up delegate support out of all proportion to his popular appeal. I remember that Oklahoma County, a conservative county in a conservative state, sent a solid McGovern bloc to our state convention. The same thing happened enough other times in enough other states to give McGovern a first-ballot victory in 1972's national convention.

Of course, his election campaign was a disaster from the start, with one mistake following another. All were irrelevant, though, compared to the original mistake: America was not going to oust a president promising (and apparently delivering) "peace with honor" in favor of a candidate said to be willing to "crawl to Hanoi." The election returns showed that, as Richard Nixon—arguably the most vulnerable sitting president since Herbert Hoover—ran up a record popular-vote margin and swept forty-nine of the fifty states. He did it in classic Nixon style by running against George McGovern, against the "peace-at-any-price" crowd that he always put at his opponent's back. It was unlike 1970 because Richard Nixon had not had to run against Congress. Just as well for him; he could not have beaten it. Though we lost a few Democratic seats in the House (most to redistricting's toll on incumbents), we still had 243 Democrats to 192 Republicans. We actually picked up two Senate seats to give us a 57-to-43 split in the other body.

Richard Nixon had the majority of votes that always had eluded him, even in 1968; we had the same majority that we always had. The war in Vietnam had elected him again. The people of America had elected us, too. He took his election as a mandate, and his self-perceived mandate became our unavoidable challenge. In little time, the resulting clash became the greatest constitutional crisis of the century. When it came, we already had our house in order.

The entire Democratic House leadership worked hard to keep that majority in the face of the Nixon landslide. I campaigned all over the country for Democratic candidates, and the other leaders did, too. In early October, a month before the election, one of them jokingly asked me if I wanted to join him on a campaign swing. "No," I told Hale Boggs, "I went there last year, so I think I'll let you make this trip to Alaska."

Hale went up with Nick Begich to campaign for Nick's reelection to Alaska's one congressional seat. On Monday night, October 17, I was resting up from one of my own campaign trips when the phone rang. It was the White House, wanting me to call Lindy Boggs. Hale's plane, with him, Nick, and two others aboard, was missing in the Alaska bush, somewhere between Portage Pass and Juneau, where the plane was last heard from twelve minutes after takeoff.

That was the hardest phone call I ever made. I told Lindy the news. All she said, in her soft Louisiana accent, was, "Oh, Cahl." Though the air force and others searched for that plane to the limit of human endurance, no one ever found it. We had lost our majority leader, and I had lost a good friend, colleague, and ally. The House had lost the man destined to be its Speaker, but Louisiana's loss was tempered when Mrs. Corinne ("Lindy") Boggs won the seat after it was declared officially vacant.

It was a shame that Hale did not live even a few months longer. He and I were the first Speaker and majority leader team born in the twentieth century. When the Ninety-third Congress convened the next January, we began the process that finally brought the House of Representatives fully into that century. When that Congress adjourned two years later, it had effected more reforms of its own procedures than had any Congress since the Cannon revolt, maybe more than in the intervening thirty Congresses combined.

Most of those reforms had been a long time coming. Nonetheless, the press and the pundits still expressed surprise at how swiftly and thoroughly each prevailed. They looked for explanations and found them everywhere. Some credited the new membership elected in 1972, though we had only sixty-eight freshmen in that class, just above average for a post–World War II Congress. Of those, only twenty-six were Democrats, and they did not make much difference in the body that sponsored most of the changes, the Democratic caucus. Other credited the Democratic Study Group, which had grown steadily to include nearly two-thirds of the Democratic membership. Despite its numbers, the DSG lost on every reform proposal that lacked the leadership's support. Within that leadership, Hale's successor as majority leader, Tip O'Neill, got a lot of the credit, and Tip took it, too. Outside the leadership, Dick Bolling, a brilliant student of Congress and a longtime press favorite, got acclaim for realizing reforms that he long had championed. Amid that praise, Dick told one of Ralph Nader's investigators that he was happy to get it and happier to see those reforms finally accomplished, but he added that there would not have been "one iota of reform if it had not been for Carl Albert. Anytime I've needed help on reform, he's always been right there."

I was right there, right there to help, right there to support, but not right there to grab the credit. I looked at it as Sam Rayburn had taught me: "You can accomplish almost anything as long as you don't mind who gets the credit." Others got the credit, but what I accomplished was a set of reforms that made the House more open to public scrutiny, more sensitive to members' needs, more amenable to its elected leadership, and more capable of meeting its responsibilities.

In early 1973, we went a long way toward each of those goals. Our vehicle was the Democratic caucus. Though long rusting, it was still the one carriage open to the entire Democratic majority. Earlier I had persuaded John McCormack to pull it out of storage. In 1973 and after, I saw to it that it became the engine pulling the entire House into its modern era.

It began with our very first caucus meetings in 1973. In January, the caucus approved the recommendations of Julia Hansen's committee to elect all chairmen automatically and to do it by secret ballot. The decision capped at least fifteen years' effort to break the hold of seniority and came after an angry debate, a debate in which many of yesterday's young reformers came forward as that day's champions of seniority. The anger outlasted the decision. In fact, a day later a second caucus meeting attempted to repeal the new rules. It might have done so except for my speech welcoming and embracing the change. The repeal effort failed, and the seniority system—for sixty-two years the single path to committee domination—died that day. Its beneficiaries still held their power (every chairman won election handily), but they knew that their power sprang not from their personal longevity but from their colleagues' institutional voice: the Democratic caucus.

That same caucus meeting agreed to place the Speaker, majority leader, and caucus chairman on our party's committee on committees. Since 1911, that committee—the committee that targeted every young member's entire career—had consisted of the Democrats sitting on ways and means. Putting us there both strengthened us as leaders and gave us a new way to lead. For the first time, we could control directly and successfully a chairman's attempts to fill his committee with members of like mind—like *his* mind. Louisiana's F. Edward Hebert, for instance, long had refused to add a black to his Armed Services Committee. In 1973, he begrudgingly agreed to accept a black member, any black member except California's Ron Dellums. He would not consider at all Patricia Schroeder, an outstanding new member for whom I had campaigned in 1972 in her first race for any office. Once enlarged, the new Democratic committee on committees put two new members on armed services. One was Ron Dellums; the other was Pat Schroeder. With their selection, both learned something about power and its ends. Eddie Hebert did, too.

In the case of one committee, the Rules Committee, I needed no educating at all. I already knew about that committee's power and its use. I knew that no Speaker since Joe Cannon had controlled it.

I knew that not even Sam Rayburn's expansion of it in 1961 had broken its power. Finally, I knew that I was going to control that committee, not for the exaltation of Carl Albert, not even for the power of the Speakership, but for the rights of the entire House membership, too often frustrated by that obstinate committee. Sitting on my party's committee on committees placed me in a position to do it. Three vacancies gave me the opportunity. All three were taken by men entirely loyal to the elected leadership: Gillis Long of Louisiana, Morgan Murphy of Illinois, and Clem McSpadden, a new member from Oklahoma.

The new Rules Committee retained its old prerogatives, and I wanted it that way. When the House subsequently considered giving the Speaker the arbitrary power to bypass the committee and put bills directly on the floor, I led the fight that beat it by a three-to-one margin. The House needed a traffic cop, but it did not need a despot. Never again would this cop signal a steady halt to frustrate the House's majority.

In each of these cases, the Democratic caucus effected the changes, since each of them applied only to the party's way of doing business. While the press and pundits looked around for people to credit, I had the quiet satisfaction of knowing that the same caucus that was a worthless instrument for most of my majority leadership was moving the entire majority party behind my Speakership. In other cases, it moved the entire House by sponsoring the very reforms I knew to be long overdue.

At the recommendation of the Democratic caucus, the House voted in early 1973 to speed the flow of legislative business by adding two days per month to clear noncontroversial bills and by giving the Speaker the power, subject to majority vote, to convene the House before noon, a hoary but inefficient tradition. More importantly, the caucus's recommendation became the House's policy to open to the public nearly all committee hearings and markup sessions (in which bills were assembled), all frequently done heretofore behind closed doors. The same source finally established a procedure to allow amendment of tax bills, a practice unknown— and thoroughly undemocratic—since the 1930s. Caucus recommendations also established a subcommittee bill of rights, which sapped the authority of tyrannical chairmen, opened legislative power to the young and able, and protected the minority's rights.

Because I had my way and because the time was right, we did all of those things and did them all in a few months in 1973. If I had had my way, we would have done even more. We would have remade what was at the very heart not only of our procedures but of our products: the standing-committee system.

Not since 1946 had anyone dared address the committee structure. The redefinition of committee lines in that distant year may have made sense, considering the Congress's old responsibilities, but by the 1970s it made less sense and still less with every passing year. Some committees, Ways and Means most noticeably, steadily had acquired awesome power, power that in the case of Ways and Means drained the energies of its 25 members and frustrated its 410 nonmembers. Other committees served no important function at all. Still others had established jurisdiction over items ill fitted to their expertise. Banking and Currency, for instance, had authority over urban mass-transit legislation, though no one knew just what that had to do with either banking or currency. Finally, new issues unforeseeable in the 1946 committee organization lay completely beyond its structure; sometimes, they lay all over its structure. Energy legislation, unknown in the cheapoil years, potentially fell within the jurisdiction of eighty-three committees and subcommittees.

None of these problems was new. What was new was a determination to do something about them, even if that something disrupted our traditional ways of doing business so that we could get our business done. Securing the Democratic caucus's approval for a study committee on committee realignment, I added the warm support of the Republican leadership, got a million-dollar appropriation to finance its work, and named a committee of outstanding members to make recommendations. At its head I placed Richard Bolling.

Bolling's committee held six months of hearings and spent seventeen days drafting its recommendations, every one of those days open to the public. On one of them, I testified to the need for complete restructuring, thereby becoming the first Speaker to appear before a congressional committee in more than a century. When it was all over, the committee had a sensible and far-reaching set of proposals. They were sensible because they balanced committee workloads, because they rationalized jurisdictional assignments, and because they adopted the House's committee structure to the nation's modern needs. They were far reaching because they transformed every committee they touched and because they touched twenty of the twenty-one standing committees. Veterans' Affairs would see no change, but three (Internal Security, Merchant Marine and Fisheries, and Post Office and Civil Service) would be abolished. Each of the remainder would have altered responsibilities, sometimes dramatically so.

It was, of course, those features that accounted for the stubborn opposition to the proposals. Members serving on committees slated to lose responsibilities—and Ways and Means was to be the big loser—rallied all of the influence that those same responsibilities gave them. Liberals heretofore intent upon remaking the House suddenly became advocates of tradition when changing that tradition would cost them their hard-won influence. Outside lobbyists, comfortably tied to the existing structure, rallied to defend those ties. The result was the otherwise inexplicable alliance of such strange bedfellows as the DSG, organized business, and organized labor in a single mighty bloc. What explained it was that politics is not about issues, it is about people, and those people had a lot to lose.

They did not lose it. Dick Bolling and I did. After a bitter debate, the caucus voted narrowly to refer his committee's proposal to the continuing Hansen committee. The latter reported a set of procedural reforms—many valuable, none affecting committee responsibilities—that the caucus sent to the entire House. All won but all fell short of readying the House for the twenty-first century. However, we had brought it squarely into the twentieth.

One final way that we had done it came back in February of

1973. At the same caucus that affirmed the election of chairmen and approved the appointment of the Bolling committee, we voted to establish a Democratic House steering and policy committee. An agent of the caucus, it was firmly under the control of the leadership. The majority leader, the caucus chairman, the whip and his deputies, joined me on the committee, with other members elected regionally. In addition, I appointed enough other members to make it the Speaker's committee. By 1974's end, that committee had taken from our Ways and Means members the role of our party committee on committees, filling every Democratic assignment to every committee except one, Rules, which the Speaker alone would fill.

As great as the procedural authority of the new steering and policy committee was, its policy powers were even more important. For the first time since Joe Cannon's one-man rule, it gave the majority party a means to recommend legislation and coordinate its passage. Cannon had done it himself, as a tyrannical czar, and his rule had created a revolt.

No one ever confused Carl Albert with Joe Cannon or with a czar, but without an "Albert revolt," I had created and now directed something bigger than any one man and more important, too. I also had seen to it that the Democratic caucus functioned for the first time since the 1920s. For the first time since 1911, the elected House leadership controlled committee assignments and the flow of bills through the Rules Committee. For the first time in too long, we all shared our power with each other and did our work in full public view.

A lot of people got and deserved a lot of credit for all of that. When I looked at it, I remembered some of Sam Rayburn's talks back at the old Board of Education. Mr. Rayburn reminisced often about how weak the office of the Speakership was for many years, his first years there, years before he became Mr. Democrat and bigger than the office. In less than four years, I had seen the Speaker's institutional authority grow to transcend even Sam Rayburn's personal influence. Mr. Rayburn could not have foreseen it, but he was right: you can accomplish almost anything as long as you do not mind who gets the credit.

"The U.S. is facing a constitutional crisis. That branch of Government that most closely represents the people is not yet broken, but it is bent and in danger of snapping." Those two sentences opened the cover article of *Time* magazine's issue as the Ninety-third Congress convened on January 3, 1973. In the article, congressmen, political scientists, and others described the impending death of an independent Congress. One senator spoke openly of the tendency toward an "Executive Monarchy." An esteemed professor saw the Congress "sliding down a razor blade, with no way to pull back." *Time's* own congressional correspondent, Neil McNeil, speculated that it would soon be necessary "to stuff a congressman and stick him in the Smithsonian in among other extinct species, so that future generations will know what a congressman looked like."

Down Pennsylvania Avenue a mile from Capitol Hill, no one was worrying about the executive's future. Richard Nixon was beginning his second term determined to reform his house, too. He had interrupted the celebration of his reelection to request letters of resignation from each of the top 2,000 officers in the executive branch. Not all were accepted, but enough were to put Nixon loyalists in charge of such heretofore semi-independent agencies as the Internal Revenue Service, the Federal Bureau of Investigation, and the Central Intelligence Agency. Unmindful of federal statutes, the president was reorganizing his cabinet by creating a super cabinet of three cabinet officers who assumed White House offices and White House titles to direct the nation's domestic affairs. Equally unmindful of statute, Nixon established a super super cabinet of three to manage the nation's foreign affairs. Not one of the new positions, unknown to law, required Senate confirmation. In the privacy of the Oval Office, men like H. R. Haldeman, John Erlichman, Maurice Stans, John Mitchell, Charles Colson, and John Dean looked with delight to four more years. Rarely did they mention a "third-rate burglary" that had occurred in June. Always, hidden tape recorders whirred along.

Politically, things seemed to be breaking well for the president, too. Exactly one week after his second inauguration, Paris negotiators formally signed an agreement that he declared secured "peace with honor" in Vietnam. In February, the first of our prisoners of war returned from Hanoi. Soon, the American military left South Vietnam but left its government with massive stockpiles of sophisticated arms and in control of 75 percent of its territory and 85 percent of its population. That government also had Richard Nixon's entirely personal "absolute assurance" of "swift and severe retaliatory action" should Hanoi renew the fighting.

No wonder the president was ready to renew his own fight with Congress.

With Indochina seemingly gone as a political issue, the president defined the contest in economic terms. Its initial skirmish involved his proposed budget, the budget of a president who had his hands in its pockets and his eyes on the ground. The hands squeezed pennies tightly, especially those devoted to domestic social needs. The eyes saw only inflation's shadow, and the president was determined to escape it. What he was still determined to do helped transform a budgetary squabble into a constitutional contest.

No one could deny that inflation's shadow was real, and no one in the Congress ignored the problem. No one could. After a modest price increase of 3.4 percent over 1972, the cost of living shot up 8.8 percent in 1973—three and one-half times the self-serving estimate of that year's budget. Food costs alone soared 30 percent, meaning that the needy, as usual, paid the heaviest price. Responding to the challenge, Congress regularly had given the president the power and tools that only the executive could use. Some this executive misused; others he used not at all. Over a four-year span, the president devised his own "game plans." Seven of them. Phase One price controls, followed by Phase Two, Phase Three, and Phase Four, all punctuated by two separate price freezes, always the talk about holding down spending. Not one of them worked.

At least, not one of them worked economically. Politically, their very failure worked to the president's advantage. They gave him the false ammunition of congressional spending and congressional irresponsibility that the White House daily fired off in televised newscasts and occasional somber speeches. They gave him an issue to rally support for his own spending priorities. They gave a basis to the charge that Congress was a bent branch in danger of snapping. Most of all, they gave the president the excuse to veto any spending bill he did not like, even if what he disliked was not the dollar sum but the program himself. And veto he did. After our 1972 adjournment, the president refused to sign twelve appropriations bills. Through 1973, his veto came steadily forth.

I thought it was all bad economics. I thought it was bad politics, too. Too often stung by a hostile president, even Republican members were backing away from Nixon's policies and failing to support his legislative requests. Enough stayed loyal that we could not override his vetoes (he won eight straight override attempts in 1973), but neither could we prevent them.

Bad economics is one thing, and bad politics is another, but the upshot of it all was worse. Even if he signed our bills, the president often refused to spend the money. "Impoundment," he called it, and that was more than economically bad, it was constitutionally evil.

Of course, Nixon was not the first president to impound congressionally appropriated money. The process dated to Thomas Jefferson, who refused to spend fifty thousand dollars that Congress had given him to purchase gunboats for the Mississippi River after the Louisiana Purchase made them unnecessary. Subsequent executives also had impounded funds, and the Antideficiency Act of 1905 gave them explicit but narrowly prescribed authority to do so. Under that law, a president could decline to spend appropriations in "some extraordinary emergency or [under] unusual circumstances which could not be anticipated at the time of making such apportionment." Within those bounds, twentieth-century presidents often impounded limited amounts of funds for limited times, always after consultation with Congress.

Richard Nixon's impoundments had none of those features. First, the sums were vast, an average of $1 billion per year. Second, the impoundments were permanent. Third, not once did he consult Congress in advance. Finally, the impoundments rested not upon even the pretense of an extraordinary emergency or unusual circumstance. The circumstance and the emergency both were the arrogant claim of the president's unrestrained right to refuse to spend lawfully appropriated monies, a right that Nixon labeled "absolutely clear." The intent was to repeal or gut social programs that dated to the Great Society and the New Frontier, even to the New Deal. The effect was to assert the executive's sole right to define public priorities, and that he could not do. It was absolutely clear.

The Constitution explicitly reserves for Congress the duty and the power to finance all national programs through "appropriations made by Law." The Constitution explicitly charges the chief executive to see to it that "the Laws be faithfully executed." Both principles grow out of the soil of colonial experience, when American assemblies had learned that only their jealously guarded power of the purse could defend their prerogatives, and their citizens' liberties, from executive despotism however asserted, whether in the name of the king or even (presumably) by the need to fight inflation.

Thus, when Richard Nixon responded to our override of his veto of a $6 billion appropriation for rural sewage treatment by simply refusing to spend the $6 billion, what was at stake was more important than country sewage and more priceless than $6 billion. When he refused to spend "appropriations made by Law" for highway construction—though that law explicitly denied any right to impoundment—he simultaneously asserted a monarch's prerogative and denied a president's responsibility to see that the laws were "faithfully executed." When he and his spokesmen proclaimed a policy to veto any appropriation passed by 535 elected members of two houses of Congress should one man disagree with its level or purposes and then to impound the money if Congress overrode that veto, he proclaimed the intent to flee the shadow of inflation by casting a pall upon the Constitution. It was absolutely clear.

The federal courts agreed. In twenty-one lawsuits, twenty-one decisions voided specific impoundments as illegal. Constitutional scholars agreed. One, William Rehnquist, the future chief justice whom Nixon himself judged qualified to appoint initially to the Supreme Court, wrote that Nixon's broad claim of an inherent presidential authority of impoundment was "supported by neither reason nor precedent." Civic groups agreed. Those as diverse as the United Auto Workers, the National Association of Home Builders, and the American Nurses Association protested the president's policy. Even conservatives agreed. Our Appropriations Committee chairman, George Mahon, and the Senate's Sam Ervin, neither some wild-eyed spender, prepared bills to overturn the impoundments and conserve Congress's constitutional heritage.

My job as Speaker was to get some bill that we could pass. Although I never wavered from the constitutional issue involved, I also knew that what we confronted was not a theory but a circumstance. The difficulty of getting a bill through both houses was part of the circumstance; the president's likely veto was another. The hardest was to address the illegitimate issue of impoundment while also dealing with an undeniable reality. The whole method of congressional appropriations lacked expertise, coordination, and direction. That lack, which had existed since George Washington, gave a gloss of apparent legitimacy to Nixon's claim of executive power. His counselor, John Erlichman, had a point when he declared that the problem with congressional control of spending was that "the right hand does not know what the left hand is doing. The fingers of the right hand do not even know what the other fingers of the right hand are doing." If we had to strengthen our constitutional hand against the president, we would have to strengthen the budgetary hand, too.

We did it by using all of the reforms that we had set in place. At our very first meeting of the steering and policy committee, I appointed Dick Bolling to head a task force on the question of impoundments. Dick had the help of John Barrier, an able professional staff man who worked for the full committee. Periodic meetings both kept the caucus informed of our progress and allowed the members to make contributions. Chairman George Mahon put his Appropriations Committee to drafting a workable bill for budgetary reform. With Mike Mansfield, I worked to keep the public informed and to get a Senate bill as close to ours as possible.

All the pieces came together in the Budget and Impoundment Act of 1973. A very complex bill, it brought order to our appropriations process. An overall budget ceiling provided a framework within which separate appropriations must fit. New budget committees in each house would reconcile separate appropriation bills and revenue bills. The new Congressional Budget Office would give us the expertise to correct White House figures. Altogether, the budget provisions of the bill finally rationalized the entire method of congressional spending by allowing us to build a comprehensive budget from the ground up rather than cheese-paring one from the top down.

They also rendered impotent the threat of a presidential veto. A president who criticized so loudly our "irresponsible" and "inefficient" ways had to sign that bill, even though it contained a separate title carefully restricting the same president's impoundments. Dick Bolling successfully joined the two in the Rules Committee, where he had the help of my three new men. Firm yet realistic, we did not forbid all impoundments under all circumstances. Instead, we provided a mechanism whereby the president would have to justify all future impoundments to the Congress. Final authority to maintain or to release the impoundments would rest firmly where the Founding Fathers had placed it: in the United States Congress. Agreeing to the bill, President Nixon tacitly bowed to the principle.

It was one of the sweetest victories of my Speakership. The victory was not mine over Richard Nixon nor even Congress's over the president. It was a victory of principle, sweetened because in winning we had acted responsibly. We were responsible to our own new procedures. We were responsible to the need to get our budget-making process in order. We were responsible to the tradition that linked the assemblies, first of noblemen, then of businessmen, and finally of common men through the ages. The executive's demands for money met again its check and its balance in the representatives' power to give money and determine its use. We had affirmed what kings had learned to their sorrow and humanity's gain since they first had turned to those assemblies for money to fight their wars.

We affirmed it again when President Nixon needed money to fight his own war.

Though President Nixon pronounced the Paris Agreements a peace with honor, they created a peace that never was in a war that would not go away. American combat troops left Vietnam, but they left hostile armies itching for battle all over Indochina. In South Vietnam itself, government and Communist forces fought for momentary advantages while each prepared for a major offensive. In neighboring Cambodia, brought into the war by Nixon's "incursion" of 1970, the government controlled only the capital. Communist armies surrounded the city and threatened to overrun it. After publicly hinting that the United States might return again to Vietnam, the president unleashed American airpower over Cambodia. Doomed to fail, the renewed bombing had one inescapable consequence. It raised again the president's claim to make war with neither congressional consultation nor consent.

It was not the first time, not even for Richard Nixon. During each of the three preceding springs, the president had widened and intensified the war in peace's name. The Cambodian invasion of 1970 had been followed by 1971's cover for South Vietnam's invasion of Laos and the American mining of Haiphong Harbor in 1973. In not one instance had the president even seen fit to inform the Congress or its leaders. In each instance, the Senate had responded with efforts to end the war by cutting off funds for it; each of those efforts had died in the House. Not one had even come within fifty votes of passing.

This time it was different. There were no negotiations to disrupt. There were no departing American troops to protect. There was only a nation sick of the war and a Congress tired of having no voice in it. In 1973, Congress raised its voice. In the House, ours was magnified by the new reforms that we had assembled. Under my direction, the Steering and Policy Committee voted overwhelmingly (eighteen to three) to join the Senate in cutting off funds for the bombing. We took the resolution to the full Democratic caucus, which voted also overwhelmingly to put the party on record. Legislative leaders and I agreed to put the issue in the form of an amendment to a military-appropriations bill. Because of 1970's requirement of recorded votes on such amendments, no one had a place to hide. On May 10, the House of Representatives passed the amendment to deny the president the money to make war in or over Cambodia by a vote of 219 to 188. Joining the majority were thirty-five Republicans, who refused to follow their president even one more bloody step. Unable to veto the measure without simultaneously vetoing all military spending, President Nixon signed it into law. In the same way, six other amendments became laws of the Ninety-third Congress and collectively erected an impassable legal barrier against any American military or paramilitary operations in, over, or off the shores of Cambodia, Laos, North Vietnam, or South Vietnam. The last still had what was left of $350 billion in American tax money spent there over the years—spent along with the lives of 57,000 of our young men. If that could not guarantee South Vietnam's independence, nothing we could do later would, either. It would be no mistake to waste not another dollar nor another life there.

There had been mistakes, many of them, and in Congress we had learned from them. The same Constitution that created our offices and gave us our power of the purse also gave us another exclusive prerogative: only the Congress could declare war. We had not declared one in Vietnam, but we had fought one. We had accepted uncritically the president's judgment—several presidents' judgments—until we had been trapped. Handing the commander in chief the power to put our forces in harm's way, we had lost any practical power to keep them and us out of war. In Vietnam we did not regain it until those forces had left the war. In the future, we would have to assert that power first. The man who made it possible was Clem Zablocki.

Outside Congress and the Fourth Congressional District in Wisconsin, few people ever heard of Clem Zablocki. Sixty years old when the Ninety-third Congress convened, Clem had come to Congress in 1949. He worked quietly but effectively on our Foreign Affairs Committee. In time, he ranked behind only Chairman Tom Morgan and headed the subcommittee on national security policy and scientific developments. There, he did the hard and unpublicized work that made possible the Peace Corps and the United States Disarmament and Arms Control Agency. I got to know him well when President Johnson sent Clem and me to represent the United States at a conference in the Philippines in 1966. We both took our wives along, and Mary, Blanche Zablocki, Clem, and I became fast friends.

In 1970 at the time of the Cambodia invasion, Clem came by my office. We both had supported every step taken in Vietnam to that point, but in 1970 I agreed with him that the widening of the war drove home the need for more congressional involvement. That day, I gave him a promise that I kept for three years: I would back his efforts to secure appropriate legislation to that end.

Through the summer of 1970, Clem's subcommittee held hearings and finally produced a joint resolution. The full committee reported it favorably, and it passed the House but died when the Senate failed to act. In 1971, he started all over. This time, differently worded resolutions passed both houses but could not find agreement in a conference committee. Undaunted, Clem Zablocki started fresh again in 1973. Again he held extensive hearings, and this time he produced a new resolution, one much stronger than the earlier versions. It passed the House. A similar version passed the Senate. Senate and House conferees agreed to a compromise, and it passed both houses handily. It was the War Powers Act.

The law acknowledged the modern president's powers in a world far removed from the eighteenth-century world of the Constitution, but it also reasserted and redefined Congress's obligations and prerogatives. Essentially, it set a sixty-day limit on the presidential commitment of American forces to combat. After that time, a president must either justify their use and secure a joint congressional resolution of approval or withdraw them. No president's hands would be tied in an emergency, but neither would Congress be powerless to do anything but silently acquiesce.

Richard Nixon would have none of it. Declaring the act both dangerous and unconstitutional, he gave it his ninth veto in ten months.

Clem Zablocki did not give up, nor did I. I knew, though, how hard an override would be. It would take a two-thirds majority, always hard, and harder still on something this controversial. We did not have a two-thirds Democratic majority in the House, and we could not expect much Republican help. Many of our Democrats were conservatives unwilling to buck a conservative president on a diplomatic issue. Others were liberals, several of whom had voted against the bill on original passage on the grounds that even sixty days was too long. This override would be the hardest yet, hard enough that I twice put off the vote.

On November 7, 1973, I finally put the question to the House. Clem and Phil Burton, a Californian who was my informal liaison with the doctrinaire liberals, had found six liberals who had voted against the bill but were approachable to switching their votes for an override. We all three approached them. My pitch was simple. "Look," I said, "Nixon has beaten us on eight straight override attempts. If you go with us, we can win on this one, and it's the biggest one of all." Each of the six agreed to stand aside while the vote was taken. If we needed them, they would vote with us. We needed them, and we got them. We repassed the bill, 284 to 135. Because of the six, we won by a four-vote margin. The Senate overrode that same day, 75 to 18.

After three years' work, Clem Zablocki had brought Congress's war-making power into the post–World War II world. As it turned out, the hardest work of all was probably done on the last day. I had not chosen it at random. A few days earlier, President Richard

Nixon had fired one of his employees, a lawyer named Archibald Cox. That made it easier to pass the War Powers Act. It also elevated a third-rate burglary into a first-rate constitutional crisis.

At the time, back in June of 1972, I thought it was a third-rate burglary, too. When the *Washington Post* first reported the Watergate break-in, I put it aside as a silly criminal act that would go no further than the district courts. Even as the newspapers began to develop the story and attach it to the White House, the only thing that aroused the slightest interest in me was that James W. McCord, one of the burglars, was said to have once lived in Waurika, Oklahoma, a friendly little town in my district.

Only in late 1972 did I begin to suspect that the Watergate affair might involve more than an isolated legal problem. One morning, Larry O'Brien, the Democratic National Committee's chairman, called and told me that there were some financial implications. Money, considerable sums of it, apparently had financed the burglars, and some of that money had been laundered in Mexico. If so, Congress might need to act. I contacted Wright Patman, chairman of the Banking and Currency Committee, and asked him to look into the matter. He did, and Republicans on the committee and elsewhere howled that we were playing politics. Wright went on along anyway, ignoring those complaints and assembling boxes of evidence. The Ninety-second Congress adjourned before he could do much with them, so Chairman Patman sealed the boxes and sent them over to the Senate. He sent them to Senator Sam Ervin.

Senator Sam. In his committee's long investigations of early 1973, America made him a folk hero, an old country lawyer with a face designed by a cartoonist. Gradually, America learned what we in Congress knew about the senator: behind that country-lawyer facade was a Harvard Law School education; behind those jowls and self-propelled eyebrows was the mind of a first-rate constitutional scholar. Gradually, too, America learned something about the break-in, more about the White House, but not enough about the president. Every passing day brought new revelations. Beneath Watergate's tip was a chilling iceberg of misdeeds, venality, and outright stupidity. Watching it all, I, too, began to wonder, in Senator Howard Baker's phase, "how much did the president know and when did he know it?" Like most, my expectation (maybe my hope) was that he had known too little too late.

Right in the middle of the Ervin hearings, the press began to report another story. This one I followed with more than passing interest. Vice-President Spiro Agnew was under investigation by a Baltimore grand jury. United States attorneys were preparing charges of fraud, bribery, and other crimes.

On September 25, Gerald Ford and Leslie Arends, the Republicans' House leader and whip, respectively, asked whether I could see the vice-president. They also asked whether I had received a call from Attorney General Elliot Richardson. I had not, but the question told me why the vice-president wanted to see me: it had to involve that investigation.

It did. Agnew came by and handed me a letter. It asked for a congressional inquiry into the allegations against him and cited as precedent such an investigation requested and given Vice-President John C. Calhoun more than 150 years earlier. We talked alone for a while, and he complained bitterly about the Justice Department's handling of the case. He added that top White House officials were pressuring him to resign, and he gave every indication that he never would.

Agnew's request was a bolt from skies grayed by the Watergate investigations. To this day I do not understand why he wanted it, but I knew instantly that the House must not involve itself in a nearly completed criminal investigation before the federal courts. I talked with Peter Rodino, chairman of our Judiciary Committee, and he agreed. He also offered to check the Calhoun precedent and report to me the next morning. When he did, he confirmed my suspicion that the cases were not at all similar. That morning, I gave the whole story to the entire House leadership, and I gave them my decision: I would steer the House of Representatives clear of the impending clash between the judicial and executive branches. Whatever Spiro Agnew's intent, he would not put the legislative branch in the breach with him.

Two weeks later, I got a second letter from Agnew. It was a copy of one informing the secretary of state that he was resigning his office. He thereby traded the vice-presidency of the United States for a suspended sentence on a single charge of income-tax evasion. As part of the deal, the Justice Department published the charges and evidence against him. Uncontested by Agnew, they documented years of sleazy kickbacks that ran straight into the vice-president's office, where Spiro Agnew had collected envelopes of cash from crooked contractors, slimy characters as crooked as he.

I was glad to see him go, but it meant a big difference in my own life. The country had no vice-president, and I was Speaker of the House. In the presidential-succession sequence, I was next in line. Carl Albert was now the one heartbeat away. For all I cared, it could have been a thousand. I worried neither that I would get the job nor that I could do it. The biggest difference for me was entirely personal: the Secret Service invaded my Washington apartment.

For invaders, they were a nice-enough occupation army. Their leader, Gil Parachos, was a fine fellow. His agents accompanied me everywhere. At home, they installed a hot line by my bed to connect me directly to the White House in the event of a national emergency. It rang two or three times, never with any news of great substance but always with an ominous sound. The agents also drew the drapes carefully whenever I was home, explaining that I made a fine target for snipers. Mary threw them open as soon as I left in the morning because she was not particularly worried about snipers. The agents also offered to help Mary carry out the garbage, but she would not allow it. Maybe they feared a bomb in the dumpster. I do not know. I do know that they X-rayed everything that entered our little apartment.

Because there were no vacant rooms around us, the Secret Service's headquarters was a van parked in the back alley. One of our neighbors returned from abroad unaware of what had happened, noticed the van, observed it, and consulted the apartment manager. A bunch of hippies had set up in the alley, he protested, and they were probably dope dealers, too, since men and women entered and left the van at all hours. Other tenants stopped Mary and told her how glad they were to have the Secret Service there; they never had felt so safe.

I was ready to get back to normal as quickly as possible. President Nixon was, too. On the afternoon of Agnew's resignation, the president summoned Mike Mansfield and me to the White House. The Twenty-fifth Amendment provided that the president would fill a vacancy in the vice-presidency by nomination, subject to confirmation by both houses. Clearly anxious to get a vice-president as quickly as possible, Nixon told us that he would ask Republican leaders at all levels for suggestions. He also said he would welcome any advice we had to offer. I thought it just a courtesy, but Mike gave him two names: Secretary of State William Rogers and a former senator from Kentucky, John Sherman Cooper. I said that since Mike had offered some choices, I knew the one who would be the easiest to confirm. "Who is it? Jerry Ford?" the president asked. "Yes sir," I answered.

Of course, House Minority Leader Gerald R. Ford was his choice, and a fine one. Although the House (unlike the Senate) had never before confirmed a presidential appointee for any office, I knew that I would assign the task to Pete Rodino's Judiciary Committee. That committee had worked on the Twenty-fifth Amendment and had general responsibility for constitutional issues. Besides, I knew that Pete's committee would conduct an impartial inquiry into the candidate's fitness, not his politics. Quite a few members, especially the younger ones, were busy advising me that we Democrats could and should block any nominee who might run against us in 1976. I thought that was nonsense. The House had a unique responsibility to the Constitution, not to my party's advantage. I knew that Pete and his committee shared that. Sure enough, the Judiciary Committee began a thorough and diligent consideration of Ford's nomination. Just ten days into it, the entire picture changed; in fact, it exploded.

On October 20, President Nixon ordered Attorney General Elliot

Richardson to fire Special Prosecutor Archibald Cox. Charged with investigating Watergate and related crimes, Cox was seeking a court order to compel the president to hand over some of the famous White House tapes for evidence. For that reason, Nixon wanted him fired, and Richardson refused to do it. So did his deputy, William Ruckleshaus. Both resigned instead. Finally, Solicitor General Robert Bork executed the order and fired Cox.

Never did I see such a spontaneous emotional eruption as the rage that greeted Nixon's "Saturday Night Massacre." Cartons of telegrams and telephone messages awaited me at my office on Monday. Resolutions of impeachment virtually rained on the House floor. I had no doubt that if one were to be called up, it would be voted through instantly.

To that point, I carefully had kept the House clear of any investigation of the president. Everyone knew that the House of Representatives alone held the constitutional power of impeachment. Any investigation, whatever its focus, would raise the shadow of that singular but ultimate sword. After the departure of the three top justice officials, all apparent victims of the president's need to conceal evidence, there was no choice. Impeachment was a possibility. Its consideration was the House's duty. How to manage it responsibly required the Speaker's decision.

I never got more unsolicited or more foolish advice. Some told me that we should strike back at the White House with our power of the purse: slash its appropriations. Otherwise sensible people saw a chance to forestall Ford's confirmation, impeach and remove Nixon, and hand the presidency to the next in line, me. Many wanted to set up a select committee to handle impeachment. Some of those wanted me to fill it with our most outstanding members; others wanted me to pack it with Nixon haters. Both pointed to precedent: the one presidential impeachment in America's history, that of Andrew Johnson, had been handled not by a standing committee but by a select committee.

I had not asked for any advice. I did not put it to a vote. I cannot even claim even to have listened very politely to such suggestions. No decision I could ever make would be more significant for my

I knew the one who would be easiest to confirm. Carl Albert with President Jerry Ford.

country. In an impeachment inquiry, two institutions would be judged, not one. We would examine the president, and the American people would examine us. I did not know what we would learn about the president, but I never doubted what the people would learn about their House of Representatives.

On Monday afternoon, October 22, 1973, I announced that I would refer all impeachment resolutions (there were twenty-five at the time) to the House Committee on the Judiciary. Whatever its eventual decision, no one could claim it rigged. Judiciary was a standing committee, most of its members serving for many years, all of them there when impeachment was just a word in civics

That was Peter Rodino. Mary Albert, Carl Albert, and Judiciary Committee Chairman Peter Rodino at the grave of Winston Churchill, in 1976.

texts. Probably not one American in a hundred could name even one of its members. They were neither particularly powerful nor prominent. By tradition, all were lawyers, but otherwise they were quite average members, average in age, average in experience, representatives of both sexes and every section, race, religion, and viewpoint in the country. I thought the average committee, if called upon to do an important job, would do it right.

Like the average committee, judiciary's most important member was its chairman, in practice the committee's most senior man. In this case, that was Peter Rodino. New to the chairmanship in 1973, he long had labored behind the famed Manny Celler. He was a quiet man of quiet talents. I suppose he was about average for a chairman. He always went about his work modestly but thoroughly, paying due regard to his committee's members and the House's traditions.

I never claimed to be much more than an average Speaker, either. I had neither sought nor received publicity. I was not a national celebrity daily before the cameras. I did not run the House, I only respected it. My job was to let Pete Rodino and his thirty-seven committee members do their job. My job was to let the House of Representatives do its work its way.

I had been in Congress nearly thirty years. For all of them, I had heard the criticism of that way: the slowness of our deliberations, the inefficiency of our procedures, the authority of our anonymous old men, the mediocrity of our members. Quite recently the critics had grown louder. The president should make decisions because all we could do was debate. The White House had to act swiftly because we took too long. The bright young men gathered there had to be loyal to the president because we were too divided. The executive branch knew what to do with power, but our branch was bent, in danger of snapping.

After clearing Ford's confirmation as vice-president, Chairman Peter Rodino and the Committee on the Judiciary of the United States House of Representatives took up a resolution of inquiry into the impeachment of President Richard M. Nixon. In the light of day, the American people would judge us all.

Yes, we were slow. Committee hearings and debates consumed nine full months. But because we were slow, we ensured that every view was aired and examined, every piece of evidence weighed and measured. Yes, we were inefficient. But because we were, we were thorough. Yes, we were divided. The thirty-seven committee members were individually loyal to no one man but were collectively bound to the U.S. Constitution and its faith in deliberative government. But no, Peter Rodino proved not to be just an anonymous old man. He became a celebrity, but only because he acted true to the House's ways. And no, his committee members proved not to be mediocrities. When Americans watched members like Barbara Jordan, Paul Sarbanes, Jack Brooks, Elizabeth Holtzman, and others wrestle publicly with their own consciences and their nation's future, America was watching representative government work. They were all average members working in a way long derided, but those people and that process worked just as well as I had expected and as the Founding Fathers had intended. Because they did, they assembled the evidence, and they debated and approved the resolutions that caused Richard Nixon to ask me to meet him in the Executive Office Building on a Thursday night in August.

With me were Senators Mike Mansfield, Hugh Scott, and James Eastland, along with John Rhodes, the new House minority leader. Collectively, we were the leaders of the Congress that the president had battled, ridiculed, and ignored over five and one-half years. There was no enmity that evening. As president, Richard Nixon told us that he would announce his resignation the next day, August 9, 1974. As a man, he talked about his inclination to stay on and fight it out, about how his family wanted him to do so, but he knew that the outcome was certain and that the country would be torn apart. Then he thanked us collectively for our support and asked us to extend it to his successor. He turned to one of us for his last words. The man who twenty-seven years earlier had asked me if I was the same Carl Albert who had won a speech contest in 1928 put his arm around my shoulders. "We've always been friends," Dick Nixon said. I could not help but be touched by it. He had been my friend, my first Republican friend in Congress. He could have been a great president, for his instincts were sure and his insights were sharp, but he was a flawed man who confused personal power with constitutional processes. His departure was not the defeat of his person but the triumph of that process.

It did not end all of our problems. The deficit still mounted. The recession worsened. Inflation increased. An old war in Indochina neared its tragic end. A new one might erupt in the Middle East at any time. My own problems did not end either. Until Nelson Rockefeller was confirmed as vice-president, I was once more next in line. The Secret Service parked its van in the alley again, installed another hot line, and started drawing my drapes. To get away, I sometimes went over to the Library of Congress and worked on some old hobbies—genealogy and translating Miguel de Cervantes's *Don Quixote*. That may have been where I encountered the diary of Frederick Muhlenberg, the first Speaker of the House. Reading it, I realized just how little America had changed since its first congressmen had ridden their horses over muddy trails to that first Congress. "The coffers are empty, the taxes almost unendurable, the people in bad humor, the money discredited," Muhlenberg had written. But he had written, too, of what was even more enduring: "However, the present Congress, believe me, consists of honest, brave, and wise men. Let us once more take cheer and be steadfast, rely on God and our own strength, and endure courageously, then we shall be sure of reaching our goals."

Like every Congress since Frederick Muhlenberg's, mine kept reaching for its goals. Like every Congress before mine (and assuredly after), we never grasped them, for it is the unending act of reaching that animates American government. Though inevitable, the process could be awfully frustrating. Our new president, Gerald Ford, was a good man and one of my best friends in Congress. He was an honest man, a decent man, a modest man. We all had smiled at his line (uttered when he became Nixon's vice-president) that he was "a Ford, not a Lincoln." But Jerry Ford also could be a stubborn man, stubborn enough to make me question whether this particular Ford was a Henry or an Edsel.

Even more tenaciously than Nixon, he clung to the determination to fight inflation by fighting Congress over the budget. A barrage of vetoes shattered the peace of our brief honeymoon. Neither the president nor the Congress won the economic fight. Only inflation did.

Politically, we won a big victory in 1974's election. Watergate had tarnished every Republican's candidacy, and Jerry Ford's premature pardon of Nixon did nothing to help them. The result was that eighty new Democrats won election to Congress in 1974, the largest turnover in membership since the New Deal. Nearly all had Nixon and Ford to thank and no one else. They certainly showed little gratitude to veteran House leaders.

Because they comprised more than a quarter of all House Democrats, the members of the Class of '74 had a lot of muscle. Sometimes they had more muscle than heart or brains. They showed the strength of the first (and, in my view, the absence of the second and third) at our organizational caucus. Three veteran committee chairmen lost their positions in a flood of freshman, antiestablishment votes. My own vote lost, too, but not as much as did Eddie Hebert, Bob Pogue, and Wright Patman. Hebert could be a pain in the neck, but I thought he deserved another term leading Armed Services. The freshmen and some others thought he had had one too many already. Pogue was a fine chairman of Agriculture, but he had goaded the professional liberals too often. Patman's loss of Banking and Currency's chairmanship pained me most. For twenty-three terms, Wright Patman had been a fighting congressman, fighting for farmers and poor people and black people. His only sin was his age, eighty-one when the Ninety-fourth Congress convened. And that was a sin to the young newcomers, who booted him out, unmindful of the fact that their own presence was ultimately traceable to those boxes of evidence that Wright Patman had assembled and given to Sam Ervin.

As Speaker, I tried to be the leader of this group that refused to be led. They wanted to build a record, not a policy, and they had the votes to pass bills that I knew Jerry Ford would have to veto. He did, but they did not have the votes to override them. The consequence too often was neither a record nor a policy. It was just frustration.

Not always, though. It was the big freshman bloc that made possible my final piece of congressional reform. In late 1976, John Brademas brought David Obey by my office. Dave was a comparatively young member himself (then forty-two, he had come to Congress in 1969), and we talked about the need for a revised code of ethics for House members. I thought it a great idea, got a resolution passed to establish the House Commission on Admin-

With Bob Pogue, George Mahon, and Wright Patman.

istrative Review, and put David Obey in charge of it. The commission did an excellent job. Its eventual fruit (harvested just after my retirement) was a comprehensive code requiring public disclosure of members' financial records, limiting their income earned outside the House, and abolishing unofficial accounts. With that piece set to be placed, I knew that I could leave a Congress remade under my Speakership, a Congress more open and more democratic but a Congress just as solid as Frederick Muhlenberg's.

I liked that aspect of my job. I liked, too, some of its perquisites.

A Speaker has many ceremonial duties here and abroad. Carl Albert in China with John Rhodes, George Bush, and Deng Xiaoping.

As leader of the legislative branch of American government, a Speaker has many ceremonial duties here and abroad. I had loved to travel since my boyhood, and I had not had such fine experiences since my Oxford days. Asked to represent the United States, I visited the Soviet Union and had long personal talks with Leonid Brezhnev. In China, I walked along the Great Wall and met Communist party leaders (there were no other kinds of leaders) at every level. No trip thrilled me more—nor, I think, meant more to America—than the one that took me back to England in 1976. I was there not as an Oxford student to receive an education but as my country's chief legislator, there to receive the physical symbol of America's inheritance from Britain. To honor our bicentennial of independence, our mother country was lending us one of four surviving original copies of the Magna Charta. The charter of liberties that English barons had forced upon King John was the tip of the taproot that had flowered into our own Declaration of Independence and U.S. Constitution.

Its loan to America symbolized the completion of a long journey unforeseeable at Runnymede in 1215. I felt that it symbolized also the completion of a long personal journey that I had begun

Now I was back in England once more to accept its gift for America but also for me. Carl Albert with Queen Elizabeth II in 1976, when Britain loaned a copy of the Magna Charta to the United States in honor of the bicentennial of independence.

about seven hundred years later. At Bug Tussle School, I had dreamed of being a congressman, even a Speaker. At McAlester High School, I had studied the Constitution and won a trip to England and elsewhere. At the University of Oklahoma, I had orated on our Bill of Rights and had won a Rhodes scholarship and a trip back to England. As a young congressman, I had been given the chance for leadership, and for more than twenty years, I had met its demands. I had done all I ever dreamed of. I had done the best I could to defend the heritage of constitutional liberty that reached back to the Magna Charta. Now I was back in England once more to accept its gift for America but also for me. I returned, my long journey complete.

A few weeks later, I announced my retirement as Speaker of the House of Representatives and member of Congress from the Third Congressional District of Oklahoma. Already (ten years earlier) I had had one major heart attack. My doctors told me that my heart just would not take too much more. I was still young enough and still healthy enough to enjoy many years with my family and friends. A lot of those friends were in Congress, and several tried to talk me out of it, but they were friends enough to know just how determined Carl Albert could be once his mind was set.

People who did not know me quite so well made me some generous offers. For handsome salaries, I could have served on the boards of dozens of corporations and associations. I knew what they wanted. They wanted me to represent them in Washington, where I would lobby my old friends in Congress. That would amount to selling myself and the Speakership of the United States Congress. Ernie Albert's boy was not for sale. So I took my unspent campaign funds of thirty years' service (seven thousand dollars) and gave two thousand dollars to the Democratic Campaign Committee and five thousand dollars to the University of Oklahoma. I turned the Washington jobs down and went back to a little community called Bug Tussle, near the town of McAlester in Pittsburg County, Oklahoma.

It was the kind of place where nobody's boy was for sale.

Where No Man Wears a Crown

In 1947, Mary and I packed everything we owned in a two-door Pontiac and drove to Washington. Thirty years later, we drove back to Oklahoma. We owned more, much of which we would have to ship, and we had two children, too. We had a Thunderbird, not a Pontiac, but the fact remained that Carl Albert was driving. I still am.

Since I had been home as much as possible over those thirty years, I knew that McAlester had changed a lot. No longer is it the booming industrial city that my parents knew, nor is it the metropolis that had so frightened a kid from country schools, but neither is it what it had been in the mid-1940s: a declining regional trade center slowly drying up with the hinterland about it. Its population has grown—grown bigger, not less friendly. The federal ammunition depot is still its major employer, but it employs more people. It has been blessed with its share (but no more than its fair share) of government projects that keep the town healthy. One fact is constant here, too: McAlester is my hometown.

The town takes a lot of pride in that. Grand Avenue, where I heard some of my first political "speakings," has been renamed Carl Albert Parkway. Amid the gas stations and fast-food franchises that line the new highway bypass, a bright blue water tower proclaims "McAlester—The Home of Carl Albert." A fine regional medical complex has revitalized the northeast part of town. One of its features is the Carl Albert Mental Health Center. So far, I have not had need of its services, but I do occasionally fill my car's tank at Carl Albert Texaco.

Down the street is the federal courthouse, renamed the Carl Albert Federal Building and United States Courthouse. At the corner of its site, there is a nice bust of Carl Albert with some awfully nice words about him; the people of McAlester put that up. The Oklahoma Historical Society put up a big granite slab several blocks away. There's not much there now, a few vacant lots and some rusting rails where the Katy Railroad once carried cars filled with coal from the Bohlen mines. The marker explains that this quite undistinguished site is the birthplace of Carl Albert, member of Congress, 1947 to 1977, and Speaker of the House of Representatives, 1971 to 1977. I guess those things strike visitors who call on me, and maybe they impress the town's occasional tourist.

One who is not impressed at all is Kathryn Marie Albert. Katy is the daughter of David and his wife, Elizabeth, and she is my favorite visitor. A bright girl of three, she must have gotten her red hair from me. When her parents bring her down from Oklahoma City, she pays no attention at all to the bust of Carl Albert at the Federal Building. Instead, she runs to my office and heads straight for a file cabinet's bottom drawer, the one that I have marked "Katy's Drawer." She knows that inside there will always be a little gift, and she gives me back a big smile.

Katy calls me Grandpa. When I walk down Carl Albert Parkway, nobody calls me Mr. Speaker. I am just plain Carl to them. I always say the best sound to a politician's ear is that of his own name. Most of the time, I know the person who stops me—know his parents, even grandparents, too— and we have a nice conversation. That pleases me more than any marker I ever saw.

I work nearly every day in McAlester. Back when I was majority leader, Congress passed a law to give retired Speakers benefits similar to those extended to retired presidents, so I have an office in Carl Albert Federal Building on Carl Albert Parkway. The government lets me hire a small staff, and for years Sara Lane and Lois

Washington have helped me with my papers, my visitors, and my obligations.

As I have grown older, one or both of them drive me to occasional events held in my honor. I am still surprised at how often these occur, and I am always proud. A very special one came a few years ago when Oklahoma put my portrait in its capitol rotunda. Charles Banks Wilson, an artist from Miami, Oklahoma, painted the portrait, as he already had done for the few Oklahomans honored there: Sequoyah, Jim Thorpe, Bob Kerr, and (later) Angie Debo. For mine, he chose to portray me in movement, stepping out of a background. That background is his reproduction of an old photograph of the Bug Tussle student body of 1914, when I was a first grader standing in the front row and dreaming of going to Congress. I was proud to be in Oklahoma City for its unveiling; I was prouder still that every living person in that painting was there, too, and I saw that they were individually introduced on the occasion that honored them.

I live now among many of them. When we returned home, Mary and I sold the house that we had kept all those years as our McAlester home. We bought the house next to my sister Kathryn's. My two surviving brothers, Earl and Noal (Budge), live in the area, too, but Kathryn and I always tease them that we are the lucky ones because they do not live in Bug Tussle; we do. In fact, my sister and I live on a piece of land that Papa farmed when we were all kids growing up in an unpainted frame house. Just down the hill from me is the very bottomland where he grew the cotton that I so dreaded to pick every year. That land is covered by water now, the water of Lake Eufaula. About ten miles northeast stands the Eufaula Dam, which created that lake.

It must be the lake that accounts for the remarkable fact that the Bug Tussle community has more people now than at any time in its history. Some of them are old-timers, folks like Kathryn and me and Manes Craighead and Bill Anderson, pals from my boyhood. More of them are newcomers, drawn by Lake Eufaula's recreation and Bug Tussle's simple country living. Quite a few live, like me, on the lake's shores, their homes backing to the waters that are there because of the dam. Every night a lot of them like to sit on their back porches and look out over the lake toward Eufaula Dam. A few know that this neighbor was one of those who helped build that dam conceived in dust, cradled in flood, and created by men. As for me, I prefer to sit on my front porch, where I can look over the hills and meadows of the old Bug Tussle community. God created those.

If I walk just a bit, I can be at the old Bug Tussle School. It is not a school any longer. Its enrollment fell below the state-required level in 1968 and it had to close. One of my saddest days was that one. I spoke at the closing, and my friends thought it would be nice if I were the one to padlock the school on its last day. I could not do it. Carrying a lunch bucket and red primer, I had walked through that same door into a world of learning and achievement. I would not be the one to lock it behind me.

Over in McAlester, the high school that I entered as a scared country kid in overalls and brogans stayed in use until recently. The old building still stands on a hill a block from my office, but the kids now go to a modern building a few miles away. Every once in a while, I have given a speech to those kids, and I find that it is just as rewarding to be in the new building as in the old. From time to time, I tutor some of those kids, helping them with their grammar or their Spanish or getting them ready for a college-entrance examination. It is partial repayment of a debt that I owe their parents and grandparents.

The University of Oklahoma has had me teach, too. Just after I retired, I offered a course on politics and congressional leadership. The young students seemed to enjoy it. Maybe one or two will one day profit from it as I did from Cortez Ewing's lectures back in the twenties and early thirties. Dr. Ewing's lectures still stand as the university's greatest gift to me, but there have been others. One has been to honor me with the creation of the Carl Albert Congressional Research Center. The only academic facility in America devoted to the study of its legislative branch, the center attracts top graduate students from all over the country and brings them

Carl Albert, from the painting in the Oklahoma Statehouse rotunda by Charles Banks Wilson.

together with outstanding scholars and major congressional figures. The center also maintains an archive filled with the papers of several congressmen from Oklahoma and elsewhere. Mine are there, all two million pages of them, the mountain of paper that records my public life and makes possible this book. From time to time, I like to visit the center and talk with the bright young people there. I am asked to give them an occasional speech, and I am always pleased to do so. In fact, I give a lot of speeches. Mary sometimes kids me that the soldier she married became a politician and turned out to be a speech maker. I just remind her that I started out a speech maker and it is what made everything else possible.

Some speeches I give before my earliest audience: the people of McAlester. They are not the same people, but I am not a high school kid, either. I do, however, sometimes use thoughts and phrases that I had even then. On July 4, 1985, I did that. I spoke at McAlester's First Baptist Church to commemorate our Declaration of Independence. I told them how, nine years earlier, I had given another speech in Washington as Speaker of the House when I welcomed England's queen and accepted her nation's gift: the loan of the Magna Charta. On that day in 1985, I was not the Speaker. I was just Carl, and I spoke the words I had used as a student orator. They were words about how our balance of powers and our Bill of Rights "distinguish Americans from the subject races of the world. They are the things that make of America a land where all are kings, but no man dares to wear a crown." The difference this time was that I had a lifetime's experience to affirm that. The constant was that I was once more in McAlester, Oklahoma, one of those places where no man wears a crown.

Lest I be tempted to forget that, I remember well one speech I gave. It was at a little country school and I was mighty glad to get its invitation. I talked to a bunch of elementary kids, and I told them about when I was a boy back in Bug Tussle School. Congressman Charlie Carter had told us all about Congress, had told us that one of us might one day become a congressman. Hoping to inspire them, I told them the same thing.

In a way it worked. I finished, and a little towheaded boy came up to me.

"Mister," he said, "that sure was inspiring."

Pleased, I asked him just what words I had said that he found so inspiring—I would have to use them again.

He answered, "It wasn't anything you said. It was watching you. I was thinking if a little shrimp like you can grow up to be a congressman, I can grow up to be president of the United States."

In this country, with that attitude, he can.

Some of my speeches are not that much fun. The people I knew as a boy are old now, and many are dying. Too often, I am asked to speak at their funerals. I spoke at one just a few months ago, that of Joe Thomas. It was at a little black church. I talked about how long I had known Joe. I talked about how we had been boys together back in Bug Tussle. I told about the day we both had started school, about how we had walked together to Kyle Tennant's meadow, how when we had gotten there, how I had angled off to the left and Joe and the other black kids had turned right. I told Joe's family and friends what I had thought about segregation back then: that it was unfair, unhuman, un-Christian. I told them how happy I was that Joe Thomas and I had lived long enough to see it end and how glad I was that Joe's grandchildren would have a better chance. I told them that I was thankful they had given me the chance to help make that true.

Then I went home.

Index